Evolving Images

Exploring Jewish Arts and Culture
Robert H. Abzug, Series Editor
Director of the Schusterman Center for Jewish Studies

Evolving Images

Jewish Latin American Cinema

EDITED BY NORA GLICKMAN AND ARIANA HUBERMAN

University of Texas Press ◆ *Austin*

Our thanks to Robert H. Abzug, series editor for the University of Texas Press, for his support.

Copyright © 2018 by the University of Texas Press
All rights reserved
Printed in the United States of America
First edition, 2018

Requests for permission to reproduce material from this work should be sent to:
Permissions
University of Texas Press
P.O. Box 7819
Austin, TX 78713-7819
utpress.utexas.edu/rp-form

♾ The paper used in this book meets the minimum requirements of ANSI/NISO Z39.48-1992 (R1997) (Permanence of Paper).

Library of Congress Cataloging-in-Publication Data
Names: Glickman, Nora, editor. | Huberman, Ariana, editor.
Title: Evolving images : Jewish Latin American cinema / edited by Nora Glickman and Ariana Huberman.
Other titles: Exploring Jewish arts and culture.
Description: First edition. | Austin : University of Texas Press, 2017. | Series: Exploring Jewish arts and culture | Filmography | Includes bibliographical references and index.
Identifiers: LCCN 2017018506
    ISBN 978-1-4773-1426-5 (cloth : alk. paper)
    ISBN 978-1-4773-1471-5 (pbk. : alk. paper)
    ISBN 978-1-4773-1427-2 (library e-book)
    ISBN 978-1-4773-1428-9 (non-library e-book)
Subjects: LCSH: Jews in the motion picture industry. | Motion pictures—Latin America—20th century. | Jews—Latin America—Identity.
Classification: LCC PN1995.9.J46 E95 2017 | DDC 791.43/652992408—dc23
LC record available at https://lccn.loc.gov/2017018506

doi:10.7560/314265

Contents

Introduction. Evolving Images: Jewish Latin American Cinema   1
NORA GLICKMAN AND ARIANA HUBERMAN

PART I. **Alternative Identities**

1. Out of the Shadows: María Victoria Menis's *Camera Obscura*   11
GRACIELA MICHELOTTI

2. Intercultural Dilemmas: Performing Jewish Identities in Contemporary Mexican Cinema   24
ELISSA J. RASHKIN

3. Incidental Jewishness in the Films of Fabián Bielinsky   36
AMY KAMINSKY

PART II. **Memory and Violence**

4. *My German Friend* and the Jewish Argentine/German "Mnemo-Historic" Context   49
DANIELA GOLDFINE

5. Dispersed Friendships: Jeanine Meerapfel's *The Girlfriend*   62
PATRICIA NURIEL

6. Revisiting the AMIA Bombing in Marcos Carnevale's *Anita*   73
MIRNA VOHNSEN

PART III. New Themes

7. *The Year My Parents Went on Vacation*: A Jewish Journey in the Land of Soccer **91**
   ALEJANDRO METER

8. Coming of Age in Two Films from Argentina and Uruguay **103**
   CAROLINA ROCHA

9. Waiting for the Messiah: The Super 8mm Films of Alberto Salomón **117**
   ERNESTO LIVON-GROSMAN

PART IV. Diasporas and Displacements

10. Geographic Isolation and Jewish Religious Revival in Two Contemporary Latin American Documentaries **133**
    ARIANA HUBERMAN

11. Negotiating Jewish and Palestinian Identities in Latin American Cinema **148**
    TZVI TAL

12. From a Dream to Reality: Representations of Israel in Contemporary Jewish Latin American Film **164**
    AMALIA RAN

13. On Becoming a Movie **178**
    ILAN STAVANS

PART V. Comparative Perspectives: North and South American Cinema

14. Jewish Urban Space in the Films of Daniel Burman and Woody Allen **187**
    JERRY CARLSON

15. Interfaith Relations between Jews and Gentiles in Argentine and US Cinema **204**
    NORA GLICKMAN

Afterword. Film Studies, Jewish Studies, Latin American Studies **225**
NAOMI LINDSTROM

Jewish Latin American Filmography **235**

Contributors **241**

Index **245**

INTRODUCTION
Evolving Images: Jewish Latin American Cinema

Movies often tell stories of a time, a place, and life experiences of those who belong to particular sectors of a culture. This certainly applies to Jewish characters in Latin American cinema. Although little attention has been devoted to Jewish films from Latin America, over the past few decades the growing numbers of publications on the Jewish presence in film reveal a growing interest in the subject. The present volume gathers together fifteen critical essays on films that focus on Jewish themes and characters[1] which show the rich diversity of Jewish cultures as they are manifested in Latin America.[2]

In spite of being demographically a very small minority, Latin American Jews, who count today for less than half a million people out of the total Latin American population—reaching 646 million—have always played a prominent role in the culture. As immigrants living in Catholic countries, Jews were engaged in film production from early in the twentieth century. All along they maintained a low profile and opted not to be identified with their religion or ethnicity. When silent features and classic film studios began to operate in Latin America, Jewish characters and narratives were barely represented. And yet, as Raanan Rein and Tzvi Tal point out, Jews played a pioneering role in various areas of artistic production: as directors, producers, scriptwriters, composers of music and lyrics, and radio and television broadcasters. Most of them, however, did not concentrate on Jewish subjects or situations.[3] Only after the second half of the twentieth century did Jews begin to appear more conspicuously as actors and directors, and by the end of the century Jewish Latin American characters and themes in movies became fully recognized.

While this collection does not attempt to be exhaustive, the bibliography in the appendix provides a comprehensive list of currently available films. The span from the second half of the twentieth century to the present encompasses many of the most representative and popular films available. While some were made in the United States and Spain, most of the films (both fictional and documentary) were produced in Argentina, Mexico,[4] and Brazil, the countries with the largest Jewish populations in Latin America. The films selected for this book were shown at national and international film festivals—a phenomenon which added worldwide popularity and exposure to Jewish Latin American cinema. They feature Jewish characters, traditions, and situations. The issues they address concern life in Latin America: how Jews—both real and fictional—interact among themselves as well as with other groups as active protagonists, and to what degree their ethnicity may be adulterated by adopting the combined identities of being Jewish and belonging to either their country of birth or their adoptive nation. With the exception of Daniel Burman—a prolific Argentinean creator who devotes most of his films to Jewish situations and characters—the directors discussed here, both Jewish and non-Jewish, do not work exclusively on Jewish subjects.

Identifying the main periods of film production in Argentina, César Maranghello's *Breve historia del cine argentino* (Buenos Aires: Laertes, 2005) distinguishes Juan José Jusid's *Los gauchos judíos* (*The Jewish Gauchos*, 1975), a musical on Jewish immigration into Argentina that was influenced by *Fiddler on the Roof* (dir. Norman F. Jewison, 1971), as appearing within the period of "militant cinema" (1967–1976). During the repressive years of the military dictatorship (1976–1983), many intellectuals sought exile, while those who remained in the country were subjected to a long period of self-imposed censorship that lasted until the return of democracy. The neoliberal reforms of the 1990s saw the growth of alternative modes of expression in "New Argentine Cinema." It gave rise to directors like Daniel Burman, who, in spite of the economic crisis that affected the production of films into the twenty-first century, centered his work on Jewish issues and characters.

In Mexico, first-generation Jewish immigrants were the founders of cinematography, with directors like Gregorio Wallerstein and Arturo Ripstein. Ripstein directed *O santo oficio* (*The Holy Inquisition*, 1973), a film about the Spanish Inquisition in Mexico. In the 1930s and 1940s, during the Golden Age of Mexican cinema, Jews kept a low profile out of fear of anti-Semitism. Only after World War II did they begin to take an active part in public life and in cinema production. Four decades later Guita Schyfter directed *Novia que te vea* (*Like a Bride*, 1994), an acclaimed film that exposes the dilemmas of combined ethnicities and identities. In the following decade Mexico produced two commercial features dealing with Jewish traditions: Alejandro

Springall's *Morirse está en hebreo* (*My Mexican Shivah*) in 2007 and *5 días sin Nora* (*Nora's Will*) in 2008. All three movies, covered in the articles that follow, show the promising direction in which Jewish cinema was heading.

With regard to Jewish films, Brazil's production is scarce yet significant. The experimental period in the 1960s, known as "Cinema Novo," gave recognition to Jewish directors Leon Hirzman, Jorge Bodanzky, and Silvio Tendler, and to the Argentinean Hector Babenco, who did not specialize in Jewish themes. In 1995 director Jom Tob Azulay made an ambitious film on the Inquisition and New Christians in seventeenth-century Brazil: *O Judeu* (*The Jew*), about the dramatist António José da Silva, accused of being a crypto-Jew and burned by the Portuguese Inquisition; in 2004 Jayme Monjardim directed *Olga*, about a German Jewish activist murdered by the Nazis; and in 2006 Cao Hamburger directed *O ano em que meus pais saíram de férias* (*The Year My Parents Went on Vacation*), which ostensibly deals with soccer, Brazil's national sport. This film remarkably reflects and translates in cinematic terms and images the preoccupations of Latin American Jews: the gradual loss of Jewish traditions, the dilemmas regarding Jewish identity, the threat of radical nationalism, and overriding political instability.

This book also treats the affinities between Jewish themes in North America and those in Latin America. US films exert an obvious influence on Latin American film directors; moviegoers who are exposed to Hollywood films are consequently aware of the multiplicity and conspicuousness of Jewish characters and themes produced in the United States. An obvious difference between North America and Latin America is that the United States, being a religiously freer society, welcomed the participation of Jewish directors earlier in the twentieth century. Some of them had previous experience in Europe, and many of them thrived in Hollywood. After World War I, as Jews became acculturated into American society, they strove to maintain their identity while grappling with issues of identity and self-assertion. In many ways, these film representations, which mirror the place of Jews in American society, share points of connection with Jews in South and Central America. The parallels and differences are reflected in the papers discussed in this volume.

The Essays

The titles of the five sections of this book represent the key themes discussed in the articles. The first section focuses on alternative identities, approaching them from different angles: the role of women in Jewish communities, death rites, a discussion on the very nature of "Jewish films," and how they are defined. It also provides valuable insights into questions of inclusion and representation of Jewish experiences in Latin America through photography and film. Graciela Michelotti's article effectively compares "La cámara oscura," the original short story by Angélica Gorodischer, with the film by the same name, *La cámara oscura* (*Camera Obscura*), directed by María Victoria Menis in 2008. The film interprets the protagonist's story as a reflection of the possibility of gaining visibility for those who live on the margins of society. Michelotti also offers new perspectives on fundamental issues of identity and belonging as delineated in Alberto Gerchunoff's celebrated text *Los gauchos judíos* (*The Jewish Gauchos*, 1910). Elissa Rashkin's essay on two Mexican films centers on mourning and funeral rites, in which Jewishness and difference confront each other. Based on performance theory, Rashkin's perspective views contemporary Jewish identities as an opportunity for the characters of the film to perform roles, and by so doing, to reinvent themselves in ways that keep their ethnic differences visible. This portion of the volume ends with Amy Kaminsky's article on the films of Fabián Bielinsky, offering a provocative view on how people perceive films created by Jewish filmmakers. Kaminsky builds a strong case for the place of films with subtle Jewish markers in Jewish Studies. She calls for an audience that is as open to looking for Jewish clues as it is to solve puzzling plots in action films.

The section of the book on memory and violence traces the connection among three traumatic historical moments in the lives of Argentineans: the Shoah, a Hebrew word meaning "catastrophe," denoting the destruction of European Jewry during World War II; the "Dirty War" (1976–1983) in Argentina; and international terrorism on Argentine soil. This section also offers a theoretical discussion of the link between history and memory. It opens with two articles on the films of Jeanine Meerapfel, a Jewish Argentine/German director. In the first, Daniela Goldfine works with the complexities of juxtaposing history and memory in the film *El amigo alemán* (*My German Friend*, 2012), the drama of a friendship and love affair between a Jewish German girl and her neighbor, the son of an SS officer. This relationship is framed in the historical context of the 1950s to the 1980s in Argentina. Goldfine's mnemo-historic reading of the film effectively depicts the multiple cultural and historical layers that bring Argentina, Germany, Jewishness, and Nazism to a crossroads.

Patricia Nuriel's analysis of *La amiga* (*The Girlfriend*) presents a very different aspect of Meerapfel's work. Nuriel explores the thematic connections between the human rights violations exerted by the military junta in the Argentine Dirty War and the Shoah. While this film also focuses on the friendship between a Jew and a non-Jew, the plot is centered on the irreparable social wounds that human rights violations inflicted on Argentine society. The differences between the female protagonists parallel and contextualize the horrific historical events that took place. Closing this section, Mirna Vohnsen analyzes the film *Anita*, directed by Marcos Carnevale in 2011, which features the 1994 AMIA bombing of the Buenos Aires Jewish Cultural Center as an event that affected not only the Jewish community but also the nation as a whole. The film approaches the attack from the point of view of a young woman with Down syndrome who wanders around the city after the tragedy has occurred in search of her mother, who was a victim of this act of terrorism.

In dealing with innovative themes, sports have only recently begun to attract attention in the field of Latin American cinema. Alejandro Meter's concern in his examination of Cao Hamburger's *O ano em que meus pais saíram de féiras* (*The Year My Parents Went on Vacation*, 2006) focuses on the perspective of a Brazilian child coming to terms with his Jewish identity through soccer. Carolina Rocha's essay discusses adolescence, a topic infrequently represented in Jewish Latin American studies. Her article covers two films in which teenage protagonists wrestle with the awkwardness of their adolescence and their Jewishness in a society that does not understand them. In the final part of this section, Ernesto Livon-Grosman's essay offers a unique view into a film corpus that has never been studied before in this context: home movies. Grosman centers on scenes in which Jewish elements appear in the films directed by Alberto Salomón. His films are composed of family events, clips from commercial movies, and staged home footage.

The terms "diaspora" and "displacement" in the title of the fourth section refer to films about Jewish life in the rural communities that flourished in the north of Argentina at the turn of the twentieth century, but they gradually disappeared as the second generation found better educational opportunities in urban centers. Since 1948, the term "diaspora" has also been linked to the concept of aliyah, or emigration to Israel. "Displacement" relates to the difficulties experienced by Jewish survivors from the Shoah while forging a new home in Israel, as well as the displacement of Palestinians resulting from repeated political conflicts. "Diaspora" and "displacement" serve as metaphors to describe an array of films that explore the tensions stemming from the lack of a sense of belonging that their characters experience while living abroad.

Ariana Huberman's article in this part examines documentaries about two "abandoned" communities—the resilience, the hybridity of their offspring, and their steps leading to aliyah. Her essay wrestles with issues of exoticism, fascination, and nostalgia in the portrayal of Jews from the community of Iquitos, Peru, and from various Cuban cities. Following the thematic thread of dislocation and negotiating identities, Tzvi Tal compares three films about the experiences of Israelis and Palestinians moving to Latin America, and Spain's contemporary struggles to integrate Islamic migrants. Even though *Seres queridos* (*Only Human*, 2004), a film about the encounter of a dysfunctional Jewish family and a Palestinian immigrant in Madrid, is not about Latin America, it is included because it fits within the larger cultural context of representations of Jews and Palestinians in the Spanish-speaking world.

In "From a Dream to Reality: Representations of Israel in Contemporary Jewish Latin American Film," Amalia Ran explores the changing image of Israel from an emblem of utopian aspirations and fantasy to a symbol of disillusion and despair in contemporary Latin American cinema. Ilan Stavans interprets three Mexican films from his own vantage point as a Mexican Jewish writer and critic. His essay highlights some of the complexities of the Jewish Mexican experience in navigating the Mexican film industry.

The last two essays of this book are comparative and center on the topics of urban dwelling and interfaith relations. Jerry Carlson writes about Daniel Burman's popular Ariel films set in the Once neighborhood in Buenos Aires, which still hosts an important Jewish population, in relation to three films by Woody Allen set in New York. While the former films take place in recent years, Allen's films are from the 1970s and 1980s. Carlson's choice of films enables him to dissect and compare how daily life in these two metropolitan centers marks the films' Jewish protagonists. Nora Glickman's article closes the collection with a comparative study of shifting attitudes toward interfaith relations in films from Argentina and the United States. Glickman follows the evolving reactions of successive generations of Jewish and Gentile parents and their offspring in romantic attachments, as represented in films produced between the 1960s and the present.

The essays gathered in this book provide insights into the intersections of Jewish experiences within Latin American cinema. They also offer a comparative overview of relevant themes from a selection of US films.[5] The themes addressed here are anchored in history, research, and personal experiences. They resonate with issues of location and dislocation, inclusion and exclusion, individual and communal identities, rural and urban life. Many of the topics and critical approaches raised in the articles are relevant to Latin American studies, Jewish studies, film studies, and history. The broad scope of the papers takes into consideration visual representations, discourses, technology, and constructions of identity. The films discussed here showcase the diversity and richness revealed in the languages and dialects of Yiddish, Ladino, Spanish, Portuguese, and English, spoken by immigrants, natives, and their offspring. Hopefully, this book will provide the reader with a sense of the richness and variety in the film production of Latin America.

Notes

1. See Isabel Maurer Queipo, ed., *Directory of World Cinema: Latin America* (Chicago: University of Chicago Press, 2013); Nathan Abrams, *The New Jew in Film: Exploring Jewishness and Judaism in Contemporary Cinema* (New Brunswick: Rutgers University Press, 2012); Toby Haggith and Joanna Newman, eds., *Holocaust and the Moving Image* (London: Wallflower Press, 2005); Eric S. Christianson, Peter Francis, and William T. Telford, eds., *Cinéma Divinité: Religion, Theology, and the Bible in Film* (London: SCM Press, 2005).

2. For a current and insightful history of the presence of Jews in Latin America, see Judith Laikin Elkin, *The Jews of Latin America* (Boulder: Lynne Rienner, 2014).

3. Raanan Rein and Tzvi Tal, eds., *Latin American Cinema and Television*, 1–8, in special issue of *Jewish Film and New Media* 2, no. 1 (Spring 2014).

4. For an interdisciplinary approach to Mexican Jewish cinema that includes literary criticism and history as well as cultural and comparative studies, see Catherine Bloch Heschel, "El cine de las migraciones judías de México," in *El cine en las regiones de México*, ed. Lucila Hinojosa Córdova, Eduardo de la Vega Alfaro, and Tania Ruiz Ojeda (Monterrey: Universidad Autónoma de Nuevo León, 2013).

5. In the post–World War II decades Jews and Jewish themes fully entered mainstream American cinema with films dealing with topics like anti-Semitism (*Gentleman's Agreement*, 1947; *Crossfire*, 1947); the Holocaust (*Trial at Nuremberg*, 1961); and Israel (*Exodus*, 1960). During the 1970s and 1980s the United States saw increasing numbers of Jewish-themed films and the emergence of renowned Jewish directors such as Woody Allen, Mel Brooks, and Steven Spielberg. For a comprehensive study on this subject that includes Latin American films, see Lawrence Baron, ed., *The Modern Jewish Experience in World Cinema* (Waltham: Brandeis University Press, 2011).

PART I

ALTERNATIVE IDENTITIES

CHAPTER 1

Out of the Shadows:
María Victoria Menis's *Camera Obscura*

GRACIELA MICHELOTTI

For so long so many of us have been invisible in the picture.
SUSAN CHEVLOWE, "FRAMING JEWISHNESS: PHOTOGRAPHY AND
THE BOUNDARIES OF COMMUNITY"

Jewish presence in Argentina's national culture started with Alberto Gerchunoff (1883–1950), who in 1910, as part of the centenary celebration of the beginning of the Argentine process of independence, published the first version of his canonical text, *The Jewish Gauchos*. In this collection, Gerchunoff re-creates the life experience of Jewish immigrants in the agricultural colonies of the Argentine interior, specifically in the Entre Ríos province. It has been estimated that at one point around forty thousand Jewish settlers lived in the five hundred thousand hectares that the Jewish Colonization Association had begun acquiring in 1891, the year the first settlement (Mauricio) was established. This organization was founded by the Jewish German baron Maurice de Hirsch with the intention of giving the persecuted victims of czarist Russia a place to reorganize their lives and an opportunity to return to the care of land as prescribed in biblical times.

The Jewish Gauchos fictionalizes the story of the agricultural settlers from the perspective of an early male inhabitant. The text has been praised and objected to in powerful terms by supporters and critics alike. But it is undisputed that, as Edna Aizenberg has argued, from the moment of its publication,

> so successful did the work become that it gave rise to multiple imitations, re-elaborations and movie[1] versions; it also became part of the standard and accepted rhetoric about Jews in Argentina: whenever anyone referred to Jewish life in the country, particularly to the *acceptance* of Jews, it inevitably

involved a reference to Gerchunoff and his Jewish gaucho "epic" of the possession of the new homeland.[2]

Nearly one hundred years after the publication of Alberto Gerchunoff's seminal text placing the Jewish immigrant experience in the Argentine popular imagination, María Victoria Menis's film *Camera Obscura* (Argentina, 2008) revisits the agricultural landscape created by Gerchunoff. She proposes a new (feminist) perspective from which to observe the process of finding and making recognizable the identity of individuals who feel marginalized, and their difficulties, failures, and successes in finding their place in the world.[3]

It has been argued that the return of democracy to Argentina in 1983 coincided with the emergence of a good number of Jewish characters and themes in the contemporary national cinema that were rescued from the shadows and began to populate the local screens.[4] Coincidently, in *Camera Obscura*, the Jewish female protagonist, Gertrudis, who with her family inhabits one of those colonies central to Gerchunoff's text, manages to escape the limited space of her environment through the eyes of an outsider. This character, like a camera obscura, reverses and projects her image into a new environment.[5] The process allows Gertrudis to see herself in a different manner and to step into the light. Using the setting of Gerchunoff's *The Jewish Gauchos* as a historic and cultural background, the director adapts a short story of the same title by Angélica Gorodischer (Argentina, 1928) and retells Gertrudis's intimate struggle for acceptance in a world she needs to create for herself.

In this essay I will explore different approaches to representing the Jew and will consider the role the gaze of the Other plays in defining Jewishness in contemporary times. The film director—like Jean Baptiste, the French character whose gaze encounters Gertrudis and liberates her—is not Jewish. Perhaps the evident references in Menis's film to Gerchunoff's *The Jewish Gauchos*, which is considered an "authentically Jewish" text, fulfills a need to legitimize her representation of Jews by a non-Jew. In any case, if there is a concern, the director chooses not to reflect it in the relationship of Gertrudis to Jean Baptiste.

Gertrudis, having been born in the nationless middle ground of a ship's gangplank at the moment her family arrives in the port of Buenos Aires, embodies the intermediate space where a sense of belonging and its relationship between past and future are generated. In addition, simply because of her status as a woman at the turn of the century, she is placed, according to Francine Masiello, "between civilization and barbarism."[6] Although she

Gertrudis, hiding from the camera's gaze. *La cámara oscura (Camera Obscura)* (2008), directed by María Victoria Menis.

has reached adulthood having lived her entire life as a Jewish member of an agricultural colony, her experience is that of a constant outsider, even in the midst of her own family. Her particular aesthetic sensitivities, her interests in ideas beyond the mundane shallowness of her familial milieu, and her perceived ugliness set her apart from her group.

In Gorodischer's short story, the narrator is Isaac Rosenberg, Gertrudis's grandson and the husband of a woman named Jaia. Isaac tells the half-dramatic and half-humorous account of a discussion he had with his wife after he asked her to remove from the mantelpiece an old photograph portraying his grandmother and her husband and children. Jaia had mounted the picture in a gilt frame and given it a place of honor in the house after Isaac recounted for her the story of the family's "tragedy": Isaac's otherwise industrious and devoted grandmother had left her philandering husband and her family and eloped with the photographer responsible for taking the picture.[7]

What is notable here besides Isaac's old-fashioned and stereotypical middle-class thinking (above all he praises his wife's beauty and excellent cooking skills), is his reluctance to display his family's photograph, an attitude which runs counter to the Jewish legacy of remembrance. This can perhaps be explained by Julia Hirsch's statement: "We do not like to preserve evidence that some of our family dreams failed in spite of the efforts we brought to them."[8] Gerchunoff's *The Jewish Gauchos* consists of several vignettes, organized as a sort of a family album of which each chapter could be considered an independent photograph. Gorodischer's story, however, encapsulates a denunciation of the kinds of strategies normally used to recount the past, such as the individual, communal, small, or large stories that shape the memories chosen to be preserved.

Jaia refuses to offer an explanation of why she has placed the photograph in such a prominent place in the house and adamantly refuses to take it down. She maintains that she cannot give details about her actions because her husband would be incapable of understanding her. Through Jaia, Gertrudis gains recognition as a grandmother, because her newly displayed image relocates her within the family sphere and gives her a place in the past. But Jaia's refusal to explain her action to her husband and children fails to celebrate Gertrudis's defiant act of fleeing the oppression she felt in her role of an invisible woman. The narrator, Isaac, never manages to understand why his grandmother abandoned her conventional life to follow the photographer and still considers her memory a shameful stain on the family.

Both the short story and the film highlight the tale of Gertrudis's birth in the port of Buenos Aires, on the gangplank of the ship that had transported her Jewish family from Russia in the late nineteenth century. Menis keeps the account of how Gertrudis got her name—it was suggested by the customs employee—and others' perception of Gertrudis as a particularly ugly young lady, who wears thick rimmed glasses and dresses all in black. This serves to explain why her marriage to the widower León Cohen brought great relief to her family. Cohen, a wealthy rancher from the Villa Clara colony of Entre Ríos (originally established in 1892), felt drawn to Gertrudis precisely because of her ugliness, since he thought it would guarantee obedience and servitude from his future wife. Both texts feature Gertrudis's elopement with Jean Baptiste, the French photographer. In both, he is a seasoned traveler, attractive in spite of a limp, who spends some time with the family, takes the photographs commissioned by Mr. Cohen, and, after a few days, surreptitiously leaves the house with Gertrudis. The two characters share bodies identified as different and are drawn to each other by their common interest in looking for beauty in the small elements in life; they share the condition of being outsiders. Gertrudis feels alienated within her own family, and Jean Baptiste, left physically and psychologically wounded by his war experiences, seems to be looking for a new place where he can start a new life, far now from the old Europe, but also removed from the *avant-garde* movement he tries to reclaim with his surrealistic photographs. The film never implies that Gertrudis's alienation originates in her being a Jewish woman, but it is not difficult to equate this feeling to the sense of identity misplacement also felt by a few other characters in the film (as discussed later) and many Jewish immigrants in the Diaspora.

The film illustrates the short story with details that focus on Gertrudis's perspective and enhances it with the specifics of the genesis of the family portraits. But the movie omits the glance into future generations provided by the short story: why Isaac, the grandson, continues to despise his grandmother's memory, which his wife has managed only to partially rehabilitate. Menis's film becomes a simpler and optimistic tale of the triumph of art and love over mediocrity and sexism. It presents us—curiously, without questioning—the beginning of a lovers' experience anticipated as carefree and joyful, without the communication conflicts that, two generations later, interfere in Isaac and Jaia's relationship and, more important, signal their struggle to define what constitutes a valid memory.

Given that in the film Gertrudis quietly disappears and in the short story Jaia's action only partially recovers the grandmother's valid presence within the family, the story seems to imply that through the agency of memory many women have been empowered, but many more still rebel in silence. Thus, the mystery of the family photograph continues to occupy an important place in the story in compliance with what Marianne Hirsch refers to when she states:

> Going beyond the surfaces, telling the stories surrounding the images, attempting to open the curtains, might offer a way out of the hermetic circle of familial hegemony. But the complicated configuration of gazes, looks, and images/screens exchanged within the familial makes any actual exposure impossible: family pictures, including self-portraits, will continue to resist understanding.[9]

It is this resistance and the movie's attempt to make it a pivotal part of how the story is told that make Menis's film especially poignant. Many feelings are left unexplained while the simple language used in the movie is artfully replaced by moving images of Gertrudis's fantasies and the reproduction of Jean Baptiste's creative surrealistic photographs. These images produce mysterious spaces that invite the viewer to participate actively in the selection of multiple, poetic meanings.

The first and last scenes in the film show an untidy dinner table with leftovers that Gertrudis has not picked up, as was her custom. The camera pans slowly over the scene and stops at the six family pictures taken only a few hours prior. These show the group in a harmonious and peaceful setting that contradicts the sense of surprise and distress experienced by Gertrudis's oldest son, who in both scenes calls three times for his mother without obtaining any response. By the end of the film, as the same scene is repeated, the audience knows the details of Gertrudis's story and understands the sense of liberation she must have felt under the gaze of Jean Baptiste, somebody who could look beyond the surface of her alleged ugliness and the unworthiness of her housewife's role. The same pictures, repeated at the beginning and end of the film, certainly tell two very different stories illustrating the point made by Julia Hirsch: "Family photographs themselves do not change, only the stories we tell about them do."[10]

The film is enriched with the presentation of Gertrudis's experience from her perspective. We feel her sense of marginality, imposed primarily by her appearance and by the patriarchal society to which she belongs. We see, for example, what she observes when she looks at her shoes at the dance where her family is offering to present its daughters to prospective marriage candidates and when she covers her face during the family portrait photo session, as her mother, who does not hide her rejection of her ugly daughter, had instructed her.[11]

The final vanishing act is anticipated in various disappearances in which Gertrudis tests her defiant attitude. She becomes voluntarily invisible to her family by obsessively devoting herself to domestic work to the point that she is missing from her own wedding party: while her husband celebrates with other community members she starts cleaning the house. Since childhood, she has enacted small personal gestures of rebellion that have helped her to take the position of an active agent against her alienation. Such gestures are related to her absence, her invisibility, as illustrated in the photographs of her past: as a child, she hides her face behind a doll in a family portrait, shifts and hides in a school photo so that she appears blurred, and looks in the opposite direction in the group photo of a party of young people, breaking the hieratic aesthetic that is standard in such pictures. As an adult she stands in the background, partially hidden behind her husband in the family portrait he has commissioned to Jean Baptiste. With her disappearance from these pictures, Gertrudis repeats the invisibility she was assigned by her family, but in actively doing so she rejects it and subverts it.

By refusing to pose submissively in those formal pictures, Gertrudis also rejects the traditional role of passive victim conventionally imposed on Jews and on women. Her actions insinuate that certain silences and absences are alternative strategies for telling one's story. The story only needs an empathetic audience to become visible and occupy central stage. The difference between her childhood gestures and that of the adult Gertrudis is that the latter has been observed by the photographer, who acts as a sympathetic witness of her marginality: "I know very well what it is not wanting to be in any picture," he tells her. Although the audience will never know for certain the story surrounding this statement, at this moment a shared secret seems to bring Gertrudis and the photographer closer together. His limp—caused by wounds sustained during World War I (Turkey, 1915), in which he was a war correspondent for four years—begins to mark him as an "outsider" like Gertrudis. The war experience has also left his spirit scarred and has trained him, having faced the horrors of the battlefield, to find hidden beauty in little things: "You have to show what you see hidden through dreams and fantasies," he says. His otherness is also a result of his foreignness (originally from Marseilles, he has been in Argentina for only nine months). This gives him a sophistication and modernity that even León Cohen appreciates, and it produces a sharp contrast with the simple and pragmatic environment of the Argentine countryside where Gertrudis and her family reside. The gaze of the Other that identifies with the protagonist's struggle is all that is needed to facilitate the emergence of the marginalized into the light. As a camera obscura, this gaze reverses conventional images and offers another perspective of the familiar.

As mentioned above, in order to illustrate the special attraction to a particular form of aesthetic expression that Jean Baptiste and Gertrudis share, Menis includes animated images of a child resembling Gertrudis moving through a dark forest that progressively becomes a colorful garden. These images give the film a distinct originality. They play out fantasies of escape into a flowery imaginary world from when Gertrudis is still a young girl and also recall the flower arrangements she prepares for the table of the family home and her attention to the flowers in her garden. For Jean Baptiste, his artistic photographs—certainly different from the "realistic" family portraits that help him make a living and the authentic archival war pictures—intertwined with other still photographs, show his creative and pioneering spirit. Interestingly, we first see Gertrudis as a child playing with the projection of her fantasies in a wooden outhouse. This intimate space foretells the other wooden room where Jean Baptiste develops his photographs, also bringing them into full light from the shadows of their negatives. At a particular moment this room becomes a camera obscura that filters and projects on its walls Gertrudis's reversed image for Jean Baptiste, who begins to feel attracted to this quiet and sensitive woman. The images remind the viewer that the gaze is always being filtered, and its exposure constructed, by photography, by movies, and by art in general. They invite the audience to bring into play other ways of seeing.

It is this ability to play with the camera obscura, to see what is not always seen, to determine—as the photographer repeats on several occasions that "things are not what they seem"—that allows Jean Baptiste to recognize in Gertrudis a beauty that goes beyond the surface. And that is what finally frees Gertrudis from the oppression of those looks that have deemed her ugly. The photographer's camera also gives her the opportunity to look through its lens and create her own images of the world, for at the end of the film we see photos taken by her, reversing the agency of the gaze, which had previously been only in the possession of her family and the photographer.

The schoolteacher and her father are the other characters who shyly perceive and appreciate Gertrudis's sensitive personality. But they are portrayed as weak individuals whose spirits are crushed by the presence of unruly students and a dominant wife, respectively. It is interesting to note the scene where the schoolteacher asks Gertrudis, with a heavy Yiddish accent, to explain God's manifested presence in the world. He asserts that this manifestation equals God's appearance to Moses and "our people in the Red Sea" and reminds his students that "we must learn to see." The scene combines the religious sphere with the concept of national historical identity as announced by the patriotic date, "1810–25 de Mayo," prominently written on the blackboard. The effect equals that of Gerchunoff's text in blending referents to the two aspects of Jewish immigrant character, their traditional religious identity and the newly acquired national one, into a new, integrated community.

In the film *Camera Obscura*, the reference to the establishment of agricultural colonies of Jewish immigrants does not bring up a questioning of how to keep the minority group's identity in a new world where: "the young people are turning into Gauchos."[12] Menis's film shows us only the inner, intimate, and personal fissures of that community, rejected by one of its members who never felt accepted and integrated.

If Gerchunoff's text aims to present a society willing to accept without prejudice the Jewish immigrant as an actively involved and recognized member of the new society, León Cohen's character is an exaggeration of this image. Gertrudis's husband is shown as a master of a world without cracks. His experience is as foreign to Gerchunoff's characters as those who reported in the Yiddish texts of the time that a trip to the pampas was "an expedition to hell."[13] León Cohen, in 1929 already a settled farmer, has a privileged economic position. With the exception of having been married to a first wife with a difficult character—"such a cute girl . . . but with such a reputation"—who had the courtesy of leaving him a widower at a relatively young age, he has no other problems.[14] He speaks Spanish without a foreign accent, as he had come to Argentina at the age of five and remembers nothing about his previous life in Europe as, one of his daughters explains: "The [paternal] grandparents never told him anything about Russia." He is a kind of feudal lord, accompanied only by his children and faithful laborers, who are meekly thankful for his good disposition: "Some *criollos* like to talk ill of the Jews, but they are very good people. We have even sat with them at the table,"[15] says a young assistant to Jean Baptiste.

Only the grave figure of Gertrudis's father connotes very slyly the vicissitudes of an immigrant not too happy in his new environment. Gertrudis mentions that, although her father was thankful to Argentina because it enabled his family to escape the deadly pogroms, he always remembered his native Russia longingly. In Russia he had been a tailor but in Argentina "as a farmer [he] was a disaster,"[16] says Cohen dismissively. However, in the film his sadness seems to come more from his submissive position in relation to a strong-willed wife than from his circumstance as an urban Jewish immigrant struggling to find his place in the new agricultural diaspora, as many others had managed to do. The film focuses more on personal conflict than on social conflict.

Cohen is an agricultural settler who stayed in the countryside, one who became a well-established landowner.[17] One photo with his sons standing against a cattle gate points precisely to the triumph of a "civilizing" project that managed to place limits on the barbarism of an open pampa without barriers. As a result, he becomes a symbol of the success of the immigration experiment organized nationwide. However, it is important to note that other circumstances of his historical context seem not to concern him. There are, for example, no allusions to the events of 1919, when Jews were savagely attacked by mobs in Buenos Aires.[18] This was ten years before the date of the events taking place in the film, but the scene of his wife reading poems by her contemporary Alfonsina Storni (Argentina, 1892–1938) is meant to indicate they are not completely isolated from the cultural milieu of the nation's capital.

Unlike Gerchunoff's text, the film presents only minimal hints at the presence of other members of the Jewish community of the historical Villa Clara settlement. There is no mention of the agricultural cooperative economy that characterized these communities. Cohen's economic success seems to be the product only of his own work, as Gertrudis's father's problems are solely his own.

Still, there are concordances with Gerchunoff's text that are worth noticing. For example, while Gertrudis and Jean Baptiste prepare their escape, Cohen is engaged in his ritual prayers. The scene points, somewhat ironically, to Gerchunoff's vignette titled "The Silver Candelabra," in which the very religious Guedalí allows himself to be robbed of the pricey object because he cannot interrupt his prayers on the Sabbath.[19]

Also, Gertrudis, as protagonist, reminds us of some of the female characters in *The Jewish Gauchos*. There is an ugly woman, Doña María, "who was in fact a little monster,"[20] and two young ladies who elope with their boyfriends. Raquel and Gabriel flee during her wedding ceremony to Pascual, the wealthy groom chosen by their parents, and Rogelio Míguez and Myriam run off because he is not Jewish and her parents would not consent to such a union. Moreover, in "The Sad Woman of the Place," graceful Jeved, sought by many suitors, falls for Lázaros, a quiet and limping musician.[21] Other characters share similarities with Jean Baptiste. For example, Nahum Yarcho, the doctor of "miracle cures,"[22] with his Epicurean outlook is, as the photographer, a removed observer of the life of the colony and the family. At one point he says to a patient: "Madam, you must look at the clouds. Believe me it is very good for the [sic] health,"[23] revealing a lyrical and creative element in himself that signals an inclination to look beyond the surface; this trait is common to both characters. In addition, the fantastic elements in Gerchunoff's stories "The Owl" and "The Witches" are echoed in Gertrudis's childhood fantasies about the Queen of Flowers. The correlations between *The Jewish Gauchos* and *Camera Obscura* become especially strong where lyric elements are used to help transform a specific geographical and social location into an oversimplified bucolic landscape.

There are no similarities, however, between female characters, as evidenced when Gertrudis's individuality is contrasted to Gerchunoff's generalizations about female characters. For example, he writes, "Raquel, I see the majestic women of ancient Scriptures in you! In the peace of the Argentine plain you suggest Biblical heroines. . . . Raquel, you are Ester, Rebecca, Deborah or Judith,"[24] identifying a category of "Jewish woman" that somehow covers all. This takes us back to Gorodischer's short story and its feminist agenda as set forth in the film. On one hand it has been shown that elements of the representation of the Jew have not changed much since 1910, for the 2008 movie repeats many of the founding story's clichés. On the other hand, the feminist theme, perhaps in a simple and triumphalist mode, attempts to establish important links between Gertrudis, a woman with a very Argentine name (as the immigration officer points out), and all other women who might still be struggling to be accepted for what they are. In this way the film establishes a strong connection between the protagonist and the general public. By integrating a Jewish character into a feminist discourse, and removing her from her family and her people, the film situates her within the common feminists concerns of any other Argentine woman, regardless of her origins. Still, Gertrudis is a woman who joins in the aesthetic pleasures shared with her father, who is aware of the conflict in his need to belong and his longing to retain memories of the past. Her father appreciates the possibility of looking for God's manifestation in the real world, as the schoolteacher had encouraged.

Family photos, as Julia Hirsch points out, are contextualized according to the stories people tell around and about them. Gerchunoff's text consists of a series of vignettes, organized as a sort of family album, in which each chapter could be considered an independent photograph. More than a century ago, "the photographer" Alberto Gerchunoff took a different set of pictures and told other stories about the lives of Jews in the Argentine countryside. Gertrudis exits the shadows of the family portrait to tell a personal story her family would have liked to erase. For Gertrudis, while it's important to remember her origins, as her father has taught her, it is also essential to be aware that, even within documented memories and family photographs, there are hidden truths—and their strengths and value come from how they are told. Such truths must be revealed, and Gertrudis refuses to be a passive subject of narratives imposed by the hegemonic nature of the genre of the family portrait and by family memories. Instead she questions them, ultimately generating new and personal images that tell the stories that have never been told. The fact that Gertrudis achieves this through her encounter with a similar Other puts emphasis on the relevance of the shared human experience among women, and among Jews and Gentiles.

Notes

1. Author's note: This movie is *Los gauchos judíos* (1975; dir. Juan José Jusid), a sugary adaptation of Gerchunoff's text that is considered a classic Argentinean film.
2. Aizenberg, *Patricide on the Pampa*, 146.
3. María Victoria Menis's previous film, *El cielito* (Todo Cine, Argentina, 2004), although in a more realistic and violent tone, also presents a marginalized character, a poor young man from the provinces who encounters a tragic end on the streets of Buenos Aires.
4. Tal, "Terror, etnicidad y la imagen del judío en el cine argentino contemporáneo."
5. The DVD cover of the film advertises the movie by saying: "One day you are looked at as never before [Un día te miran como nunca te habían mirado]" (my translation).
6. Masiello, *Between Civilization and Barbarism*, 9.
7. In contrast, in María Luisa Bemberg's film *Momentos* (1981), which covers the subject of infidelity within marriage and was produced during the last years of the dictatorship, the protagonist returns to her husband after having an affair.
8. Hirsch, *Family Frames*, 13.
9. Ibid., 107.
10. Ibid., 5.
11. The rejection of her daughter's body by Gertrudis's mother reminds viewers of Doña Leonor, Carlota's mother in María Luisa Bemberg's film *De eso no se habla* (*I Don't Want to Talk about It*) (1993). Both mothers play the role of the repressor, which is characteristic of patriarchal societies. Here the protagonist also abandons her family to escape with an itinerant circus at the end of the film. In this moment the camera focuses on Carlota's perspective and the audience sees what she sees.
12. Gerchunoff, *Jewish Gauchos of the Pampas*, 46.

13. Stavans, "Yiddish South of the Border," 144.

14. Ironically, after abandoning León and her family, Gertrudis also acquires a "bad reputation."

15. In Jusid's movie a scene shows the peons having lunch in the kitchen with their Jewish employers, making this a token of integration and elimination of class distinctions.

16. Note the pun in Spanish: "Habrá sido un buen sastre allá, lo que es aquí, como campesino, era un desastre."

17. Brailovsky, "Las colonias agrícolas," 33.

18. "La semana trágica," Buenos Aires, January 1919: a violent repression of workers' protests organized by the Argentine Patriotic League. Its members targeted the Jewish population of Buenos Aires, whom they considered representatives of "foreign" forces.

19. Gerchunoff, *The Jewish Gauchos of the Pampas*, 147–149.

20. Ibid., 138.

21. Ibid., 25.

22. Ibid., 140.

23. Ibid., 137.

24. Ibid., 30.

Works Cited

Films

Bemberg, María Luisa, dir. *Momentos*. GEA Producciones. 1981.

———, dir. *De eso no se habla*. Aura Film-Mojame S.A. Oscar Kramer S.A. 1993.

Jusid, Juan José, dir. *Los gauchos judíos*. Film Cuatro. 1975.

Menis, María Victoria, dir. *La cámara oscura*. Sophie Dulac Productions, Todo Cine S.A. 2008.

———, dir. *El cielito*. Primer Plano Film Group. 2004.

Articles and Books

Aizenberg, Edna. *The Aleph Weaver: Biblical, Kabbalistic, and Judaic Elements in Borges*. Potomac, MD: Scripta Humanistica, 1984. [As cited in Edna Aizenberg, "Patricide on the Pampa: Deconstructing Gerchunoff and His Jewish Gauchos." *Essays on Foreign Languages and Literatures* 17 (1987): 24–29.]

Brailovsky, Antonio Elio. "Las colonias agrícolas y el encuentro con la utopía en Argentina." In *El imaginario judío en la literatura de América Latina: Visión y realidad: Relatos, ensayos, memorias y otros textos del Tercer Encuentro de Escritores Judíos Latinoamericanos*. San Pablo: Agosto, 1990.

Chevlowe, Susan. "Framing Jewishness: Photography and the Boundaries of Community." In *The Jewish Identity Project: New American Photography*, ed. Susan Chevlowe, 1–26. New York: Jewish Museum, 2005.

Gerchunoff, Alberto. *The Jewish Gauchos of the Pampas*. Repr. Albuquerque: University of New Mexico Press, 1983.

Gorodischer, Angélica. *La cámara oscura*. Buenos Aires: Emecé, 2009.

Hirsch, Julia. *Family Photographs: Content, Meaning, and Effect.* Oxford: Oxford University Press, 1981.
Hirsch, Marianne. *Family Frames: Photography, Narrative, and Postmemory.* Cambridge, MA: Harvard University Press, 1997.
Masiello, Francine. *Between Civilization and Barbarism: Women, Nation, and Literary Culture in Modern Argentina.* Lincoln: University of Nebraska Press, 1992.
Stavans, Ilan. "Yiddish South of the Border." In *Singer's Typewriter and Mine: Reflections on Jewish Culture*, 142–145. Lincoln: University of Nebraska Press, 2012.
Tal, Tzvi. "Terror, etnicidad y la imagen del judío en el cine argentino contemporáneo." nuevomundo.revues.org/58355?lang=en.

CHAPTER 2

Intercultural Dilemmas: Performing Jewish Identities in Contemporary Mexican Cinema

ELISSA J. RASHKIN

In his 2015 article "Judíos, indios y el mito del crimen ritual," Misgav Har-Paled shows that negative social representations of Jews came to the Americas with the Conquest, where they played a key role in determining how the European Catholic colonizers imagined indigenous populations. Myths of human sacrifice and cannibalism used in Europe to justify the persecution of Jews were reinvigorated in New Spain, where the enslavement of natives was viewed as a just punishment for supposed savagery (128). Some writers went so far as to suggest that the similarity between the words "judíos" and "indios" indicated a direct link: Amerindian peoples were descendants of Israel, and therefore deserved to suffer for the killing of Christ as much as their European Jewish relatives (127–128). In the colonial Catholic imagination, distinct forms of cultural difference fused into one grotesque Other, whose phantasmagorical, malignant nature served to justify domination.

While seemingly archaic, the paradigm of violent, self-serving intolerance toward nondominant cultural identities described by Har-Paled continues to inform social relations in Mexico today, insofar as indigenous citizens continue to be marginalized, abused, and frequently blamed for the very conditions of poverty and marginality that the colonial system of caste stratification created and perpetuated long after Independence and the revolutions and reforms of the modern era. It is more difficult, however, to judge how the sixteenth-century "black legend" may or may not haunt contemporary Jewish experience. To be sure, Mexico continues to be seen as a Catholic country, its national identity synonymous with the worship of the Virgin of Guadalupe; yet nineteenth- and twentieth-century anticlericalism, educational reform, the increasing presence of non-Catholic Christian denominations, and other historical factors have served to displace the overt anti-Semitism of the Inquisition and legitimize religious diversity.[1]

Contemporary media such as *Diario Judío* attest to the vibrancy of Mexican Jewish life and highlight Jewish achievers, including figures from the film world such as producer Alfredo Ripstein. Moreover, Mexico City's International Festival of Jewish Film celebrated its thirteenth year in 2016 and consistently attracts audiences beyond the Jewish community, reflecting a tendency to project Jewish culture beyond its traditional institutions. A historic downtown synagogue, for instance, has become a cultural center whose installations are not restricted to explicitly Jewish content. The acclaimed Museo Tolerancia y Memoria serves as a reminder of past atrocities—the Holocaust among others—even as it attempts to educate in favor of pluralism.

On the museum's website, a section on "El otro y yo" (The other and I) reads in part: "Debemos ser capaces de reconocer que lo que nos hace iguales es que todos somos diferentes, esta variedad enriquece nuestros conocimientos y nuestra sensibilidad [We should be capable of recognizing that what makes us equals is that we are all different, this variety enriches our knowledge and our sensitivity]."[2] That there is a perceived need for such statements in today's social environment suggests that the notion of diversity as enrichment has yet to be naturalized in the contemporary psyche; however, in contrast to the virulent racism that members of the urban ruling classes have expressed toward rural indigenous Mexicans,[3] the prevalent attitude toward the Jewish minority would seem to be less one of recognition of *difference*, whether positive or negative, than one of occasionally puzzled *indifference*.[4]

Are twenty-first-century Jews "different" from other Mexicans? What might constitute Jewish identity in an era of cultural fragmentation and dissolution, and how is this identity, or "difference," viewed by non-Jewish Mexicans, as well as by Mexican Jews themselves? The present chapter explores these questions through two films made in the first decade of the current century: *Morirse está en hebreo* (*My Mexican Shivah*, 2007) and *Cinco días sin Nora* (*Nora's Will*, 2008). Both films center on death (surreptitiously reversing, perhaps, the "black legend" of Jewish murderousness through the tragicomic depiction of mourning and funeral rites), and both constitute cultural performances in which "Jewishness" is invoked, emphasized, and acted out in juxtaposition to its absence or otherness. Drawing on performance theory as an analytical framework, I propose that these films represent intercultural dilemmas, confronting *indifference* and *difference* in an attempt to salvage historical identities threatened by postmodern forms of invisibilization.

Identity and Intelligibility

Judith Butler, in *Gender Trouble: Feminism and the Subversion of Identity*, asks, "To what extent is 'identity' a normative ideal rather than a descriptive feature of practice?" (16), and posits the existence of a "matrix of intelligibility" through which identities are culturally recognized and legitimized, or conversely, rendered invisible and unspeakable, thus inexistent (17). While Butler's work refers primordially to gender and sexuality, her questioning of the existence of fixed identities before or outside of the processes by which they are produced is relevant to other situations in which the boundaries between "I" and "Other" delimit relationships of power and domination: "Clearly, the substantive 'I' only appears as such through a signifying practice that seeks to conceal its own workings and to naturalize its effects" (144). The films studied here are, I argue, part of a "signifying practice" that seeks to make visible Jewish difference—in the positive sense recommended by the Museo Tolerancia y Memoria—even as the conventions of narrative cinema work to conceal the numerous ways in which that difference is produced in and by processes of representation, including those of the films themselves.

That the two films considered here center on death and funeral rites is not a casual circumstance; as Joseph Roach points out, "In any funeral, the body of the deceased performs the limits of the community called into being by the need to mark its passing."[5] The notion of "community" is recreated in the rite itself as a performative action, yet as this "community" is not a preexisting fact but rather the result of a socially motivated invocation, it is subject to reinvention as well as contradiction. Roach, continuing his analysis, writes, "That is why performances in general and funerals in particular are so rich in revealing contradictions: because they make publicly visible through symbolic action both the tangible existence of social boundaries and, at the same time, the contingency of those boundaries on fictions of identity, their shoddy construction out of inchoate otherness, and, consequently, their anxiety-inducing instability" (39).

As we shall see, each of the deceased central figures in *Morirse está en hebreo* and *Cinco días sin Nora* has a privileged relationship to performance: in the former, Moishe is a member of a theater troupe, and in the latter, Nora scripts not only her own death but also the events that follow from it. The process that Roach calls *surrogation*, referring to the futile yet transformative attempt to fill the void left by the deceased through memory, forgetting, and substitution (2), comes to the fore as a way of reflecting on Jewish identity in twenty-first-century Mexico: a set of stories to be told and also, through the medium of commercial cinema, a conscious performance for outsiders.

Specters of Jews Past

Morirse está en hebreo, directed by Alejandro Springall and written by Jorge Goldenberg from a story by Ilan Stavans, was released in English as *My Mexican Shivah*. This translation highlights its easy fit into the subgenre of ethnic drama-comedies such as *My Big Fat Greek Wedding* (dir. Joel Zwick, 2002) and others centered on family conflicts and reconciliations as well as the display of ethnicity in ritual settings such as weddings or, as in this case, funerals.[6] Like Springall's previous feature, *Santitos* (1999), the film exhibits a fascination with popular religious traditions that, in this case, include not only folk Catholicism but also manifestations of contemporary Judaism, whose incorporation implies intercultural reconciliation, however partial, within a postmodern and multicultural society.

Bypassing many central plot elements, my interest in this film lies in its display of processes of identity construction, especially as these unfold during key intercultural encounters. From its opening moments, *Morirse está en hebreo* situates itself in the realm of performance: the initial scene takes place in a theater, where Moishe Szelewiansky (Sergio Kleiner), prominent cultural figure and Ashkenazi community leader, and friends are celebrating the fiftieth anniversary of their theater company, Di Maske. While the group dances to a mariachi ensemble playing Jewish music, the otherwise empty audience space is occupied by Aleph (Enrique Cimet) and Bet (Max Kerlow), rabbinical spirit figures in Chassidic dress, who, after Moishe's sudden death during these same festivities, will follow the proceedings closely, attempting to determine whether the deceased will be accompanied in his journey by the angels of light or those of darkness. These internal, spectral spectators function in the narrative as a Greek chorus, offering commentary, yet they also sit in judgment not only over Moishe's moral worth but also over the competing notions of Jewishness that the film brings into play. These figures, and the association with theater, underscore that the film is less an "objective" depiction of Jewish cultural identities than a participant in their production, a performative discourse associated via drama and humor with cultural masquerade.

As the news of Moishe's death circulates, the characters move into ritual time, with its attendant ceremonies. Discomfort caused by Moishe's known relationship with a non-Jewish woman (Blanca Guerra) is the first of numerous awkward elements and situations. The wearing, or not, of ritual garments is clearly a part of the performance; humor is generated by the enthusiasm of the paid *chevreman* (Lenny Zundel) as he works to exchange guests' flamboyant shoes for mourner's slippers, by the donning of yarmulkes by Gentiles such as security guard Sargeant Antúnez (Gustavo Sánchez Parra) and the mariachi musicians, and by the *chevreman*'s sarcastic response to the information that Moishe probably didn't own a *tallit*: "So what did he use for praying, a serape?"[7]

Like gender transvestism, the use of these garments suggests that Jewishness, to be visible, must be externalized and therefore converted into costume; yet this process implies mishaps and exaggerations. When Moishe's grandson Nicolas (Emilio Savinni) arrives in Orthodox dress, his new look is viewed with suspicion, and his cousin Galia (Sharon Zundel) jokes about whether he still takes a toke now and then, "or can't you get weed in Israel?" Her disbelief is borne out later, when Nicolas is arrested on drug-related crimes and we learn that his migration to Israel, arranged by Moishe, was not a matter of faith but rather of escape from the law. In Nicolas's case, outward orthodoxy would seem to be a cover, thus false; yet in jail, when a fellow inmate demands his blessing for a dying prisoner and he explains that he can only offer words in Hebrew, the prayer in what the prisoner calls "the language in which God spoke to Christ" provides for a moment of transcultural identification.

Points of identification and dissonance between popular Catholic and Jewish practices are a main theme in both *Morirse está en hebreo* and *Cinco días sin Nora*. Representing Catholic practice in Springall's film are the two domestic workers, Nati (Rosa María Hernández) and Trini (Vicky de Fuentes). Doña Nati takes pride in her familiarity with the shivah rules, yet quietly and out of view of her employers, she maintains a parallel ritual practice; an early scene shows her praying for Moishe's soul at an eclectic home altar, an intimate rite intercut with the collective prayer in Hebrew carried out in the main space of the shivah. Trini, new to Jewish ritual, bursts in to share the revelation that "they"—the Jews—also say "amen": "Qué padre, ¿no? [Cool, huh?]."

Apart from this discovery, little about the shivah makes sense to Trini.

Conflict comes to a head when Esther (Moishe's daughter, played by Raquel Pankowsky) visits the kitchen and finds Trini mixing dairy and meat on the serving tray. Esther flies into a rage and, yelling that mixing the two is a grave sin, dumps the food into the garbage. Trini, shocked, boldly counters that throwing away food is also a sin. Esther replies that, in the end, everything ends up being a sin, while the *chevreman* offers to resolve the situation by ordering from "Kosher Specialties," a delivery service whose color-coded trays are unappetizing yet unambiguously correct for the occasion.

According to data from the Comité Central Israelita de México, the majority of Mexican Jews belong to the country's upper income brackets.[8] The Szelewiansky family is no exception, and thus Trini's critique acquires an ethical dimension that goes beyond the clash between cultural practices: in a country where millions live below the poverty level, does keeping kosher justify the wanton waste of food? Between the intense moments of interaction among the characters, the camera keeps us attentive to the ritual of shivah using wide shots of the apartment-as-stage, and in most of these scenes characters can be seen eating. Food is abundant, if no more so than at a Catholic wake; in any case, although the film does not develop the argument, Trini's anger at the seemingly arbitrary disposal of food, followed by Esther's biting suggestion regarding the inevitability of sin, reflects the difficulty of maintaining traditional ethical stances in a multidimensional, intercultural environment.

Another dissonant encounter occurs when "the widow Wolf" (Margo Wagner), a member of Di Maske, arrives on the third day of the shivah with a guest, the engineer Herman Neuburger. Proud of her acquisition, Wolf introduces him as "brilliant . . . too bad you all don't speak German." The scene is blatantly comic; the engineer is so tall that his head stretches out of the frame except when he bends down to greet the other guests, and Rosa, puzzled, asks if he is Jewish, to which the widow replies, "Yes, but a category of Jew that we rarely see around here." Neuburger's supposed superiority is challenged when Trini leaves the room and an eyeline match shows us the visitor following her derrière with his gaze. Upon noticing his interest, his host remarks in German: "The girl is an absolute Diego Rivera, don't you think?" The phrase invokes the long-standing association of indigenous Mexicans with colorful folkloric and artistic traditions in the dominant social imagination, even as they are marginalized and excluded from full citizenship on practical and political levels. Here Trini, who has been put upon to serve the guests in proper kosher style with little attention paid to her opinions, is dehumanized as an exotic object of contemplation.

Later that night, an oneiric scene shows Doña Nati amid the shadows, cleansing the house with incense and herbs. The rabbinical spirits look on without comment, while she is indifferent to their presence. The performance of this ritual without the knowledge of the apartment's occupants or the shivah guests suggests a subterranean current of resistance and at the same time an intercultural convergence, in that two mutually exclusive spiritual traditions are brought into play in the service of the same goal: Moishe's transition to the afterlife. Indeed, it is clear that Moishe, in life and in death, is at the center of an eclectic cast of Jewish and Gentile personalities, from orthodox to New Age, from elite professionals and their gossipy wives to a fervent Communist, mariachi musicians, and others. Their link to the deceased, however ambivalent, allows them to rise above the personal and social differences that otherwise push them apart.

By the end of the film, the experience of mourning has seemingly transcended the specificity of Jewish ritual (and its multiple violations during the shivah), allowing the audience to celebrate diversity and, at the same time, elide any potential discomfort caused by the history of forced and voluntary separatism: or as the director commented in an *El Universal* interview with César Huerta, regarding public response to the film: "Donde se ha presentado . . ., el público dice: 'Oye, pero si tus judíos son bien mexicanos' [Wherever it's been shown, the public says, 'Hey, your Jews are totally Mexican']." In this sense, the film constructs its spectatorial relationship to the Other first by highlighting difference and then by appealing to sentiments of universality, thus incorporating Mexican Jews into an easily accepted matrix of intelligibility.

Scripts in Collision

Richard Schechner, in his pioneering work on performance as "restored behavior," considers that performative acts are those that follow a predetermined sequence that is reinvented, or "restored," via its (re)enactment in new contexts.[9] The same processes operate in a theatrical script, a civic or religious rite, and many other events in which individuals assume their roles in a situation whose repetition ("twice-behaved behavior") implies the production of an identity that is "transindividual," that is, generated as an effect of the performance (36–37). At the same time, one performance is never identical to another: a circumstance that allows for ruptures, fissures, and interventions on the part of participants, spectators, and other actors.

As we have seen, *Morirse está en hebreo* depicts a performance—shivah—whose script comes from Jewish tradition yet whose contours are developed by the idiosyncrasies of the individuals involved, forcing the viewer to recognize the diversity of perspectives and the discrepancies put into play by the repetition of this ritual in a postmodern, intercultural context. In *Cinco días sin Nora*, written and directed by Mariana Chenillo as a semi-autobiographical first feature, what is shown is not the attempt to perform a traditional script that may or may not be suited to contemporary circumstances, but rather the disruption of the script via various gestures of disidentification that begin with Nora's suicide and continue in the acts of conformity and resistance performed by members of her family and community as they attempt to cope with her death in both existential and practical terms.

The format of the two films is similar in its episodic division; in the case of *Cinco días*, however, the time frame is not the ritual time of shivah, but rather an imposition caused by the convergence of numerous prohibitions. Because her death occurs just before the onset of Pesach, the burial must be postponed for two days (even though Jewish law states that burial must take place within twenty-four hours), and the fact that the following day is Shabbat adds another day to the wait. The fact of suicide further complicates the issue, but the delay sets the stage for a kind of reverse shivah in which the script scrupulously drawn up by Nora (Silvia Mariscal) and the resistance presented by her ex-husband, José (Fernando Luján), clash with other scripts imposed by figures such as Rabbi Jacowitz (Max Kerlow), who underlines the performative element from the outset through actions such as handing José a printed questionnaire about the deceased in order to be able to provide a more authentic and "moving" homily at her burial. Even as the recalcitrant José and others display conflicting interpretations of Jewishness, the presence of non-Jewish domestic staff again figures prominently as a strategy for performing cultural difference and dissent.

The relevant figure in this case is Fabiana (Angelina Peláez), Nora's cook and former nana to Rubén (Ari Brickman), Nora and José's son, now an adult married to the daughter of a prominent Ashkenazi community leader. The cultural battle over Nora's corpse ensues between the specter of the absent in-laws, whose public visibility (more than faith on the part of any particular family member) mandates "correct" handling of the burial, and Fabiana, whose personal loyalty to Nora motivates her to follow a script appropriate to "one of her own": placing a rosary around Nora's neck and making her up for burial in defiance of the Jewish prohibition on such adornments. Fabiana is also charged with preparing Nora's Passover dishes, her "last wish" according to the cook; yet in spite of Nora's directions, Fabiana also alters the recipes to incorporate flavors from her home village.

Fabiana (Angelina Peláez) and Moisés (Enrique Arreola) find common interests in cooking. *Cinco días sin Nora* (*Nora's Will*) (2008), directed by Mariana Chenillo.

Interestingly, this cultural hybridity brings together Fabiana and Moisés (Enrique Arreola), a young Jew sent by Jacowitz to pray and also keep watch over the proceedings. While seemingly a holier-than-thou agent of the meddlesome rabbi, Moisés turns out to be a liminal figure, converted to Judaism at age eighteen for reasons that remain unstated, in defiance of his now-estranged Catholic family. Fabiana's dishes call up distant memories as well as his own love of cooking, and the two characters turn out to be from neighboring villages rather than different worlds.

While these characters enact competing scripts out of allegiance to their personal faith and/or ideologies, José attempts to thwart Nora's pre-scripting of her own funeral by sabotaging both her directives (switching the Post-it notes on the plastic containers of food in the refrigerator) and, as if in passing, Jewish mortuary tradition. Realizing that the burial has to take place before the onset of Pesach or wait for days, he contacts a Catholic cemetery, which offers a "wake to go"; soon, cemetery employees arrive with a shiny polished coffin (in contrast to the plain wooden box in which Nora will be buried at the film's end), enormous floral arrangements, including one in the shape of a cross, equally large candlesticks, and an air conditioner to maintain the apartment's temperature during the wake.

Although this plan is quickly canceled, José continues to take delight in sabotaging Nora's posthumous Passover plans and the edicts of Rabbi Jacowitz, notoriously ordering a pizza with ham, bacon, and chorizo, and inviting the rabbi to this scandalous repast. In conversation with Moisés, he declares that "all religions are about the same thing: manipulation and money," and that God doesn't exist. Jacowitz's hypocrisy would seem to justify José's rebellion, even though it is clear that his complex feelings toward Nora (especially the discovery of a long-ago infidelity) constitute the deeper motivation for his intransigence. In the end, when hope of a Jewish burial for Nora is almost extinguished, it is José who reinvents tradition in order to close the circle, giving up his own family burial plot in collaboration with a sympathetic rabbi who agrees that "what goes on in another person's mind is a mystery that is not to be judged." As in *Morirse*, the film ends with the dead laid to rest and the living in a state of harmonious, if precarious, reconciliation.

As a narrative of memory, forgetting, and substitution, *Cinco días sin Nora* illustrates Roach's reading of funeral rites as events that reveal "the tangible existence of social boundaries and, at the same time, the contingency of those boundaries on fictions of identity, their shoddy construction out of inchoate otherness, and, consequently, their anxiety-inducing instability" (39). The willingness of José's young granddaughters to play in the empty coffin without any sense of abhorrence signals one possible disruption of, or *indifference* to, the shoddy constructions of social difference, as does the unlikely convergence of Fabiana, Moisés, and Aunt Leah (Verónica Langer) in the kitchen. Also interesting is the extratextual connection between the two films generated by the repetition of actors: Max Kerlow, the atheist Rubinstein in *Morirse*, is the intolerant Jacowitz in *Cinco días*, whereas Martin LaSalle embodies rational tolerance as, respectively, Doctor Isaac Fisher and Rabbi Kolatch (who finally oversees Nora's burial).

Does the repetition of funeral themes, shared locations, and cast in two widely circulated feature films—both black comedies filled with personal and cultural conflict but ending in harmony—contribute to defining Mexican Jewish identity within a "matrix of intelligibility" for general audiences? *Cinco días*, whose camera focuses from the beginning on intimate gestures and personal melancholy—the "mystery" alluded to by Rabbi Kolatch that eventually overrides the rule of "community"—would seem to be the more complex of the two films, while *Morirse*, with its Jewish-worldbeat soundtrack by the Klezmatics, seems more deeply invested in its appeal to reconciliation and, ultimately, universality. Yet the two films, each built around competing notions of difference and indifference, constitute a large part of the small corpus of Jewish-themed Mexican cinema produced to date;[10] their success implies not only the extension of visibility to a "minority community" but also, more important, the examination of contemporary Mexican Jewish identities as an indefinite sequence of performances, invented and reinvented onscreen and off.

Notes

1. For an analysis of long-range impacts of modernity on Jewish thought and experience, see Bokser Liwerant, "Los dilemas del judaísmo."
2. Translations are mine unless otherwise indicated.
3. This racism was enacted in public responses, including on the part of prom-

inent cultural and political figures, to the disappearance and presumed murder of forty-three students from the teaching college in Ayotzinapa, Guerrero, on 26 September 2014, as well as many similar incidents in the country. The disdain of the privileged toward the rural poor found expression, in this case, in social networks; notoriously, Francisco Victoriano Pagoaga Lamadrid, a high-ranking official in the National Science and Technology Council (Conacyt) in charge of assigning scholarships to students at public universities, dismissed the crime as "morenacos matando a otros morenacos . . . un parricidio morenaco," a gross racist-classist slur that cost him his position after public outcry but nevertheless raises questions about the private views of those in power, including those in the education bureaucracy. In May 2015, a similar scandal arose when the president of the National Electoral Institute was recorded using ridicule and vulgar language to describe his meetings with indigenous leaders and representatives of the forty-three missing students.

4. For relevant reflections on ethnicity and public space in recent Jewish Latin American film, see Tal, "Etnicidad y espacio público."

5. Roach, *Cities of the Dead*, 14.

6. The title of Zwick's film became *Casarse . . . está en griego* in Mexico, perhaps inspiring the title of the Stavans story and Jewish-themed film under discussion.

7. Translated dialogue for this film is taken from the English subtitles.

8. Bokser Liwerant, "Latin American Jewish Identities," 98.

9. Schechner, "Restauración de la conducta," 36.

10. See FitzGerald, "Mexican-Jewish Life through a Lens," for a 2009 assessment of the two films' place in Mexican Jewish cinema.

Works Cited

Films

Chenillo, Mariana, dir. *Cinco días sin Nora (Nora's Will)*. Perf. Fernando Luján, Max Kerlow, Angelina Peláez. Cacerola Films/Fidecine/IMCINE. 2008.

Springall, Alejandro, dir. *Morirse está en hebreo (My Mexican Shivah)*. Goliat Films/Elevation Filmworks/IMCINE/Springall Pictures. 2007.

Articles and Books

"Alfredo Ripstein, productor y pionero del cine mexicano." *Diario Judío*, 29 April 2014. http://diariojudio.com/opinion/personalidades/alfredo-ripstein-productor-y-pionero-del-cine-mexicano/6658.

Balfour, Brad. "Exclusive Q&A: The Jewish-Mexican Experience via Mariana Chenillo's Award-Winning Film." *Huffington Post*, 15 October 2010. http://www.huffingtonpost.com/brad-balfour/exclusive-qa-the-jewish-m_b_764653.html.

Bokser Liwerant, Judit. "Los dilemas del judaísmo en la modernidad." *Fractal* 7, no. 26 (2002). http://www.mxfractal.org/F26bokser.html.

———. "Latin American Jewish Identities." In *Identities in an Era of Globalization and Multiculturalism: Latin America in the Jewish World*, ed. Judit Bokser Liwerant, Eliezer Ben-Rafael, et al., 81–108. Leiden: Brill, 2008.

Butler, Judith. *Gender Trouble: Feminism and the Subversion of Identity*. New York: Routledge, 1990.

FitzGerald, Tara. "Mexican-Jewish Life through a Lens: Can Film Help Create Acceptance and Tolerance?" *Inside México* 25, April 2009, 14–15.
Har-Paled, Misgav. "Judíos, indios y el mito del crimen ritual: El caso de Chamula, Chiapas, 1868." *LiminaR: Estudios Sociales y Humanísticos* 13, no. 1 (2015): 122–136.
Huerta, César. "Organizan un velorio judío muy especial." *El Universal*, 26 October 2007. http://www.eluniversal.com.mx/espectaculos/79486.html.
Museo Tolerancia y Memoria. "El otro y yo." 2015. http://www.myt.org.mx/tolerancia/el-otro-y-yo.html.
Roach, Joseph. *Cities of the Dead: Circum-Atlantic Performance*. Social Foundations of Aesthetic Forms. New York: Columbia University Press, 1996.
Schechner, Richard. "Restauración de la conducta." In *Estudios avanzados de performance*, ed. Diana Taylor and Marcela Fuentes, 31–49. Mexico: Fondo de Cultura Económica, 2011.
Tal, Tzvi. "Etnicidad y espacio público: La imagen del judío en películas de México y Chile." *Estudios Interdisciplinarios de América Latina y el Caribe* 24, no. 1 (2013). http://www7.tau.ac.il/ojs/index.php/eial/article/view/320.

CHAPTER 3

Incidental Jewishness in the Films of Fabián Bielinsky

AMY KAMINSKY

At his death in 2006 at age forty-seven, Fabián Bielinsky left a body of work consisting of two feature films and two shorts. Say it aloud, roll the words around a bit, and the unhappy pun emerges. Bielinsky's two major works, *Nueve reinas* (2000) and *El aura* (2005), released in the United States as *Nine Queens* and *The Aura*, are rich, beautifully crafted movies whose international success makes them central to the New Argentine Cinema of the early 2000s. They can help us answer crucial questions about the place of Argentine film in the transnational economy of culture and about the specificity of Argentine cinema, insofar as Bielinsky's work taps into an Argentineity that is both rooted in the local and legible transnationally. His first short film, *La espera* (*The Wait*, 1983), is based on a story by the iconic Jorge Luis Borges; and his leading man, Ricardo Darín, is the internationally recognized face of Argentine cinema. All this notwithstanding, the fact that Bielinsky lived to direct only two feature films makes both moot and futile questions that only a fully developed body of work created over decades could answer.

Looking at Bielinsky's films in the context of this book's focus on Jewish cinema may intensify the impulse to imagine the director into a future he did not have, in which Jewish themes might have emerged more visibly or centrally in his work. It seems more interesting to me, however, to take this opportunity to explore what might constitute an entity that could be called "Jewish cinema."

The very notion of Jewish cinema in Latin America (or anywhere else, for that matter) rests on a presumption of something recognizably Jewish that is discernible in one or more aspects of a body of films. Most often, it is a matter of mutually reinforcing Jewish elements attached to a particular movie or set of movies. These elements may include a filmmaker who self-identifies as Jewish, who makes one or more movies that contain visible signs of Jewishness, and who explores themes that resonate with questions of interest to Jewish spectators *as* Jews. Daniel Burman's Ariel films—*Esperando al Mesías* (*Waiting for the Messiah*, 2000), *El abrazo partido* (*Lost Embrace*, 2004), and *Derecho de familia* (*Family Law*, 2006), along with his later, related Ariel film, *El rey del Once* (*The Tenth Man*, 2016)—serve as prime examples. The main character in each of these films both is and is not the same individual. Played in the earlier films by Daniel Hendler, all four characters share the same first name, and they represent a kind of Argentinean Jewish everyman, even as their particular stories diverge.[1]

Then again, a screenplay that foregrounds Jewish characters, especially if the plot centers on Jewish identity, might also be included under the rubric of "Jewish cinema," even if its director is not identifiably Jewish. Eduardo Mignogna's *Sol de otoño* (*Autumn Sun*, 1996), which functions as a veritable pedagogy of Jewishness, falls into this category. In it, the main character is a Jewish woman who teaches a Gentile man the fundamentals of Jewishness so she can pass him off as a Jew to her visiting brother. Films that seem unproblematically categorizable as Jewish often stake a claim to full participation in Argentina *as* Jews, as is the case of the cinematic version of *Los gauchos judíos* (*The Jewish Gauchos*, 1975); or undertake pedagogies of Jewishness, like *Esperando al Mesías* and *Sol de otoño*; or function as a technology of memory in the face of violence aimed at the Jewish community, as do Marcos Carnevale's *Anita* (2009) and *18-J* (2004), both of which deal with the 1994 bombing of the AMIA Jewish center in Buenos Aires.

But to what extent can a movie *be* "Jewish"? What is the meaning of the adjective, after all? This question gets even more complicated if we pause to take account of the way the adjective works in each of the languages we are dealing with here: Spanish, in which the adjective and the noun are identical (judío/judía) and English, in which the adjective (Jewish) has taken the place of the noun (Jew) in much polite conversation. The slippage between the nominal and the adjectival in Spanish (which "judío" shares with other adjective/noun pairs concerning ethnicity, race, and nationality) implies a kind of solidity, an essential core of Jewishness that irrevocably marks both Jew (i.e., the Jewish subject) and any noun it modifies. Although for the purposes of this volume, such solidity would seem to be at least desirable, if not a precondition of its being, I would like to suggest that the very instability of this key term underlies our whole project. Within the Jewish community, the anxiety about maintaining a Jewish identity in the face of a dominant culture that both embraces and threatens Jews and Jewishness is at the core of the response to books, music, art, and films made by and about Jews.

If Burman's Ariel films exemplify an apparently unambiguously Jewish

Argentine cinema in which the Jewishness of the writer/director, the main characters, and the thematics coincide, and Mignogna's film complicates it, Fabián Bielinsky's directorial oeuvre raises still another question concerning this not-so-simple taxonomy. Bielinsky, like many of his cinematic colleagues, is representative of a particular Jewish history in Argentina—urban, well educated (at the prestigious Colegio Nacional Buenos Aires and the Escuela Superior de Comercio Carlos Pellegrini), and assimilated. Neither of the two feature films Bielinsky wrote and directed before his death concerns itself with Jewish history, Jewish ethnography, or Jewish identity. This lack allows us to push at the edges and prod at the center of what might be called Jewish film and ask what happens to this category when a film contains some reference to Jewishness without centering on overtly Jewish themes, that is to say, when Jewishness is incidental.

Carolina Rocha maintains that, as a director, Bielinsky follows the path of Jewish filmmakers who avoid Jewish content in their films. By claiming that Bielinsky and others like him merely pay lip service to Jewishness in their movies, Rocha implies that they somehow disappoint the filmgoer, whose expectations of a Jewish experience in the movie theater are frustrated. Nevertheless we may question the implication that autoethnography is a responsibility of the filmmaker. To the extent that autoethnography is defined as a narrative of the self whose deployment is an acknowledgment of difference and made in response to and using the tools of a dominant culture to make oneself comprehensible to that culture, the assumption that Jewish-identified filmmakers should be held to it is deeply problematic.[2]

To be fair to Rocha, her project is to highlight the work of filmmakers who choose to put Jewish identity and Jewish concerns at the center of their work. Still, films made by Jews that have no Jewish content but that leave a Jewish calling card do not turn their backs on Jewishness. Instead, they function as a reminder that Jews, too, live here. Hernán Goldfrid's *Tesis sobre un homicidio* (*Thesis on a Homicide*, 2013) is one such movie, a mystery thriller that questions the nature of law and justice. The film's main character is a law professor who suspects one of his students (who is also possibly his son) of murder. Another of the students in the professor's class is named Maia Weistein. He calls out her surname when he is taking attendance, but that brief mention is the only overt indication of her Jewishness. Her part is minimal, but she stands as a marker for the presence of Jews in the world of the film.

Fabián Bielinsky's *Nueve reinas* lies somewhere between Burman's films and Goldfrid's *Tesis sobre un homicidio*, among a group of films that clearly mark Jewishness, incorporating it into the story in a significant but secondary way.³ This group of movies includes Julia Solomonoff's *El último verano de La Boyita* (*Last Summer of La Boyita*, 2009) and Paula Markovich's *El premio* (*The Prize*, 2011). In both these films, an assimilated Jewish child is offered a figure of the Virgin Mary by a well-meaning Catholic, in one case another child at school and in the other a servant. These Catholic characters—who, for reasons of age or class, are not expected to be sophisticated about religious difference—represent the unfiltered national unconscious, reminding the viewer that normative Argentineity remains a challenge for Jews. In both cases the mothers somewhat uncomfortably find a way to allow their daughters to incorporate the figure of the Virgin into their lives, reinforcing a sense of Jewish marginalization that echoes the sexual and political marginalization that is at the center of those films.

Although Jewishness emerges under very different circumstances in Bielinsky's *Nueve reinas*, just as in the films by Solomonoff and Markovich it is neither central nor trivial. It is, quite literally, incidental. That is, a single incident in the movie relies on an interchange in which Jewishness is fundamental to meaning. *Nueve reinas* is a fast-paced urban film about two con men, the more experienced Marcos (Ricardo Darín) and the younger Juan (Gastón Pauls), who come together to swindle a Spanish banker in what turns out to be a double cross. Among the large group of people involved in the scam are an elderly Jewish forger named Sandler and his sister. Cristina Gómez Moragas argues that the film is about Argentina's cultural collapse, that it is a snapshot of the nation as it disintegrates. This is a national allegory that incorporates, but does not highlight, Jews and Jewishness.

In *Nueve reinas* the viewer's discovery is that no one is to be trusted, and nothing is what it seems. The film's implicit critique of late capitalism in general and of Argentine politics of the moment is another instance of its appeal to transnational as well as local audiences.⁴ The nine queens of its title refers to a block of rare Weimar Republic stamps in the possession of an elderly Jewish woman, forged copies of which the protagonist hopes to sell to the Spanish businessman. The vicissitudes of the plot make it necessary for the con men to obtain the original stamps, and the crucial scene— the incident—in which this interchange occurs hinges on one of the grifters' knowledge of Argentine Jewish history.

In the late nineteenth century, the German Jewish philanthropist Baron Mauricio von Hirsch was persuaded to buy land in rural Argentina that could be leased by Jews escaping the pogroms of Eastern Europe. Hirsch's Jewish Colonization Association brought thousands of Jews to Argentina over a period of several decades and has become a central feature of what we might call the Argentine Jewish origin myth. The first widely acknowl-

Detail of Jewish Colonization Association certificate. *Nueve reinas* (*Nine Queens*) (2000), directed by Fabián Bielinsky.

edged piece of Argentine Jewish literature, Alberto Gerchunoff's *Los gauchos judíos* (1910) is a fictionalized memoir about life in one of the JCA settlements; and narratives of the Jewish colonies remain a force in Argentine Jewish cultural memory.[5] Like so many others, Gerchunoff eventually left the agricultural settlements in favor of life in the city. In *Nueve reinas*, the Jewish Colonization Association certificate on the wall of the old woman's apartment in Buenos Aires encapsulates this entire narrative: the historical migration from Eastern Europe to Argentina, the creation of Jewish institutions and a Jewish community under the leadership of a beloved rabbi, and the subsequent dispersal of the vast majority of the Jews of the Hirsch colonies into the urban life of the capital.

In the con-within-a-con, Juan immediately grasps the importance of this history and improvises a family history of his own in which he claims an affiliation with the same rabbi whose name appears on the old woman's JCA certificate. This performance of inventing a Jewish connection is meant to convince both Marcos and the audience of Juan's extraordinary agility as a grifter. Nothing has indicated that Juan is Jewish up until this moment, nor is the audience expected to believe him to be Jewish now. The point of Juan's performance is to make the elderly Jewish woman—the ostensible mark of the scam—believe so. Indeed, everything we have seen up until now leads us to believe that Juan's great gift as a confidence man is to invent and inhabit roles and convince other people they are real. By presenting himself as authentically Jewish to the old woman, Juan is proving himself a credible scam artist to Marcos (the intended audience within the fiction) and to the audience viewing the film.

This scene is highly suggestive of the ways that Jewishness both permeates Argentina and yet remains inassimilable, for although Bielinsky does not directly engage in the production of Jewishness in *Nueve reinas*, either by foregrounding Jewish characters or focusing on problematics of Argentine Jewishness, *Nueve reinas* assumes that its audience has at least a rudimentary knowledge of the rural roots of Jewish Argentina.

The reason that the multilayered con works is that the affective meaning of the JCA certificate is limited to a knowing audience deeply familiar with the Jewish history of Argentina. Not only does Juan know that history, but he understands its emotional content, and this knowledge makes him credible. It is not just a matter of having lived in the colonies himself or of having family there, but also of being able to claim a close connection to the rabbi, establishing a set of credentials that rely on both affect and status. This intimate knowledge of what counts in Juan's ability to read the certificate and extract what is important from it derives, ultimately, from the filmmaker. That knowledge is, moreover, communicated to an audience whose members include those (primarily Jews) who immediately understand the complexity and depth of the relationship being claimed, and others (predominantly Gentiles) for whom that connection may be less stunning. In this sense the film's Jewish incident is an inside reference, most meaningful to its Argentine Jewish viewers. The Jewish incident is differentially experienced not because of any essential difference between Jews and Gentiles, but because members of these groups are likely to have different affective responses to this particular slice of Argentine history. Nevertheless, both groups are expected to have a background awareness of at least the broad outlines of this history. In other words, the in-group story of the Argentine Jewish origin myth must already be legible to the film's wider audience.

Nueve reinas is both deeply Argentine, and, in that one incident, specifically Jewish Argentine. Its locations are the streets and neighborhoods of Buenos Aires, and its geographical references are the pampas as well as the urban spaces of the city.[6] It taps into the nation's nineteenth-century policy of encouraging immigration with its allusion to the Jewish agricultural settlements, and it echoes the integrationist ethic propounded by Gerchunoff. Moreover, as Gabriela Copertari points out, Sandler's sister lives in a building identified with established wealth, in contrast to the new globalized wealth of the international hotel where the Spanish businessman is staying.[7] Bielinsky underscores the fact that the Spaniard's stay is temporary; the scam has to take place quickly, before he leaves the country. In an interesting but not uncommon inversion, the Spaniard is a token of transnationality, of that which is not-Argentine, while the Jewish woman, resident in the site of old money and oligarchy, represents deep-rooted Argentineity.

Sandler's sister can be conned only because Juan knows the story of the colonies and understands the trustworthiness that claiming to know her rabbi confers on him. With nothing else overtly Jewish in the film, this scene taps into an underlying knowledge available pretty much only within Argentina and suggests that Juan, who sees the certificate on the wall and instantly knows how to use it to his own advantage, might also be Jewish. But the point here is that his Jewishness (if it is there at all) is utterly incidental to his character. Juan is a great con man, so he knows what buttons to push to make people trust him, or to get them to think they can take advantage of him. As the victim of the double cross, Marcos is taken in by Juan's ability to take advantage of this bit of esoteric knowledge. In the end, this nugget of Jewish history is so fully integrated into the story line that it functions to establish Jewish Argentine history as constitutive of Argentine history tout court.

As Cynthia Tomkins has convincingly argued, Bielinsky's second feature film, *El aura*, is thematically linked to *Nueve reinas*. They play in very different tonal registers, however. Whereas *Nueve reinas* is a caper film, viewed for the pleasure of the ride, *El aura*'s complex criminal plan plays out on a darker screen, quite literally. The location shifts from brightly urban settings to a threateningly rural space, from a city with convenience stores and luxury hotels to a wooded landscape, a rundown hunting lodge, and a dark and telluric feel, from urbane confidence schemes to violent confrontations. By linking the two films, Tomkins suggests that Bielinsky might be understood as an auteur with a consistent underlying worldview that, as an artist, he might have developed into a coherent body of work. Seeing echoes of one film in the other authorizes a sensitivity to a range of echoes, including Jewishness, especially since the first criterion of Jewishness has already been fulfilled: the director's name locates him somewhere in the Jewish community. By the same token, there is the risk of finding Jewishness where you search for it, of the projection of Jewishness onto the screen.

The Jewish incident in *Nueve reinas* may indeed have raised expectations about engagement with Jewishness in Bielinsky's films among those responding to something that might be thought of as an implicit "Jewish pact," loosely akin to Lejeune's "autobiographical pact."[8] Seekers of this pact suppose that Jewish writers and filmmakers who once make mention of Jewishness in their work invite their audience to expect Jewish resonances in all their work. Although there are considerable pitfalls in the notion of the Jewish pact, among which are its tendency toward essentialism and a temptation to read Jewishness where it is not, the idea does suggest that a writer or filmmaker who manifests some sense of him or herself as a Jew authorizes reading his or her work through Jewishness. Underlying the notion of the pact is the sense that upbringing in a Jewish milieu gives one a framework for understanding the world, a sensitivity to certain kinds of nuance. Such a framework offers a set of coordinates for reading the world.

Read through the admittedly problematic, but still suggestive, framework of the Jewish pact, *El aura* resonates with Argentina's Nazi past.[9] The secretive, violent German man whose criminality becomes evident as the protagonist begins to put together pieces of a crime easily forms a chain of signification that includes a history of Nazis taking refuge in southern Argentina. Moreover, the claustrophobic atmosphere of the film, its dark palette, and its pervasive threat of violence all help to produce the effect of anxiety in a situation that threatens to become unstable.

The film's protagonist, once again played by Ricardo Darín, is introduced in a moment of loss of bodily control, unconscious in front of an automatic cash machine. Bielinsky plays with our expectations: a man unconscious next to an ATM should signify a robbery, but this man's wallet has not been stolen. Only slowly do we realize that Darín's character has epilepsy, and that the seizure's most significant moment is not its height, but rather the moment between control and loss of control; the moment between that is the aura that gives the film its title. Only the Jewish pact makes it even conceivable that this sense of anxiety and accompanying heightened awareness can have anything to do with Jewishness, and I am loath to suggest an overt connection. Nevertheless, the sense of precariousness that Darín's character experiences as an epileptic at the mercy of his body resonates with the precariousness of Jewish security and safety at the mercy of the dominant body politic.

The protagonist's friend and colleague who takes him to Patagonia on a hunting trip bears the German Jewish name Sontag. In contrast, Dietrich, the violent, mysterious hunter accidentally killed by the protagonist early in the film, has a German Gentile name; his shady life, his penchant for violence, and his residence in Patagonia all suggest a reference to Nazis hidden in the depths of rural Argentina. Sensitivity to such cues is a mark of the specific subaltern sensibility that characterizes Jewishness in Argentina.

The sensitized filmgoer is receptive to overtones of Jewishness in the film's haunted atmosphere of foreboding.

When Roland Barthes developed the notion of the punctum, the incidental detail that compellingly draws and keeps the viewer's attention in *Camera Lucida*, he was writing about still photography in the context of his own mother's death, not about the communal experience of cinema. Barthes's photographic punctum inadvertently affects the viewer, and it triggers a deeply private memory. While they are not true examples of it, both the subtle cues of *El aura* and the incidental Jewishness of *Nueve reinas* may be likened to Barthes's punctum. Bielinsky's cinematic punctum, like Barthes's photographic one, creates an intimate connection between the viewer and the object portrayed. Although it may be deliberately included and not inadvertent at all (as in *Nueve reinas*), the cinematic punctum is true to its origin in that it is incidental to the larger, public, story it tells. In the absence of an overtly Jewish incident in *El aura*, the film's perhaps subtle, and perhaps unintentional, references to Jewishness echo the closed intimacy of Barthes's photographic punctum. In any case, both films open up the absolute hermeticism of the punctum to a group that shares a response to the telling detail that is no longer utterly idiosyncratic but still limited to those bounded and bonded by a particular history.

In a paradigmatic scene in *Nueve reinas*, Marcos surveys what is apparently an ordinary street scene in Buenos Aires and systematically points out to Juan one scam or illegal transaction after another. The scene has quite aptly been compared to the unsavory machinations of political and economic institutions in the Argentina of the 1990s, just under the surface but visible to those who know how to see and what to look for. Bielinsky delighted in the knowledge that after watching his film, audiences were suspicious of everything going on around them in the streets of the city when they left the movie theater. They had been made to see what might be right in front of them. Seeing what is in plain sight but visible only to those who know the signs, and teaching the audience to see those signs, is not unlike seeing the Jewishness of the film and of the world from which it emerges. For those sensitive to the signs, they are easy to find. Like the audience members who, once made aware of the possibility of criminality, suspect that it exists all around them, Jewishness is perceptible to, and thereby called into being by, those who have the proper receptors.

Notes

1. Hendler and Alan Sabbagh, who play Ariel in the last film, are also Jewish, adding one more layer cementing the Jewish identity of the film.

2. See Pratt, "Arts of the Contact Zone," for a discussion of autoethnography.

3. Still, it is instructive to remember that, like *Nueve reinas, Esperando al Mesías* explores the economic crisis of the moment, and a significant parallel plot concerns non-Jewish characters. One film ends where the other begins, with the protagonist among a crowd of people trying fruitlessly to get into a closed bank.

4. See Gómez Moragas, "Representación fílmica del universo posmoderno," for a full discussion of *Nueve reinas* as a critique of Menemism and as an exploration of the specifically Argentine fusion she calls "barbarie posmoderna," with its implicit references to both Sarmiento and global culture. Gómez Moragas calls the film "a national allegory of the ethical crisis in the exercise of political power in late capitalism [una alegoría nacional de la crisis ética en el ejercicio del poder político en el capitalismo tardío]" (31).

5. Scenes from the play based on Gerchunoff's text decorate the lobby of a theater in Buenos Aires's Barrio Once, where so many Jews settled in the first half of the twentieth century, and the book was turned into a movie in 1975.

6. Martín, "Los laberintos del simulacro," highlights the representation of Buenos Aires in *Nueve reinas* as a multifaceted, real-life city. She points out that the camera takes in gas stations, cafes, newspaper stands, neighborhood restaurants, and busy streets and avenues, as well as luxury hotels and fancy neighborhoods. Humor, she says, "floods every nook and cranny of urban life [el humor inunda cada recoveco de la vida urbana]" (131). Martín does not, however, mention anything Jewish about the film, not even its sardonic humor, as Jewish as it is Porteño.

7. Copertari, "*Nueve reinas*: A Dark Day of Simulation and Justice," 286.

8. I am grateful to author Esther Bendahan for introducing me to the idea of the Jewish pact (personal conversation, Madrid, April 2013).

9. Gómez Moragas, "Representación fílmica del universo posmoderno," points out a connection to Nazi Germany in *Nueve reinas* as well, in the chain of associations that begins with the Weimar stamps and ends with the Argentine military dictatorship and state terror of the 1970s and 80s, both of which link to the Nazi regime and therefore to Jewish concerns.

Works Cited

Films

Bielinsky, Fabián, dir. *El aura*. Buena Vista. 2005.
———. *La espera (The Wait)*. Escuela Nacional de Experimentación y Realización Cinematografica. 1983.
———. *Nueve reinas (Nine Queens)*. SONY Pictures Classic. 2000.
Burman, Daniel, dir. *Derecho de familia (Family Law)*. IFC First Take. 2006.
———. *El abrazo partido (Lost Embrace)*. BD Cine et al. 2004.
———. *El rey del Once (The Tenth Man)*. BD Cine/Pasto. 2016.
———. *Esperando al Mesías (Waiting for the Messiah)*. BD Cine et al. 2000.
Burman, Daniel, Adrian Caetano, et al., dir. *18-J*. Aleph Productions. 2004.
Carnevale, Marcos, dir. *Anita*. Shazam S.A. 2009.
Goldfrid, Hernán, dir. *Tesis sobre un homicidio (Thesis on a Homicide)*. BD Cine et al. 2013.
Jusid, Juan José, dir. *Los gauchos judíos (The Jewish Gauchos)*. Film Cuatro et al. 1975.

Markovitch, Paula, dir. *El premio* (*The Prize*). Elite Studios et al. 2011.
Mignogna, Eduardo, dir. *Sol de otoño* (*Autumn Sun*). V.C.C. 1996.
Solomonoff, Julia, dir. *El último verano de La Boyita* (*Last Summer of La Boyita*). Travesía Productions et al. 2009.

Books and Articles

Barthes, Roland. *Camera Lucida: Reflections on Photography*. Trans. Richard Howard. New York: Hill and Wang, 1981.
Copertari, Gabriela. "*Nueve reinas*: A Dark Day of Simulation and Justice." *Journal of Latin American Cultural Studies: Travesía* 14, no. 3 (2005): 279–293.
Gerchunoff, Alberto. *Los gauchos judíos*. La Plata, Argentina: Joaquín Sesé, 1910.
Gómez Moragas, Cristina. "Representación fílmica del universo posmoderno, un caso ilustrativo: *Nueve reinas*." *Ciencia Ergo Sum* 16, no. 1 (March–June 2009).
Lejeune, Philippe. *On Autobiography*. Theory and History of Literature. Minneapolis: University of Minnesota Press, 1989.
Martín, Marina. "Los laberintos del simulacro: Técnicas borgesianas del suspense en Alejandro Amenábar y Fabián Bielinsky." In *Historia & cinema: 25 aniversario del Centre d'Investigacions Film-Història*, ed. José María Caparrós Lera, 121–132. Barcelona: Universitat de Barcelona, 2009.
Pratt, Mary Louise. "Arts of the Contact Zone." *Profession* 91 (1991): 33–40.
Rocha, Carolina. "Jewish Cinematic Self-Representations in Contemporary Argentine and Brazilian Films." *Journal of Modern Jewish Studies* 9, no. 1 (2010): 37–48.
Tomkins, Cynthia. "Fabián Bielinsky's *El aura* (The Aura): Neo-noir Inscription and Subversion of the Action Image." *Confluencia* 24, no. 1 (Fall 2008): 17–27.

PART II

MEMORY AND VIOLENCE

CHAPTER 4

My German Friend and the Jewish Argentine/German "Mnemo-Historic" Context

DANIELA GOLDFINE

When given the opportunity to reminisce, people talk as if their memories were there, waiting to be given the opportunity to be expressed in words.
ELIZABETH JELIN AND SUSANA G. KAUFMAN, "LAYERS OF MEMORIES: TWENTY YEARS AFTER IN ARGENTINA"

You don't have to be German, or German Jewish, to relate to it. It has to do with us as human beings and about love and what love can do for you.
JEANINE MEERAPFEL (INTERVIEWED BY HOMA NASAB)

Film director and screenplay writer Jeanine Meerapfel was born in 1943 in Buenos Aires, Argentina. Her parents, German Jews, had survived and escaped the Shoah and found a new home in this South American country. Meerapfel grew up speaking both Spanish and German and in the 1960s went back to her parents' country of origin, where she studied film and started her productive career. Her latest feature-length film, *Der Deutsche Freund* (*My German Friend/El amigo alemán*, 2012), is a semi-autobiographical account of her life and her attempt to create what, according to her, is the first film to address the relationship between Germans who escaped the Shoah and the ones who escaped justice.[1] Meerapfel says: "I always found it astonishing that nobody has told the story of the families, the Jewish German families, that came to Argentina, escaping from the Holocaust. . . . And then, some years later, after the war, came the Nazis. . . . So, that's something that nobody has told, what happens with the children."[2]

My German Friend provides a space where the "mnemo-historic" context—a concept in which memory and history are intersected by the mediation of the reproductive view of memory—surpasses the tight frame of both history and memory: Meerapfel's technique of mixing real-life events

Sulamit Löwenstein (Celeste Cid) and Friedrich Burg (Max Riemelt) discover the painful past of their families. *My German Friend* (2012), directed by Jeanine Meerapfel.

(including background scenes of historic events projected onto a virtual reality TV set) and fiction creates a crossroads that allows for the analysis of the formation, reconstruction, and recording of memory. Maurice Halbwachs—a well-known scholar who has extensively studied collective memory—explains, referring to the reconstitution of the past:

> We preserve memories of each epoch in our lives, and these are continually reproduced; through them, as by a continual relationship, a sense of our identity is perpetuated. But precisely because these memories are repetitions, because they are successively engaged in very different systems of notions, at different periods of our lives, they have lost the form and the appearance they once had.[3]

Meerapfel highlights historical events in order to support her story, which is based on her own memories. This binding of two streams—memory and history—results in the significant concept of "mnemo-history." It is in this Jewish Argentine/German context that *My German Friend* develops its ideas and comments on the fate of Jews worldwide. As Sulamit (Celeste Cid) states: "I just learned how to fit in. Like all good Jews . . . My parents taught me, what possibly all Jews teach their children: to survive anywhere, anytime, to adapt."

Meerapfel created the characters of Sulamit Löwenstein, who, like the director, was born in Argentina to Jewish German parents, and her next-door neighbor, Friedrich Burg (Max Riemelt), the Argentine son of an SS officer, to tell the story of how collective memories shape lives—in this case, the lives of the people who lived in Argentina and Germany from the 1950s to the 1980s—and how these memories vary in changing contexts. In this film, history and memory are intertwined as a means not only to question the collective history of Jewish and German émigrés to Argentina but also to uncover the consequences of the earlier generations' choices—consequences that drive both Sulamit and Friedrich into exile and propel the latter into political involvement, including the guerrilla movements of the 1970s. By utilizing Daniel Levy's concept of "mnemo-history," I propose to analyze the way the past is remembered and recorded in this film.

"Mnemo-History" and Its Nuanced Approach

Daniel Levy's take on "mnemo-history" is based on Jan Assmann's exploration of the subject.[4] Expanding on the concept, Levy asserts that

> it is not about the exploration of the past per se but rather concerned with how particular pasts are being remembered over time and how the conditions for their appropriation are subject to changes. . . . The past is invented, shaped, and reconstructed in a dialogical relationship with the present, past constraints, and future possibilities. How histories are remembered (and by extension distorted over time) emerges as the main focus of our analytical pursuits. . . . By historicizing memory as a contingent phenomenon, this process-oriented approach suggests "memory is not only storage of past 'facts' but the ongoing work of reconstructive imagination. In other words, the past cannot be stored but always has to be 'processed and mediated.'"[5]

This is the basis of *My German Friend*: Jeanine Meerapfel methodically processes and mediates her memories to uncover the painful political and historical events that surrounded life after World War II, while returning to the topics of identity and self-discovery she had already explored in other films (like *La amiga* [*The Girlfriend*], 1988, and *Amigomío* [*Friend of Mine*], 1995). The main characters coming of age politically in the 1960s cannot help getting involved, but, most of all, they cannot avoid confronting what their parents did in the past. As Friedrich discovers his father's involvement with the Nazi regime, his feelings of frustration and shame envelop him. He needs to find his own path in life and do more research about his family, so he travels to Germany, where he will still feel lost and powerless. Both Friedrich and Sulamit will have to wander aimlessly for decades before understanding each other. This is, after all, a film where history supports memory (and vice versa) and where the ideological sways of a generation of Argentines are depicted by a knowledgeable director who lived through these vicissitudes.[6]

As a "mnemo-historical" approach is developed and further validated, Meerapfel's strategy is to undertake a reflection on history from the standpoint of fiction imbued with factual memory to achieve productive discourse. "Mnemo-history" presents itself as remarkably dynamic and able to destabilize the static notion(s) provided by unmediated history. The alternative narration of memory/history allows for a space where the film director can consider and later take to the screen the challenges that encompassed her life and her two countries of residence for many years. The issues surrounding what/who remembers (or forgets) provide a space to recognize the relevance of re-creating memories and the importance of remembering emphasized by Jewish tradition. It is the responsibility to remember (*zahor*, in Hebrew, as in "remember the Sabbath day" in Exodus 20:8), no matter what the relationship is between and the effects of the past and the present, or the fissures of the past, or whatever remains the past might have left in the present. The repercussions of the past have a role in the present. The "mnemo-historic" context provides a venue for peeling layer after layer of memory to rediscover how this same memory has merged with history in other time frames, and to show as well that any revision of the past is not without fault, as forgetting is encompassed in the act of recollection.

"Memory was, as ever, creation," says writer Jay Neugeboren,[7] and that is what Meerapfel does in *My German Friend*: she finds a way to tell her story at the fine intersection of memory and history. In her creation, she is aware of the pitfalls of memory and the use of historical facts. For her film, the director reinvents the language employed to tell a story as she attempts to present a record of the 1950s–1980s in Argentina and Germany. Simultaneously, she transforms the interstice produced by her remembering and forgetting. In this crevice she manages to acknowledge the inaccuracies of memory and discloses the processes that lead to a creation that blurs the lines between memory and history. The two neighbors that became friends and then lovers live separately much of their lives but keep finding a way to reunite through the bond they had formed when they were children. Their families' past haunts the relationship, and Friedrich's obstinacy contrasts sharply with Sulamit's patience. It is not Meerapfel's goal to merely tell a love story: it is her duty to also leave a legacy for those who did not live through those tumultuous decades. Life in the twentieth century was filled with contradictions and incessant searches; it was also a time to reassess what had been inherited and what was to be left to future generations.

The Byroads of Memory

My German Friend follows the chronological story of Sulamit and Friedrich from their time in elementary school to their adulthood. The film resembles a chain in which every scene is a link, each connected to what happens before and after but also able to function as its own individual unit. The thread that keeps the action going is the story of the main characters, but there is also the chronological order of historical data that is inserted throughout the film. This factual information frames the fictional account and works toward a veneer of authenticity. Meerapfel is conscious of this attempt, as she explains: "After all, this is, above all, a love story developing against the historical background of victims and victimizers converging on the same place after ravages and atrocities of war."[8]

The filmmaker, then, utilizes her own memories to construct Sulamit's character while Friedrich's, on the other hand, is based on knowledge Meerapfel had of some of her neighbors—although she never truly met the son of a Nazi officer when growing up in Buenos Aires. For her film, however, these circumstances—her lack of personal knowledge—are irrelevant, as she does not contextualize her story within a historic frame or within a mnemonic one.[9] By bringing the future into the "mnemo-historic" context of the film Meerapfel establishes a connection with younger generations, as she presents young Sulamit and Friedrich as the universal young lovers that struggle to find a happy ending (a representation of love with which audiences can easily identify).

The circumstances surrounding this love and its constant setbacks are the historical events of the 1950s to the 1980s in Europe and South America. From the overthrow of President Perón to the student movements in Germany in 1968 to the brutal government repression in Argentina in the 1970s, political and historical events mark Sulamit and Friedrich's love story.[10] The story follows Friedrich through his desperate attempts to make sense of his father's choices in the past.[11] While immersed in this quest to, in some way, elucidate his forebear's wrongdoings, Friedrich cannot see that Sulamit loves him for who he is, without concern for his family's past.[12]

Aware of the weight her name carries (great-aunt Sulamit was killed by the Nazis), Sulamit's family errs on the side of silence about their past: there are few references to the Shoah, and Sulamit is confused by the ceremony and the Jewish ritual carried on at her father's funeral.[13] It is her aunt Else with whom she has the only conversation about her family's past:

—This ring used to belong to your great aunt Sulamit. It's for you.
—For me?

—You got your name from her.
—Why do we never talk about her?
—Because it's difficult. Perhaps she could have been saved. If only she'd not been so stubborn. I shouldn't talk so much. I'm just a bit *meshugge*.
—You're not, aunt! You can talk to me about anything, always.

Sulamit has been put in a position where her family's past and her own present are disassociated. Because of this, she is able to separate Friedrich from his past—as well as his actions from his father's—resulting in her decades-long unconditional love for him.[14]

The first scene in the film shows Sulamit holding a key while traveling by train through the vast Patagonia. She is going to visit Friedrich, who has settled there after being imprisoned in Rawson, Chubut (a southern Argentine province) during the dictatorship (1976–1983). We eventually find out that the key was given to her by Friedrich when they were both children and wanted to meet without supervision (the key accessed the attic in Friedrich's house). This key could also be a symbol of their love: Sulamit keeps it throughout her life, but before embarking on that final train ride, she finds out that the attic door does not exist anymore. When Friedrich gave it to her, there was a chance for their love to flourish. However, Friedrich has not reciprocated Sulamit's love for years.

In one scene, Sulamit, already a university professor in Germany, is teaching a poem by the Jewish Romanian Paul Celan (1920–1970):

With a changing key,
you unlock the house where
the snow of what's silenced drifts.
Just like the blood that bursts from
Your eye or mouth or ear,
so your key changes.

Changing your key changes the word
That may drift with flakes.
Just like the wind that rebuffs you,
Clenched round your word is the snow.

Friedrich also reads Celan's work during his long imprisonment under the dictatorship.[15] Patricia Nuriel associates this reading with Celan's focus "on the universal condition of persecution that exists beyond national, racial, ethnic, religious, or political affiliation."[16] This is the condition in which

Friedrich finds himself at the moment of imprisonment, but it may also provide him a way to begin understanding Sulamit and her family's plight. Friedrich has spent his life struggling to grasp the logic behind his father's decisions and, even though he commits to numerous political and social movements with the goal of addressing social injustice, it takes him several decades to genuinely engage with his own values and principles.

Although Meerapfel does not dwell on the Shoah, she provides glimpses of its consequences and the (mostly silenced) burden that second generations carry. The "mnemo-historic" context that frames her film presents her memories as a child of survivors/escapees and combines them with real-life events like the kidnapping of Adolf Eichmann in 1960. In the film Sulamit writes about this historical incident in her high school newspaper, and here Meerapfel has utilized her own memories of writing in a student newspaper, transposing the name of that newspaper (*El espolón* [*The spur*]) into the fictional world.

By employing a universally understood narrative device, the love story, Meerapfel manages to connect to audiences worldwide. Furthermore, by inserting autobiographical references, she challenges audiences by showcasing how the historical events of the Shoah have shaped two nations (and touched numerous others) and will continue to affect many generations into the future.[17] The director concedes: "Cuento historias. Que en el mejor de los casos pueden llegar a conseguir que esas cosas no se repitan [I tell stories, that in the best case scenario, can prevent those things from happening again (my own translation)]."[18] There is the underlying desire to leave testament to world history, as well as to lay to rest personal memory.

Otherness Multiplied

In her 1981 documentary *Im Land meiner Eltern* (*In the Country of My Parents*), Jeanine Meerapfel says in voice-over: "If Hitler had not existed, I would have been born a German Jew, more German than Jewish, in a small village in southern Germany."[19] Like her creation, Sulamit, Meerapfel felt like an outsider growing up. Being Jewish and speaking German with her parents in Argentina meant being marked as a foreigner. When moving to Germany in her youth to study film in Berlin and Ulm she was met by the skepticism of her peers, who had not met "a Jew" while growing up in postwar Germany. As Shawn Magee states: "Jeanine Meerapfel is an outsider. As a woman in a patriarchal age, as a foreigner in a xenophobic country, as a direct descendant of a race nearly eradicated a generation ago by genocide, she stands apart from the mainstream of German society" (63). The feeling of not belonging followed the filmmaker, and she pours that feeling into her cinematic alter ego.

In a scene toward the beginning of the film, Sulamit is attacked when leaving her high school building, called "Dirty Jew!" and threatened with "We'll slit you up" (this is an autobiographical event included by the director). This is one of two remarks signifying anti-Semitism in Argentina in the film and provides a context for understanding the society in which Sulamit grows up.[20] (Haim Avni maintains that Argentina has never been welcoming to a Jewish sense of communal or ethnic identity. Therefore, Jews have never been viewed as "equal Argentines."[21])

Even though Friedrich also speaks German at home with his family, the film does not showcase any feeling of estrangement that comes from the outside. Friedrich's alienation comes rather from within, born after he finds out what his father was and what he did in Germany. The revelation of his father's dreadful past disturbs him with such force that, a few years later, he decides to travel to Germany to unearth more about it.[22] Without being able to cope with the true identity of his father—and, therefore, his own—Friedrich spends his life supporting political causes. He involves himself in such a manner that he loses himself—a coping mechanism for dealing with the tainted blood running through him. He seems to chase ghosts throughout his life, and when his support of German students' demands in 1968 does not feel drastic enough, he goes back to Argentina to fight with the armed guerrilla movement which is starting to publicly oppose the government.

Meerapfel explained that when she went back to Germany in the early 1960s, she met German students her age who fanatically tried to debunk their parents.

> These young men and women were so ashamed of the Nazi atrocities that they would conceal their German passports, or would blindly join extreme leftwing parties. They all had to go a long way before learning to love themselves and to love others.[23]

The persona of Friedrich in this film is informed by these young people Meerapfel encountered in Germany. The twist she adds to her male protagonist is his returning to Argentina, joining an armed guerrilla movement, and being detained by the police. Friedrich does not become one of the many disappeared (*desaparecidos*) because his location is known—he is transferred to a prison in the south for many years. When set free, instead of moving back to Buenos Aires or Germany, he stays in Patagonia to help the indigenous people of the area (the Mapuches) reclaim their land. Through Friedrich, the director tries to represent the lack of direction this guilt-ridden generation possesses: Friedrich's shame and loneliness cloud his judgment and do not let him see Sulamit. And Sulamit, the Other *par excellence* in this story, is actually the one who thrives in Germany, eventually realizing her potential as a college professor. (In her personal life, her relationship with Michael Tendler [Benjamin Sadler] collapses as she cannot let go of her feelings for Friedrich.)

Conclusion

Jeanine Meerapfel's *My German Friend* crosses the Atlantic back and forth in a story that evolves over decades and transforms itself into a semi-autobiographical account set within the framework of historical events. This approach to both history and memory—to looking at the past through the lens of "mnemo-history"—gives the director the necessary freedom to explore various themes within the work. The film was shot in Spanish and German, and it touches on such topics as immigration, exile, memory, and identity.[24] Meerapfel taps into her own memory to re-create settings and wardrobe in minute detail—the countries' customs, the domestic items in a room, and even the stores and cars are carefully portrayed, allowing the audience to connect with that past time. The director commented that the original name of the film was "Children of . . ." ("Hijos de . . ."), in reference to the children who have to bear the weight of their parents' past. This emphasizes another of the film's central themes: the personal and political acts in a transnational context.[25] Both Sulamit and Friedrich become involved in political causes not only because of the ideas behind them but also to establish the distance between their own and their parents' generation. These children of immigrants torn apart by conflict are now citizens of a new nation and are eager to work on the restoration of humanity as a whole—as well as of their families and themselves—to prove that there can be a future even after the grimmest past.

Most of all, this film utilizes "mnemo-history" to show the connection between memory and history, between the present and the past. Meerapfel repositions her memories onto the screen, privileging events meaningful to her and utilizing historical events to support her picture. The challenge of reconstructing her story through fiction frames the experiences for what is remembered through both space (Argentina and Germany) and time (1950s through mid-1980s). The resignification of these two axes through a love story is what allows present-day audiences to connect to this seemingly distant past. "Here memory and its association with a particular past are not an impediment for the future but a prerequisite to enunciate a narrative (bridge) over the present."[26] The director/screenwriter succeeds in situating her film on a myriad of crossroads, where languages, nationalities, cultures, identities, temporalities, and geographies intersect. Above all, *My German Friend* is a film embedded in the "mnemo-historic" context, a space where memory and history—and where Jews, Argentines, and Germans—coalesce.

Notes

1. Here Meerapfel is referring to the Nazi officers who fled Germany at the end of World War II and were never tried for their crimes. In an interview by Homa Nasab, Meerapfel talks about the fact that both Jews and SS officers came to the same country: "It is very ironical this destiny, somebody has to tell it and that's what I did." The irony is the fact that both Jews and Nazis sought refuge in the same South American nation—not the only place where this happened, but the setting of this film.

2. In an email communication with the author, Meerapfel adds that the plot is not entirely fiction and that it is based on real events: she emphasizes the fact that children of Jewish escapees and Nazi officers did meet and interact in real life. However, the director clarifies that she fictionalized these real-life interactions to create her story.

3. Halbwachs, *On Collective Memory*, 47.

4. In "Changing Temporalities and the Internationalization of Memory Cultures," Daniel Levy analyzes Jan Assmann's text *Moses and the Egyptian: The Memory of Egypt in Western Monotheism* (Cambridge, MA: Harvard University Press, 1997).

5. Levy, "Changing Temporalities" (quoting Assmann), 21–22.

6. Further expanding the notion of "mnemo-history," Levy explains that memory and history are intersected by the mediation of the reproductive view of memory and emphasizes the interconnectedness that is established between past, present, and future. Memory does not happen in a vacuum, but instead represents the cultural and epochal distinctiveness of its time. It is the fairly recently conceptualized global worldview that allows contesting the notions of nation and culture—challenging the space these two concepts encompass and allowing for an alteration of memory. In Levy's words: "This transformation of memory corresponds to the fragmentation of memories and their related privatization, a process which manifests itself in a changing relationship of memory and history" (26).

7. Neugeboren, *News from the New American Diaspora*, 58.

8. "*My German Friend*: The Byways of Memory."

9. Levy suggests that an individual, instead of attempting to discern between fact and fiction, between past and present, be "attentive to the different relationships of the temporal triad of past, present and future" (24).

10. Juan Domingo Perón was president of Argentina 1946–1952, 1952–1955, 1973–1974.

11. Friedrich's and Sulamit's trips to Germany bring to mind Eva Hoffman's account: "Still, the visit helps. It helps in measuring the distance between the past and the present, and in anchoring that swirling childhood knowledge in solid actualities. And perhaps a kind of task has been fulfilled, for it is not good not to know where your parents came from, and where your ancestors died or were murdered. This was for my sister and me to do: to keep this fragment of a larger story in mind, and perhaps, in some way, pass it on" (*After Such Knowledge*, 220). Curiously, it is Friedrich who is defiantly inquisitive about his family's past (actually, he is haunted by it) and it is Sulamit who finds in Friedrich an excuse to go to the land where her family perished. While in Germany she makes no attempt to find out what happened to her ancestors or to visit her parents' hometowns. Her lack of curiosity may be traced back to her family's silence: a silence that was very common among Holocaust survivors and escapees, who wanted to start anew in a new land and not burden their children with horror stories.

12. In contrast to Friedrich's feelings, his father is not ashamed of his past. When Friedrich finds a bread basket with a swastika stitched in it, he asks his father about it and the answer is: "It's a decor. A relic from other times." The use of the word "relic" implies the sentimental value this object has for the former SS officer. Friedrich seems to react in shock both to the unearthing of this part of his family's history and to the nonchalant way his father acknowledges his past.

13. Sulamit has attended a private French school but is forced to switch to a public school after her father dies, leaving Sulamit and her mother in a perilous economic situation. In her elementary school, we see that she is excluded from religious studies and directed instead to ethics. There are only two references to Judaism in Sulamit's life: one is during the high holidays, when her extended family suggests she celebrate "Chrismukkah, then. Christmas and Chanukkah" as a compromise between her family's tradition and the acknowledgment that Sulamit is growing up in a reality different from that of her parents. The other instance occurs at the synagogue when Kaddish is being said for her father. Sulamit asks why she and her mother are separated from the men and she also complains: "I don't understand a word, anyway." It is not only Hebrew that has not been passed on—Sulamit cannot speak German either and will have to learn that language as a young adult when she travels to Germany to study.

14. In an interview with Homa Nasab, Meerapfel states her point of view about this love: "Only through love he [Friedrich] will really heal himself, he cannot do it through hate." Nevertheless, Friedrich spends decades loathing who he is and what his family did, and is not able to see Sulamit and the sacrifices she has made for him, like traveling from Germany to Patagonia (south of Argentina) to visit him in prison after he is jailed as a political dissident. The final scene shows a form of realization of these efforts and an acknowledgment by Friedrich, but it is open to interpretation: after years of going back and forth between two continents Sulamit (who has established herself as a university professor in Germany) asks: "Are you coming with me?" to which Friedrich (who has settled in Patagonia after spending many years in prison there) answers: "Are you staying here?"

15. When Friedrich returns to Argentina after several years of living in Ger-

many, he voices his desire to use action to provoke change in his country. He then gets involved in a guerrilla movement which prepares an attack on Junta forces. The assault backfires, Friedrich is taken prisoner, and he is sent to the southern province of Chubut to bide his time. Life under a military dictatorship meant no trial and no sentence. Therefore, his long time in prison was dictated by the whim of those in power. Meerapfel shows how, ironically, Friedrich (the son of a Nazi officer) decides to fight against the Junta government and, as a result, ends up in prison. This reinforces his lifelong commitment to differentiate himself from his father in all circumstances.

16. Nuriel, "On Meerapfels' *My German Friend,*" 108.

17. Noticeably, at the moment the film ends—when Friedrich and Sulamit are in their forties—neither one has had children, and therefore they are disrupting generational continuation and transmission of memory.

18. Chiesa, "Jeanine Meerapfel estrena 'El amigo alemán.'"

19. Magee, "*Malou. In the Country of My Parents*: Cross-Cultural Examination," 64.

20. In the background of the film, there is also a brief reference on the news to Graciela Narcisa Sirota, a nineteen-year-old college student who, in 1962, was kidnapped from her hometown of Buenos Aires and whose kidnappers carved a swastika on her breast. Unfortunately, without previous knowledge of this fact, the remark is lost on most viewers.

21. Haim Avni explains that Jewish presence pointed both to Argentina's conflicting goals of immigration and to its widespread intolerance toward religions other than Catholicism (*Argentina and the Jews*, 87).

22. Friedrich is distressed and can only think about himself and uncovering his family's hidden past. This hurts Sulamit, who realizes she is not part of Friedrich's present or future. Friedrich tells her: "I got a scholarship to study politics in Frankfurt. Please understand! I've got to know who my father was, what he did. And my own position in this."

23. "*My German Friend*: The Byways of Memory."

24. Nuriel, "On Meerapfels' *My German Friend,*" 108.

25. Ibid.

26. Levy, "Changing Temporalities," 16.

Works Cited

Film

Meerapfel, Jeanine, dir. *Der Deutsche Freund* (*My German Friend*). Perf. Celeste Cid, Max Riemelt, Benjamin Sadler. Neue Visionen Filmverleih, 2012.

Articles and Books

Avni, Haim. *Argentina and the Jews: A History of Jewish Immigration*. Tuscaloosa: University of Alabama Press, 1991.

Chiesa, Nicolás. "Jeanine Meerapfel estrena 'El amigo alemán,' con Celeste Cid." *Suite 101*, n.p., 3 July 2013.

Halbwachs, Maurice. *On Collective Memory*. Trans. Lewis A. Coser. Chicago: University of Chicago Press, 1992.

Hoffman, Eva. *After Such Knowledge: Memory, History, and the Legacy of the Holocaust*. New York: PublicAffairs, 2004.

Jelin, Elizabeth, and Susana G. Kaufman. "Layers of Memories: Twenty Years after in Argentina." In *The Politics of War and Commemoration*, ed. T. G. Ashplant, Graham Dawson, and Michael Roper, 89–110. London: Routledge, 2000.

Levy, Daniel. "Changing Temporalities and the Internationalization of Memory Cultures." In *Memory and the Future: Transnational Politics, Ethics, and Society*, ed. Yifat Gutman, Adam D. Brown, and Amy Sodaro, 15–30. Hampshire, England: Palgrave Macmillan, 2010.

Magee, Shawn S. "*Malou. In the Country of My Parents*: Cross-Cultural Examination." *Jump Cut: A Review of Contemporary Media* 30 (1985): 63–64.

Meerapfel, Jeanine. "Homa Nasab in Conversation with Jeanine Meerapfel, Director of *My German Friend*." FirstPost, 2013.

"*My German Friend*: The Byways of Memory." *Buenos Aires Herald*, 4 October 2012.

Neugeboren, Jay. *News from the New American Diaspora and Other Tales of Exile*. Austin: University of Texas Press, 2005.

Nuriel, Patricia. "On Meerapfels' *My German Friend*." *Jewish Film and New Media* 2, no. 1 (April 2014): 106–108.

CHAPTER 5

Dispersed Friendships: Jeanine Meerapfel's *The Girlfriend*

PATRICIA NURIEL

La amiga (*The Girlfriend*), directed by Jeanine Meerapfel, is a West German–Argentine co-production released in 1988. Born in Buenos Aires in 1943, the director has lived since 1964 in Germany, the country her parents had fled during the period of Nazi rule. There she studied cinema at the Ulm School of Design under Alexander Kluge and Edgar Reitz, important figures in the New German Cinema. As filmmaker, screenwriter, producer, and professor, in 2015 she became president of the Academy of Arts, Berlin. Meerapfel's films illuminate stories of exile and immigration, inquiries concerning memory and identity, struggles for justice and human rights, and explorations of the margins of society and gender issues. *The Girlfriend* develops a feminist view of resistance and survival during the military dictatorship of 1976–1983 in Argentina, examining the depth of friendship in the face of repressive military rule. In this particular historical context, I will focus on aspects of the film as they relate to the Jewish tradition and experience through scattered, often implicit, motifs. While not always at the center of the plot, the Jewish predicament lies beneath and contributes to the story.[1]

The Girlfriend can be seen as part of a series of post-dictatorship Argentine films that explore and shed light on the regime, the crimes of which included thousands of forced disappearances and deaths, widespread torture, and other human rights violations. With the return of democracy in 1983, the imperative of giving an account of this traumatic experience led the country to a reassessment of its national identity, a process in which Argentine cinema played a significant role.

Raúl Alfonsín (1983–1989) was the first democratically elected president following the dictatorship. During the first few years of his administration, the National Institute of Cinematography and Audiovisual Arts (INCAA) provided public financing to the national film industry. The institute intended to promote the industry both domestically and abroad, and Argentine films did in fact achieve international recognition. For example, *The Official Story* (*La historia oficial*), directed by Luis Puenzo, won the Oscar for best foreign film of 1985. However, state funding dried up with the deterioration of the economy in 1987, and with passage of the Full Stop Law (Ley de Punto Final) and Law of Due Obedience (Ley de Obediencia Debida) in 1986 and 1987, respectively, immunity was given to the military officers responsible for the crimes committed during the dictatorship. The amnesty contributed to a climate of forgetting which, together with the impact of the economic crisis on the film industry, led to a loss of interest in making the dictatorship a theme for films.[2] In order to develop film projects despite these adverse conditions, filmmakers turned to international co-productions.[3]

The Girlfriend was made during this period of economic crisis and in the wake of the amnesty accorded to military officers; part of its funding came from Germany. The Norwegian actress Liv Ullmann, famous for her roles in Ingmar Bergman's films, starred in the movie along with the well-known Argentine actors Cipe Lincovsky and Federico Luppi. Among the many recognitions earned by this film, it is worth noting the best actress awards Ullmann and Lincovsky received at the 1988 San Sebastian International Film Festival. After it premiered in Argentina, *The Girlfriend* was the country's entry for the Oscars the following year.

Meerapfel wrote the screenplay for *The Girlfriend* with the Argentine filmmaker Alcides Chiesa. The story takes place between the height of the dictatorship and the beginning of democracy. The friendship that gives the title to the film refers to María and Raquel, childhood friends who meet again after their lives have taken different paths. María, played by Ullmann, is a Catholic housewife who lives in a modest neighborhood in Quilmes, on the outskirts of greater Buenos Aires. She is married to an unemployed factory worker, Pancho (played by Luppi), with whom she has three children. Raquel, played by Lincovsky, is a Jewish middle-class intellectual. She is a stage actress, unmarried, and does not have a family. State terrorism affects both their lives. María tenaciously searches for her son Carlos, who was involved with leftist groups and later abducted. Her mission leads to her joining and later becoming a leader of the Mothers of the Plaza de Mayo, a movement founded during the dictatorship made up of mothers seeking to find their abducted sons and daughters. For her part, Raquel stages Sophocles' *Antigone*. Because of this, she is threatened and forced to leave Argentina immediately. She chooses to go to Germany, the country her parents had fled during Nazi rule. Because Raquel's parents were German, she has the right to settle in West Germany.

In showing *Antigone* onstage, the film brings attention to an intertextual

María (Liv Ullmann) at a Mothers of the Plaza de Mayo rally. *La amiga* (*The Girlfriend*) (1988), directed by Jeanine Meerapfel.

exchange with literature. Indeed, such commerce between film and literature has been a constant since the development of the Argentine film industry. In her study on the relationship between Argentine cinema and fiction, María Gabriela Mizraje notes that film "usually occupies a space previously won over by text," but there are also cases where literature advances on the film's domain.[4] In *The Girlfriend*, this exchange can be seen in the use of a female character from Greek mythology to stage opposition to a tyrannical regime. Bertolt Brecht did much the same to question Nazi Germany; in the context of Latin American theater, the figure of Antigone has also been used to investigate and unpack various historical periods.[5]

Raquel's role as Antigone in the play is a mise en abyme of the path the characters of *The Girlfriend* take. But while it is Raquel who plays Antigone onstage, María is closer to Sophocles' heroine in the film. Beginning in her childhood, she shows empathy for those whose rights have been violated. Many years later, María leaves the private space of the home when she joins the Mothers of the Plaza de Mayo. Despite her husband's rebukes for neglecting her duties as a housewife, she becomes a more and more politicized figure in the public sphere, gradually assuming the role of Antigone. Unlike the Antigone of myth, whose act of disobedience is to bury her brother, John King describes María as "an Antigone in reverse" (378) because she refuses to bury her son's bones when they are exhumed from a mass grave.

Burials are central to both the film and the myth of Antigone. Cemeteries play a key diegetic role, because they are the settings in which the main themes and debates of the film are conveyed. It is in these themes and debates that the film takes up issues related directly or tangentially to Jewish tradition and experience. Christian Gundermann notes that cemeteries are "places at the center of the work's approach to political, cultural, and affective issues."[6] King alludes to the "sense of identity, of genealogy, of history, of place" (378) that cemeteries give. There are three scenes in graveyards, and in all three both friends are present. The first takes place at the beginning of the film, during the characters' childhood; the second is in the middle, during Raquel's exile in Germany; the third takes place toward the end, when the remains of disappeared people are exhumed from mass graves.

The opening scene of the film is set in a cemetery in which a group of children, including María and Raquel, hold a Catholic funeral for a canary. The children throw Raquel out of the ceremony and insult her by calling her "rusa de mierda [fucking kike]." María, however, defends Raquel and invokes her universal right to participate in the ritual. This leads to a physical confrontation between Raquel and one of the boys. Meanwhile, the canary is forgotten and, in the end, trampled. The scuffle thus goes beyond merely sidetracking the initial purpose of the ceremony and leads to an outright sacrilege. The incident can be seen as an allegory of the violation of human rights, including those of ethnic minorities. It thus alludes to the crimes the military regime committed systematically while it promoted a discourse of national unity.

Later in the film, Raquel is the target of anti-Semitic abuse by the regime's various agents and plainclothesmen, who make disparaging comments such as "a tu putita moishe la vamos a hacer jabón [We're going to turn your little Jewish whore into soap]," "judíos bolches [Jewish pinkos]," and "judíos a la horca [Jews to the scaffold]." It is worth noting that the only times the word "Jew" is used in the film is as part of a phrase of abuse. The film thus reflects critically on the inclusion of Jews in Argentina and on the continued use of an anti-Semitic discourse permeated by Judeo-phobic tropes. In these insults and threats, racist and misogynist tropes commonly draw on the archetype of the Jew as a threat conspiring against the nation. In the view of Albano Harguindeguy, the Minister of the Interior during the dictatorship, whose words are heard in the background of the film, the nation is the "víctima . . . de coaliciones oscuras [victim . . . of dark alliances]." Beyond recreating the climate of the period, the voices of the military officials on mass media help the viewer experience the discourse the regime contributed to and produced.

In addition to her heroism and sense of equality, María, as a child, shows that she is also unlike others in the curiosity she shows toward what is different. In a scene shortly after the incident at the cemetery, María is interested in the Yiddish she hears in Raquel's house, where her parents "hablan en raro [talk weird]." She enjoys listening to Raquel sing in Yiddish and trying on the clothes Raquel's family brought from Europe. During this scene of cultural exchange in Raquel's house, the girls drink *mate*, a symbol of traditional Argentine culture. While Raquel is linked to Yiddish and to her parents' culture, she is also linked to Argentina whether or not others accept her. This scene shows a member of an ethnic minority demonstrating a genuine interest in being part of the nation. It can thus be interpreted as an appeal for a place for those different from the dominant culture. Later in the film, other products symbolic of Argentine culture will reinforce the connection between Raquel and Argentina. The song in Yiddish also activates an intertextual dialogue with other Argentine and Latin American pieces of music, both diegetic and extra-diegetic. It contributes to a web of associations that, in counterpoint to the story, manages to bring Yiddish and the Argentine and Latin American traditions into harmony, thus reconciling Raquel's dual identity.[7]

The second cemetery scene occurs in Germany, the birthplace of Raquel's parents and where she chooses to live in exile as a result of a death threat due to the performance of *Antigone*. The film thus highlights the reversal of roles between the two countries. Argentina has become an unstable country whose regime expels its citizens while West Germany has restored democracy after the end of Nazism; the latter now admits immigrants and accepts cultural pluralism and multilingualism. Seeing both countries onscreen brings together and makes an association between the two regimes that have marked Raquel's life, namely Nazism and the Argentine dictatorship.

In Argentina, the military regime made use of Nazi-inspired discursive elements in combination with the practice of torture and other violent methods employed for interrogation and elimination of suspected members of the political opposition. This has led the Argentine imaginary to develop parallels between the dictatorship and the Holocaust. Florinda Goldberg distinguishes two levels in this construction. The first concerns the actions themselves: similarities in mechanisms of repression upon that sector within society differentiated as a threatening group seen as the "other," in the experience of political exile manifesting in a diasporic awareness of their loss of country, and in the general indifference shown by the public.[8] The second level takes up the very possibility of representing either experience, a theme that draws on the debate concerning the problem of fictionalizing the Shoah.[9] Faced with the inadequacy of realistic mimetic strategies for representing the atrocity that was the dictatorship, a need for new literary mechanisms arises. Since the mid-1970s, Argentine literature has called for a different metaphoric and symbolic mimesis. It turns to the experience of the Holocaust and the Jews not only as, in Goldberg's words, the "prototype of socio-historical events" but also as the "paradigm of emptying to express, symbolically, the emptying of paradigms" (142). Turning to the Holocaust then leads to further questions about the ethical implications of this very move, a debate which we will not delve into here.

In the film, the regime's methods of repression—threats, break-ins, abductions, and murders—and the rhetoric it employed are presented openly and with an almost documentary verisimilitude. The dictatorship is shown in action and in speech, but the film also calls for, as Goldberg says, an "allusive and symbolic mimesis from a new die." It does so by employing the myth of Antigone and, even more so, by turning to the paradigm of the Shoah. In constructing the Holocaust as unsayable and inexpressible, the film makes silence itself a commemoration of the horror of a past that should not return: that of the Shoah and the dictatorship. In effect, Raquel is afraid that "todo vuelva a repetirse [everything will happen again]."

In Berlin, Raquel takes María to visit the grave of her great-grandparents, who died in Germany at the beginning of the twentieth century. At this point of the story, some distance has already grown between the two friends. María does not accept Raquel's decision to live in exile, which she considers equivalent to abandoning the political struggle. As Catherine Grant correctly argues, María is "no longer able to identify with [Raquel's] situation as a Jewish woman under attack" by the military (320). She is reluctant to give weight to the persecution that forced Raquel to flee, and goes so far as to ask her "¿Qué sabés vos sobre el miedo, . . . las amenazas, las persecuciones? [What do you know about the fear, . . . the threats, being followed?]." She also seems unaware of the similar situations Raquel's family must have experienced. Shortly after this, María refers to those who saved themselves in an accusatory and suspicious tone, which hurts Raquel and leads her to ask "¿Me estás diciendo que todos los que se salvaron son unos trai . . . ? [Are you telling me that all the people who saved themselves are trait . . . ?]." It is difficult not to associate this exchange with the stigmatization of those who were saved in the Shoah, as analyzed by Primo Levi in *The Drowned and the Saved* (1986): "The worst survived . . . all the best died." Those who were spared were thus faced with the task of perpetually justifying their survival to themselves and to others as not having been achieved at the expense of others (82).

The film sketches a family history for Raquel in which her grandparents' generation is neither mentioned nor shown. Based on Raquel's age, we know that her parents would have lived and suffered under the Nazis, which explains their having left Germany for Argentina. At the cemetery in Berlin,

Raquel says of her great-grandparents that "por lo menos ellos tienen sus tumbas [at least they have their graves]." This refers indirectly to those who have no graves, including possibly her grandparents; Raquel's comment may then allude to those who perished in the Shoah and were thus denied burial. While Raquel's relationship to Judaism is not explicitly shown in the film, it is present precisely in the act of remembering her ancestors, which can be understood as a collective act of identification with the Jewish people. María is unable or hesitant to understand the link Raquel maintains with her ancestors: "Cómo hinchás con tus antepasados, ¿eh? [You're such a pest about your ancestors, you know?]." In order for remembering to be possible, Raquel insists that the dead must have a proper burial. This theme is developed in the scene in the third cemetery and points to the unidentified remains of thousands of disappeared victims of the dictatorship that were left in unmarked mass graves.

This third scene takes place in Argentina precisely when what might be the remains of María's son are exhumed. In one of the strongest clashes between the two friends, María opposes the exhumation; she is at odds with the authorities as well as her husband and friend. The latter insist that the remains must be unearthed for two reasons: because the dead need a proper burial, and because the living need a place to mourn. Pancho and Raquel thus feel a need for closure and maintain that the act of disappearance needs to be given material form in a place for remembering: "María, no sabés lo que decís; los muertos tienen que tener un lugar. Nosotros tenemos que tener un lugar donde poder ir a llorar [María, you don't know what you're saying; the dead need to have a place. We need to have a place where we can go to cry]." For her part, María will not accept the death of her son until she can see his murderers.

Gundermann emphasizes the testimonial intention of the film. In analyzing its depiction of the experience of the dictatorship and the activism of the Mothers of the Plaza de Mayo, he argues that this scene refers to the split in the organization. Because of disagreements among the Mothers, the organization was divided into two factions in 1986. One of the reasons for the split concerned exhumations, with the Founding Line faction comprising those who accepted them and sought to identify the remains of the disappeared. Gundermann interprets María's centrality in the film as "taking a position on the side of Hebe de Bonafini's hardline, revolutionary ideology" (45).[10] He explains that the exhumations effectively silenced the families of the disappeared. In shifting the place of mourning to the private sphere, this undermined activists' demands for prosecution of those responsible (50).[11]

María and Raquel's disagreement over the issues of amnesty and exhumations, among others, corresponds to their fundamentally different outlooks: María is idealistic whereas Raquel is pragmatic.[12] Raquel says "el mundo no es blanco o negro, María, lo que pasa que hay cosas que vos no entendés, que simplemente no sabés [The world isn't black and white, María. There are just some things you don't understand, you simply don't know]." Raquel's insistence that María does not understand everything may be an oblique allusion to the persecution her family suffered and, ultimately, to the Shoah. Raquel's pragmatism seems to be the product of that family history. The differences and disagreements between the two friends derive from their opposing political and life outlooks, and lead to a growing distance in their friendship. In reference to the fact that those responsible for the disappearances are not punished, María condemns the act of giving in. For her part, Raquel fears that if the officers are not given immunity, the dictatorship may return; she thus alludes to the reiteration of other pasts, regimes, and persecutions. Each in her own way, María and Raquel are both connected to the myth of Antigone, as Grant shows, in that both struggle against "the lack of respect for the dead" (321). The struggle to preserve their memory is imperative for both of them, even if they respond to it differently.

The three scenes in cemeteries—the first Catholic, the second Jewish, and the third a mass grave in which the dead are deprived of their names and identities—lay out problems proper to various spheres: politics (state terrorism and the Mothers' activism during the dictatorship and subsequent restoration of democracy), history (the military regime in Argentina), ethnicity (the role of memory and genealogy in the construction of identity), gender (the prominence of female characters and the politicization of a mother), and the personal (the estrangement of two friends). These scenes work as milestones in the story that highlight the sequence of the film—its beginning, middle, and end—and mark moments of key logical and chronological importance.

The film thus presents a clear narrative structure that lays out several axes along which the characters move. These axes include past to present, friendship to estrangement, foreigner to local, totalitarianism to democracy, threat to protection, idealism to pragmatism, career to family, and anonymity to prominence, among others. The coexistence of the Jewish and Argentinian aspects of Raquel's identity, which her adult life in Argentina renders uneasy, is one of the many oppositions Meerapfel lays out in the film. Some of these pairings are inverted over the time span the film covers, which is laid out in various aspects of María and Raquel's friendship. The film thus sets up leading roles for both Raquel and María, but at different times; this is already suggested in the resonance of their names with the Torah and the

New Testament, respectively. The first reunion of the two friends takes place during the dictatorship, in the dressing room of a theater, where Raquel is surrounded by fans after the opening of *Antigone*. Raquel is at the apex of her career, while María is a housewife facing the tragic abduction of her son. Afterward, Raquel returns to Argentina with the restoration of democracy, but she is no longer a prominent artist. Meanwhile, María has undergone a transformation and has become an important political activist with the Mothers of the Plaza de Mayo.[13] As the plot progresses, María develops as a character and gains prominence. Raquel undergoes the opposite process, and during this progression her diasporic characteristics are highlighted. Indeed, Grant brings up Meerapfel's intention to create an antagonist for María in order "to provide a productive dichotomy for the film's structure," because in prior drafts of the script, "María was turning out to be an ultra-'saintly' and uninteresting character" (318).[14]

Raquel's diasporic character is in fact a crucial difference that separates her from María. In analyzing how Raquel's character is developed in the film, it is useful to consider Georg Simmel's notion of the stranger as a figure who "is fixed within a certain spatial circle . . . but [whose] position within it is fundamentally affected by the fact that he does not belong in it initially and that he brings qualities into it that are not, and cannot be, indigenous to it."[15] As the daughter of Jewish immigrants, Raquel is seen as newly arrived. She is thus singled out as different, and she is not entirely incorporated into Argentina even if she does feel Argentine. In addition, she does leave the country: asylum in Germany is a viable possibility for her, which is precisely why María reproaches her. However, the experience of exile accentuates Raquel's wandering characteristics. In Germany, she feels uprooted and foreign: "Esta es la tierra de mis padres pero no la mía [This is my parents' land, but not mine]." But when she returns to Argentina, her loss of economic status and social capital makes her feel out of place there, too. Raquel does not have family, but rather ancestors. Nor does she take part in the life of the Jewish community; she is the only Jewish character in the story. By contrast, María is, above all, a mother. This gives her a clear place within the family and society at large. It is in fact as a mother that María evolves and becomes a political actor. It is even María's motherhood which gives Raquel a certain genealogical continuity: María's daughter is named Raquelita, and Raquel's namesake is working in theater.

At the end of the film, the tension between the two friends, which had reached a breaking point in the scene at the mass graves, begins to subside. However, they do not succeed at reconciling their friendship despite Raquel's attempt to approach María. The last scene of the film takes place at night, with the two friends sitting on a pier on the Río de la Plata. They once again lay out their different points of view. While they had once sealed their childhood friendship at the very place where they are sitting, it now becomes the stage for their final estrangement. In their childhood, what was different about them had helped solidify their friendship. Decades later, however, and in the context of military repression, the two protagonists' reactions become polarized. As mediated by María and Raquel's different memories, personal histories, and cultural backgrounds, the experience of the dictatorship finally disperses their friendship.

Notes

This essay was translated from Spanish by Jozef Engel Szwaja-Franken.
1. For more information on Meerapfel's life and work, including *La amiga*, see www.meerapfel.de.
2. Burucúa, *Confronting the "Dirty War" in Argentine Cinema*, 1–4.
3. Grant, "Camera Solidaria," 312–313; King, "Assailing the Heights of Macho Pictures," 363. Grant's and King's articles take up the issue of international coproductions in Argentina from the end of the 1980s through the mid-1990s.
4. Mizraje, "El doble sueño: Literatura y cine argentinos," 26. *Translator's note*: all translations in quotes are mine.
5. González Betancur, "Antígona y el teatro latinoamericano," 77–79. In the case of Argentina, Leopoldo Marechal turned to Sophocles' character in *Antígona Vélez* (1951) in order to reconsider a more remote historical period, namely the Conquest of the Desert in the late nineteenth century. Like Meerapfel's film, Griselda Gambaro's play *Antígona furiosa* (1989) questioned and criticized a much more recent period, namely the dictatorship's many crimes and abuses.
6. Gundermann, *Actos melancólicos*, 50.
7. Grant, "Camera Solidaria," 326, and Burucúa, *Confronting the "Dirty War" in Argentine Cinema*, 138–139, analyze the intertextual role of music in the film.
8. Goldberg, "'Judíos del Sur': El modelo judío en la narrativa de la catástrofe argentina."
9. The vast discussion around the problem of representing the Shoah and the ethical implications that go along with this includes questions ranging from the "authenticity" of the images shown and the "permissible modes of representation" to the "aestheticizing of the Holocaust" (Lang, *Holocaust Representation: Art within the Limits of History and Ethics*, ix).
10. Hebe de Bonafini is one of the Mothers' founders.
11. In analyzing the activism of the Mothers of the Plaza de Mayo, Gundermann employs the lens of melancholia. In this reading, they refuse to accept the death of the disappeared; correspondingly, the fact that the bodies were not found does not lead to resignation, but rather to greater resistance and militancy. In contrast, the work of mourning accepts loss. The theoretical approach informing this reading is derived from Judith Butler's work, among others (11–22).
12. Grant, "Camera Solidaria," 318.

13. Burucúa, *Confronting the "Dirty War" in Argentine Cinema*, 140.
14. Grant's source for this assertion is an interview with Meerapfel held on 12 February 1997.
15. Simmel, *On Individuality and Social Forms*, 143.

Works Cited

Film

Meerapfel, Jeanine, dir. *The Girlfriend*. Neue Visionen. 1988.

Articles and Books

Burucúa, Constanza. *Confronting the "Dirty War" in Argentine Cinema, 1983-1993: Memory and Gender in Historical Representations*. Tamesis: Woodbridge, 2009.
Gambaro, Griselda. "Antígona furiosa." In *Griselda Gambaro: Teatro 3*, 195–217. Buenos Aires: Ediciones de la Flor, 1989.
Goldberg, Florinda F. "'Judíos del Sur': El modelo judío en la narrativa de la catástrofe argentina." *Estudios Interdisciplinarios de América Latina y el Caribe* 12, no. 2 (2000-2001): 139–152.
González Betancur, Juan David. "Antígona y el teatro latinoamericano." *Calle14* 4, no. 4 (2010): 72–84.
Grant, Catherine. "Camera Solidaria." *Screens* 38, no. 4 (1997): 311–328.
Gundermann, Christian. *Actos melancólicos: Formas de resistencia en la posdictadura argentina*. Rosario: Beatriz Viterbo, 2007.
King, John. "Assailing the Heights of Macho Pictures: Women Film-Makers in Contemporary Argentina." In *Essays on Hispanic Themes: In Honour of Edward C. Riley*, ed. Jennifer Lowe and Philip Swanson, 360–382. Edinburgh: Department of Hispanic Studies, University of Edinburgh, 1989.
Lang, Berel. *Holocaust Representation: Art within the Limits of History and Ethics*. Baltimore: Johns Hopkins University Press, 2000.
Levi, Primo. *The Drowned and the Saved*. Trans. Raymond Rosenthal. Repr. New York: Vintage International, 1989.
Marechal, Leopoldo. *Antígona Vélez*. Villa Constitución, Córdoba: Ediciones Clásicas Literarias, 1998.
Mizraje, María Gabriela. "El doble sueño: Literatura y cine argentinos." *Hispamérica* 42, no. 124 (2013): 21–30.
Simmel, Georg. *On Individuality and Social Forms*. Trans. Donald Levine. Chicago: University of Chicago Press, 1971.

CHAPTER 6

Revisiting the AMIA Bombing in Marcos Carnevale's *Anita*

MIRNA VOHNSEN

On 18 July 1994, at 9:53 a.m., the headquarters of the most important Jewish community center in Argentina, the Asociación Mutual Israelita Argentina (AMIA), located at 633 Pasteur Street in the historic Jewish neighborhood of Once, Buenos Aires, was the target of the deadliest bombing that has ever occurred on Argentine soil.[1] Eighty-five people were killed and three hundred were injured. Although twenty-four years have passed since the attack, no one has been convicted and the case remains unsolved.

This unhealed wound in Argentine history has spawned numerous cultural expressions, among which is the Argentine feature film *Anita* (dir. Marcos Carnevale, 2009). The film revisits the AMIA bombing from the viewpoint of one of the victims, a childlike protagonist who in the aftermath of the bombing is left to wander the streets of Buenos Aires. With a nonprofessional actress in the lead, the film is a telling commentary on the hardships of "a real person" who is searching for her missing mother. In the remainder of this essay, the protagonist, despite being an adult, is referred to as a child because she undertakes a journey that is the reverse of the search for the child (or the truth about the child) in films such as *La amiga* (*The Girlfriend*) (dir. Jeanine Meerapfel, 1988), *Garage Olimpo* (dir. Marco Bechis, 1999) and *La historia oficial* (*The Official Story*) (dir. Luis Puenzo, 1985). There is a metatextual connection between *La historia oficial* and *Anita*: the renowned Argentine actress Norma Aleandro plays the mother in both films. Whereas in the former Aleandro searches for her child's true identity, in the latter the child searches for her mother.

Informed by cultural memory, this essay argues that although *Anita* is a fictionalized memory narrative of the AMIA bombing, the film establishes a dialogue with the search for the disappeared under the last repressive governmental regime in Argentina (1976–1983). To further this argument, two related issues are explored: the child's wandering in search of her missing mother and her own status as one of the disappeared. While the protagonist embarks on a journey that echoes the search undertaken by the Mothers of the Plaza de Mayo (henceforth the Mothers) for their own missing offspring, her brother searches for her. Facing adversity, displacement, and exclusion, the child embodies the memory of the victims of both atrocities and their resistance to invisibility. Furthermore, mindful of the image of the AMIA bombing as solely a Jewish problem, the essay aims to demonstrate that by strategically charting a map of the Argentine family, the film makes the AMIA bombing a national experience and ultimately a constitutive part of the nation's cultural memory.[2]

Anita inscribes itself within the discourse of cultural memory in three related ways. First, it is one of the many cultural expressions that fashion the cultural memory of the AMIA bombing, such as commemorations, art exhibitions, literary works, the AMIA Wall (a billboard displaying the names of the victims), and Memoria Activa (an association formed by relatives and friends of the victims of the AMIA which gathers every Monday in front of Buenos Aires Supreme Court to ask for justice).[3] Second, in reenacting and recalling the AMIA bombing, the film can be regarded, in the words of Edna Aizenberg, as a "keeper of contemporary memory."[4] Although Aizenberg alludes in her study to literature and not film, both cultural expressions fulfill, in the context of the AMIA bombing, the same function, namely, that of keeping alive the memory of the atrocity. Third, through the theme of the search for missing family members, the film taps into the memory of the disappeared during Argentina's Dirty War.

Anita

Inspired by the AMIA bombing, Marcos Carnevale produced, directed, and wrote *Anita*, his fifth feature-length film.[5] With a viewership of 125,548, *Anita* was the ninth most popular film in Argentina in 2009.[6] It was declared to be of social interest by the government of the Autonomous City of Buenos Aires, and the film garnered numerous accolades at different international Jewish film festivals as well as the award for best film at the International Latino Film Festival held in Los Angeles in 2009. Moreover, it received positive reviews by national and international film critics. *Clarín*'s critic Diego Lerer, for example, points out that "*Anita* se aprecia debido a su contención emotiva (el atentado está manejado fuera de campo) y a una protagonista que calará a fondo en los espectadores [The strength of *Anita* lies in its emotional restraint (the attack is handled off-screen) and in a protagonist who will make a deep impression on viewers]."[7] *La Nación*'s Adolfo Martínez, for his part, praises the work of Carnevale with these words: "Con enorme calidez y permanente emoción, el director y coguionista Marcos Carnevale relata esta historia que posee, además, el recuerdo de uno de los hechos más luctuosos ocurridos en la Argentina [This story, which commemorates one of the most tragic events to have occurred in Argentina, is told with enormous warmth and constant emotion by director and co-scriptwriter Marcos Carnevale]." In the same vein, Dave Robson from *Sound on Sight* remarks that "*Anita* is a lovely film with an unorthodox—and resultantly refreshing—look at tragedy."

Anita narrates the story of Anita Feldman, a young Jewish woman with Down syndrome, who lives in Once with her mother, Dora.[8] Anita and her mother run a stationery store located in the same building where they reside. On the morning of 18 July 1994, Dora leaves Anita alone in the store while she goes to the headquarters of the AMIA, situated nearby. On that day, the AMIA is blown up. As a consequence of the blast, Dora perishes and their store is completely destroyed, but Anita survives the explosion with minor injuries. Amid the confusion, Anita starts roaming the streets of Buenos Aires in search of her mother, but she gets lost. Anita's meanderings lead her to encounters with several strangers. In the meantime, Anita is the subject of a search by her brother, Ariel, who finally finds her.

There are three issues around the character Anita that deserve further attention: her Jewishness, her understanding of what she has experienced, and the actress's performance. The ethnicity of Anita and her family is downplayed to such an extent that we see only a smattering of Jewish objects in the family's dwelling. Additionally, the family does not take part in any communal or religious activity. The few cues that disclose that this is indeed a Jewish family are, first, the Yiddish words *mayn feygele* (my little bird), a term Anita's mother uses to awake her daughter; second, the surname, Feldman, written on the sign of their stationery store; third, the Star of David and the Hebrew characters carved on the gravestone of Anita's father; finally, the mention of the AMIA in a conversation Dora has with Ariel. Metaphorically speaking, Anita's Jewish identity is given by the family setting and, once this setting vanishes, her Jewishness is attenuated, too.

Concerning Anita's experience of the attack, it should be highlighted that she cannot understand what has happened. When asked the reason for her bruises and blood-stained clothes, she replies that she has fallen off a ladder in the stationery store. Despite being a victim of the attack, Anita does not realize it. Therefore, what the film plays out is the limited comprehension

Anita (Alejandra Manzo) and Dora (Norma Aleandro) in front of the stationery store. *Anita* (2006), directed by Marcos Carnevale.

that Anita has of traumatic events, thus signaling that there is no room for such an atrocity in her memory.

The film does not explain the tragedy by dissecting its causes. Instead, it focuses on the consequences of the attack as experienced by the central character, played by Alejandra Manzo, an adult with Down syndrome. Manzo delivers a believable performance thanks to her guileless appearance, and there lies the key to the success of the film. As Karen Lury argues, "audiences are less likely to be manipulated if they believe that the child actor is genuine or (a) natural."[9] Manzo's interpretation of Anita is indeed genuine and natural. Despite being an adult, Manzo is able to show her character exhibiting characteristics related to childhood: namely innocence, vulnerability, and a dependence on adults, as well as behaving and dressing in a childish fashion. In this regard, it is illustrative to note that Anita's innocence, vulnerability, and dependence highlight the cruelty of the attack, leading the audience to empathize with her. Carnevale has deftly crafted the film as a child-centered narrative through which he compares and contrasts Anita's life before and after the AMIA bombing.

Life before the AMIA Bombing

The explosion, which becomes the turning point in Anita's life, splits the story into two parts. The first part reveals the highly ritualized life of Anita and Dora in a seemingly safe environment. The film opens with an establishing shot of a dormant Buenos Aires, followed by a sequence of shots portraying the family's daily routine. Whereas this portrayal exudes harmony and unity, it also unveils Anita's complete reliance on her mother. Her reliance and their ritualized family life are further emphasized in the two bathroom scenes, played out in the first segments of the film. In the first, the camera captures mother and daughter in the bathroom and, while Dora does her hair, she instructs Anita on how to brush her teeth. In the second, Anita takes a bath, and Dora, while sitting nearby looking over some invoices, tells her child each body part she should wash. The ritualization of these actions, which are based on a trustful relationship, is conveyed by a comment Anita makes in the second bathroom scene. Busy with the invoices, Dora forgets to mention that Anita has to wash her ears, to which Anita says, "Te olvidaste las orejas, ma [You forgot to mention my ears, mom]." Anita's comment shows that these actions are conducted routinely in the same manner at every bathtime, which permits the child to predict the order in which they are performed and eventually to do them independently.

A preference for shooting interiors in the first segments of the film overshadows the portrayal of the neighborhood where mother and daughter live. The neighborhood of Once has been widely portrayed as a place bustling with people but scarred by the AMIA bombing, especially in the filmography of Jewish Argentine director Daniel Burman. A case in point is Burman's untitled short in the anthology film *18-J* (dir. Burman et al. 2004), which depicts the neighborhood of Once as a place where the memory of the attack runs deep through all its spaces. Privileging the private over the public, Carnevale does not give the same prominence to Once as Burman does. His preference for showcasing the domestic sphere in the narrative underscores two motivations of the film: the link that exists between Anita and her mother and Anita's estrangement from the outer world. In the first part of the film we see Anita outside the domestic sphere only on one occasion, namely, when she and her mother go to the Jewish cemetery where Anita's father is buried. Whilst the domestic sphere is highly ritualized, the outside world represents an unbounded, unpredictable space, and the scene in the cemetery eloquently displays this unpredictability.

Once in the cemetery, Dora, who has been busy tending her husband's grave, looks around but cannot see Anita. Concerned about her daughter's whereabouts, Dora looks for Anita and finds her playing with some stones. Play is normally associated with freedom and autonomy, and according to Amanda Holmes, "as an activity, play incites the exploration of ideas; it allows participants to push past the structured boundaries that define their day-to-day identities."[10] Indeed, Anita's unsupervised contact with the outer world is marked by exploration through play and stands in stark contrast to her ritualized life in the domestic sphere. This first diegetic detachment from her mother and her surveying of an unfamiliar space foreshadow the imminent change that surfaces after the explosion, namely the destruction of her family and her consequent orphanhood, two events that entail the charting of unknown territory. In sum, the first part of the film seeks to reconstruct the memory of a "happy childhood" that the bomb disrupts.

The Explosion: Destruction, Death, and Destitution

The key motif of loss pervades the scene of the explosion, in which Anita loses not only her mother but also her familial milieu. Prior to the bombing, from the moment Anita is awoken by her mother, she is never left alone. The shots are framed in such a way that Anita is flanked by her mother at all times. Nevertheless, on 18 July 1994, Anita's life suffers the impact of terrorism and undergoes a dramatic transformation. Because Dora has to run an errand to the AMIA building, she makes the decision to leave Anita alone in their stationery store. Insofar as this is the first time that Dora leaves Anita, the plot builds up an expectation of change in Anita's life. To put it differently, Dora's departure from Anita's side prefigures the fact that the child will eventually lose the person who is closest and dearest to her.

The scene of the explosion explicitly portrays Anita's loss of her familial milieu. From the moment Dora leaves Anita, the audience shares Anita's point of view in that we only have access to what takes place inside the store. Carnevale sutures the audience's viewpoint into this traumatic moment in Anita's life. The camera follows Anita's feet and the bottom of the ladder she is pushing, a synecdoche that may represent Anita on her way to autonomy. Before leaving, Dora tells Anita not to climb the ladder, but Anita is determined to challenge her mother. The cut to a close-up of Anita's hands picking up a box of pencil cases confirms her determination to put the pencil cases on one of the top shelves of the store. Next is a close-up focusing on Anita's feet going up the steps of the ladder, which symbolizes her movement toward a different stage in her life. The following shot is a close-up of the hands of the wall clock moving to 9:53, a reminder to the viewer of what would take place a few seconds later. A long shot next captures the tidiness of the shop, and Anita, who is a part of that order, is seen from behind on top of the ladder. The mise en scène positions Anita as the central element of a well-known, protective world. Even the colors of her clothes match the surroundings, which enhances a sense of belonging.

This is the last shot in which Anita is an integral part of a safe environment, and the last instant before her world is, quite literally, shattered. The last glimpse of this prior existence is a medium shot of Anita's happy face forming the foreground of an overexposed background, which produces a sort of chiaroscuro where all colors have practically vanished. Hence the intent of this shot is to direct the audience's attention from the interior to the exterior of the store. The silence of the scene is broken by a terrible blast, Anita falls off the ladder, and a cloud of ash covers everything. The scene ends with a black frame that signifies that a major shift has taken place and even that Anita could have suffered a blackout.

Expelled from her home by the explosion, Anita ventures out into the unknown. The first steps she takes unveil an alien environment covered by conspicuous grey ash and peopled by the injured, a scene shot in slow motion and accompanied by a buzzing sound as well as monotonous music. This mode of filming conveys Anita's mental state, which is one of total confusion and inability to comprehend the ghastly situation she is faced with. In fact, not only Anita but also Once itself has fallen victim to a terrorist attack. The representation of Once evokes a locus of suffering and destruction but at the same time of solidarity, as images of people helping each other are juxtaposed with images of Anita's bewilderment. In this respect, it is worth recalling Aizenberg's words on the attack: "Ironically, the pluralistic solidarity so often elusive in Argentine society has partially been achieved through shared suffering."[11] The solidarity displayed on the street reinforces one of the ideologies of the film: Once is a district where Jews and non-Jews stand together and help each other in the most traumatic situation ever experienced there. This, in turn, evokes the contentious issue of the extent to which the AMIA bombing is a problem affecting all Argentines: the motif of solidarity confirms the attack as a shared national event and not as an entirely Jewish problem.

Cultural memory, then, is articulated in the reenactment of the explosion in two distinct ways. First, Carnevale memorializes not only the traumatic event but also its devastating impact on Once. Insofar as destruction, death, and destitution are experienced not only by Anita but also by the rest of the victims, the figure of the child becomes a metonymy for wider suffering. Through the individual story of Anita, the film echoes the metamorphosis of Once from a neighborhood where people lived and developed their commercial activities agreeably to a place where people are killed and their means of living crushed. Second, the film mediates one of the most traumatic episodes in Argentine history by making it a national experience and ultimately a constitutive part of the nation's cultural memory. Because the explosion is reenacted in the film, it becomes part of the public arena, thus creating a sense of shared participation in the victimhood of the bombing. So, while cultural memory is evoked in the representation of the bombing in the first part of the film, in the second part, it is constructed through the depiction of the search for the disappeared.

The Search for the Disappeared

The search for disappeared family members is a theme utilized in films dealing with the traumatic events of the Dirty War. With its thirty thousand disappeared, the Dirty War left such a profound impact on Argentine society that it continues to haunt the Argentine psyche. Although its influence is particularly tangible in stories produced in the aftermath of the repressive governmental regime, *Anita* echoes the trauma of the period by establishing a dialogue with the search undertaken by the Mothers for their missing offspring. Focusing on the search for two females, *Anita* reimagines the search for the disappeared through a double voice.

The AMIA explosion tore families, a neighborhood, and by extension, a nation apart, and it affects the narrative structure of the film by dividing the story into two juxtaposing narrative strands: one hinges on Anita's search for her mother, and the other engages with Ariel's search for his sister. Their search is analogous to the situation experienced by the Mothers, who persistently sought (and still seek) information about their kidnapped family members. This is skillfully represented in *Garage Olimpo*, when María's mother first sells her house and then loses her own life in the effort to obtain information about her disappeared daughter. At the same time, *Garage Olimpo*, like *Anita*, depicts the child's futile search for her mother when María, who is unaware of her mother's death, repeatedly phones her, but to no avail. It is the contention of this essay that by turning the camera on the search undertaken by Anita and Ariel, Carnevale intends to build bridges between the AMIA bombing and the Dirty War. Accordingly, by incorporating the theme of the search for missing family members, *Anita* protects the memory of the disappeared during the Dirty War against the corrosive action of time. Hence, the film constructs cultural memory by drawing on the memory of another traumatic event in the history of Argentina.

After the explosion, the outer world displaces the inner world represented in the first part of the film, and what emerges is a hostile and decadent Buenos Aires, where hurried passers-by, graffiti-covered walls, and closed stores form the backdrop to Anita's wandering. This cityscape undoubtedly mirrors Anita's own hardships, but it also signals the legacy of an inefficient state.

In an article on the image of Buenos Aires as a threatening city in nine key Argentine films, Catherine Leen concludes that the films she discusses "share a sense of disillusionment and even despair with the city in which they are set."[12] In *Anita*, too, there is a sense of disillusionment and despair with Buenos Aires; although the film captures instances of solidarity immediately after the attack, these are contested by images of an urban environment that displaces the central character. More important, the hostile cityscape alludes to the inability of the state to protect its own citizens, whether they are minors or adults, and ensure a safe society, a critique that links *Anita* to *La amiga* and *Garage Olimpo*, films in which the state is not only inefficient in aiding its citizens but also the perpetrator of violence.

Anita, motherless and homeless, is left to fend for herself in an estranged city. Anita is treated at the Hospital de Clínicas, where she witnesses the suffering of the survivors of the blast. Situated two hundred meters from the AMIA, the Hospital de Clínicas played a pivotal role in assisting the victims of the attack in 1994, so the inclusion of the hospital in the narrative functions as a remembrance of collective suffering.

After leaving the hospital unnoticed, Anita embarks on her urban wandering. Carnevale portrays Anita's fruitless quest and disorientation through high-angle shots in which she appears almost to be an invisible person ensnared in the immensity of the city. Her invisibility is further accentuated by passers-by who take no notice of her presence. During the city scenes, the film lapses into a narrative standstill which suggests Anita's incomprehension of the traumatic events that have taken place in her life. Her bewildered state resonates with that of the survivors of the AMIA bombing, who almost twenty-four years later cannot grasp why they were the target of such a heinous attack. In this sense, the film constitutes a critique of a society that has failed its own people. Because it has been unable to protect its people and find those responsible for the bombing, the state still owes a debt to its citizens.

Anita's journey through the city entails the meeting of various individuals who, albeit not readily, come to her aid by offering her shelter, food, and clothing. In light of this, it can be argued that the strangers she encounters act as her surrogate family. The first person Anita makes contact with is Félix, a drunken photographer who gives her shelter for two nights. Worn out from her aimless walking, Anita falls asleep in a decrepit hallway but is awoken suddenly by the voice of a boy talking to his mother on a public phone next to her. On hearing him utter the word "mamá" several times, Anita approaches the phone but the boy hangs up and leaves. Immediately afterward, Félix, who wants to make a phone call, lifts the receiver to talk to his ex-wife and Anita exclaims "mami" while pointing to the phone. This is the first time that Anita makes an explicit reference to the fact that she is looking for her mother.

Heedless of Anita's presence, however, Félix engages in a heated argument with his ex-wife over their son, whom he is not allowed to see. Félix's conversation reflects the disintegration of the family in Argentine society, a theme that has pervaded Argentine cinema since the 1980s as a result of the impact of the most recent military dictatorship and the implementation of neoliberal practices in the 1990s.[13] Enraged by the argument, Félix breaks the receiver by hitting it repeatedly against the phone. Suddenly realizing that Anita is standing next to him, Félix excuses himself and asks her if she has to call someone, to which Anita nods. Félix offers to take her to a bar nearby where there is also a phone, but neither that one nor the one in his home works. As if the phone constitutes the only means through which Anita may contact her mother, the broken phones symbolize the severing of the bond between mother and daughter and the impossibility of restoring this bond given that Dora has been killed. The symbol of the phone hints at the unanswered phone calls that María makes in *Garage Olimpo*. María, unlike Anita, has access to phones but cannot be reunited with her mother, because her mother, like Dora, is dead.

Despite his personal problems, Félix tries to help Anita: he takes her to his home and asks Anita for her personal details. Anita, however, cannot give him a satisfactory answer, or at least an answer that may prompt a reconnection with her family. Not knowing what to do, Félix decides to let Anita stay overnight in his messy apartment and promises her that they will find a solution the following day. In spite of all his defects, Félix acts as a surrogate father through his role as provider of shelter and food (Félix cooks dinner for Anita). The house of an alcoholic father is the setting in which Anita spends her first night outside her home, but she does not seem to mind. The fact that Anita accepts this person who is so alien and different from her family can be qualified as remarkable. Her unprejudiced reaction helps her to meld into whatever milieu she is in, and this is vividly portrayed in the dinner scene, in which Anita and Félix share not only the same space but also their experiences of the day. This cinematic device invites viewers to draw a parallel between Anita's family life before and after the AMIA bombing.

Echoing the fragmentation of the family in Argentine society, Félix ultimately fails Anita. Breaking his promise to help her, Félix tries to get rid of her the following morning. Anita's resilience persuades him to give her accommodation for a second night, but on the following day he abandons her on a bus. Félix's reluctance to continue helping Anita suggests two readings:

on the one hand, Félix embodies the destabilization of the traditional type of masculinity, which upholds men as breadwinners, moral leaders of their families, and heads of households. The implementation of neoliberalism in Argentina under the Menem Administration (1989–1999) led to high unemployment among men, a situation that transformed men's traditional roles.[14] Those men who were unable to adapt to the new system proved less able to fulfill their roles as fathers, and that seems to be precisely Félix's case. Félix's ex-wife indeed accuses him of being incapable of taking care of anybody. On the other hand, Félix's behavior mirrors that part of Argentine society that has turned its back on the victims of the AMIA bombing. Anita's determination, conversely, represents the voices of the victims who insist on being heard.

Anita's strength of will emerges once again in her encounter with a Chinese family who run a grocery store. This encounter reinforces the fact that the child accepts her hosts' hospitality openly and without reservations, but it is not a certainty that they will accept the child. It is Anita's relentless patience that defeats their reticence, and this is depicted in the scene that portrays Anita's incorporation into the Chinese family. A long shot of Anita sitting on some wooden boxes across the street from the Chinese grocery store speaks of her orphanhood and exclusion while the shopkeepers—a Chinese matriarch and her daughter—argue in the foreground of the frame about whether they should take her in or not. By highlighting Anita and placing her between the two women, Carnevale anticipates her inclusion in the Chinese family. The next scene, then, shows Anita sitting at the table with the entire family and sharing their dinner, just as she did with Félix. If Félix acted as Anita's surrogate father, the Chinese family represents a surrogate extended family composed of a grandmother, a mother, a son, a daughter, and a baby. Interestingly, there is no father figure in the Chinese family, another allusion to the failure of men's traditional roles in the family as providers and protectors. As if putting together the pieces of a familial puzzle, the story gradually constructs a picture of the multiethnic Argentine family.

Pursuing the idea of the Argentine family, the film delivers the figure of the surrogate mother in the shape of the last person Anita meets on her journey, the nurse Nori. Anita helps the Chinese family at the grocery store, but a robbery at the store frightens her, and she therefore runs away. As a result, she again gets lost and starts sleeping rough. The film captures once more Anita's alienation as a critique of an inefficient state that is not capable of providing for its citizens. Anita falls ill and is picked up by a group of men, who take her to a disadvantaged neighborhood in the suburbs of Buenos Aires. There she is cared for by Nori, a frustrated, middle-aged nurse who lives alone and seems to have problems with alcohol. Nori cures Anita but is not interested in letting Anita stay with her. Nonetheless, Anita's extraordinary patience and persistence break down Nori's barriers. Consequently, she ends up caring so much for Anita that she treats her as if she were her own child, and thus a mother-daughter relationship is forged between them. Nori, as the rest of the people Anita meets on her journey, is not aware that the child is a victim of the AMIA bombing. One day, however, Nori sees Anita's brother appear on television searching for his sister, and, understanding who Anita is, she contacts Ariel.

Having embarked on a quest to find her mother, Anita comes across an array of people who epitomize the multicultural national family, and she thus becomes the child of this wider family. Accordingly, the child's search for her mother conveys not only her own hardships but also the hardships of an entire society, which has been badly hit for decades by socioeconomic and political issues. In other words, the characters Anita encounters form a metonymy of a society that has been affected by the long-term effects of repression, disappearances, exile, neoliberalism, and financial crises. This has rendered society fragmented, dysfunctional, and at times unable, or not always willing, to protect its most vulnerable citizens. Nevertheless, by taking Anita in, the Argentine family exhibits that there exist remnants of solidarity in Argentine society. Being simultaneously the victim of the AMIA bombing and a disappeared child in search of her missing mother, Anita concurrently embodies the cultural memory of the AMIA bombing and the Dirty War. As Carolina Rocha and Georgia Seminet correctly observe, the cinematic representation of youth "as the repository of cultural memory and the guardians of hope for the future has become a staple of films seeking to give voice to those who were unjustly murdered, tortured, or disappeared by dictatorial regimes."[15] These words indeed resonate with Anita's case.

Following Nori's call, Ariel goes to her house, where he is finally reunited with his sister. After this reunion and to give closure to the narrative, brother and sister go back to the stationery store, where Anita recalls her past life the moment she enters. The final scene compels the viewer to be participant of this moment of growing realization. Ariel explains to Anita what has happened and informs her that their mother perished in the AMIA bombing. Anita's understanding of the traumatic event that she has experienced is accompanied by soft music and verbalized by her when she raises the question, "¿Por qué explotó la bomba? [Why did the bomb explode?]," to which Ariel answers, "Porque alguien la puso ahí, porque está todo mal, no sé por qué, no sé [Because someone put it there, because everything is wrong, I don't know why, I don't know]." Anita's genuine curiosity coupled with Ariel's helplessness denounces not only the attack but also the lack of justice surrounding the event and the frustration felt by the families of the victims.

As a recollection of what Dora had said to her before leaving the store, "Cuando la aguja larga esté en el número de arriba, mami vuelve [When the long hand of the clock is at the top, mom comes back]," and ultimately as a call for Dora's return, Anita places the long hand of the wall clock on the number 12. The film concludes with a close-up of the siblings' profiles looking at the stopped clock, which is a clear symbol of death and, by extension, of their deceased mother. Writing about the victims of the Shoah and drawing on psychoanalysis, Dominick LaCapra explains how survivors of traumatic events may react in relation to those who perished: "One's bond with the dead, especially with dead intimates, may invest trauma with value, and make its reliving a painful but necessary commemoration or memorial to which one remains dedicated or at least bound."[16] LaCapra's observation sheds light on Anita and Ariel's reaction. The closing of the film, which conflates the siblings' reunion with the memory of their mother, can be construed as a painful but necessary commemoration that forges their familial bond and seeks to repair the fracturing of their family.

Conclusion

In reenacting trauma and its aftermath through a child-centered narrative, *Anita* may be viewed as one of the memorials that retrieve the cultural memory of the AMIA bombing and the Dirty War. Although the film is a fictionalized story, it cannot be separated from culture at large in that it is based on a real-life event, has been publicly screened, and therefore has been shared with others. The film thus contributes to the construction of a common culture that has been affected by trauma.

Anita is an embodiment of victimhood that justice has forgotten but cinema memorializes. It is in the reenactment of personal memories that are made public and therefore collective experiences that enables film to keep alive the cultural memory of such traumatic events. In addition, the apt theme of the search for the disappeared permits Carnevale not only to revisit the AMIA bombing and the plight of the Mothers but also to survey the wider social ills of the country. Through the creation of a multiethnic national family in which the Jewish female has found her place, the film rectifies the damage done to a whole society by the attack. Ultimately, the ideology of the film conveys that Jews and non-Jews are part of the same national family.

Moreover, the casting of a person with Down syndrome in the leading role provides viewers with a new perspective from which to grasp the AMIA bombing. The character of Anita not only is a vulnerable person but also has an intellectual disability, yet she overcomes all the challenges she faces, thereby becoming a role model for the Argentine people. Thus, the portrayal of the child vis-à-vis the Argentine family constitutes a call to a nation that should not remain indifferent to the suffering of its fellow citizens. Belonging to the same genre as *La historia oficial*—the family melodrama—*Anita* shares with *La historia oficial* the combination of emotional manipulation and hard-hitting exposé of harsh realities in Argentine history. Melodramatic but nonetheless gritty, *Anita* brings a message of hope to a society that needs to deal with the traumas of its past.

Notes

The author is grateful to Dr. Catherine Leen for her insightful comments on this paper.

1. The AMIA has its roots in the Chevra Kedusha Ashkenazi (Jewish Mutual Aid and Burial Society), created in 1894 with the purpose of founding a cemetery for the Jewish Argentine community. Between 1910 and 1915, the number of Jews doubled from approximately fifty thousand to one hundred thousand (Feierstein, *Historia*, 117). Due to the increase of the Jewish population, the Chevra Kedusha Ashkenazi gradually expanded and diversified to include philanthropic and educational programs. On the eve of the celebration of its hundredth anniversary, a terrorist attack took place on the headquarters of the AMIA, and the seven-floor building was leveled by the explosion. In 1999 a new building was opened on the same ground, and today the AMIA boasts a range of programs, including social, communal, educational, job placement, and burial services.

2. In the interview provided on the DVD version of the film, Carnevale says that he regards *Anita* as a means of reflecting on the traumatic event, and, moreover, he stresses that with *Anita* he intends to demonstrate that the AMIA bombing is an event that affects all Argentines regardless of their ethnicity.

3. Aizenberg, *Books and Bombs in Buenos Aires*, 11.

4. Aizenberg, "Argentine Space, Jewish Memory," 112.

5. Carnevale, born in 1963, is a relatively young yet renowned industrial auteur in the Argentine film industry. Aside from *Anita*, Carnevale has directed eight feature films to date. In general, his films have been well received by the Argentine public.

6. DEISICA, *Informe sobre los aspectos económico-culturales*, 20.

7. This and all subsequent translations are my own.

8. The name Anita alludes to one of the survivors of the AMIA bombing, namely

Anita Weinstein, head of the Center for Documentation and Information on Argentinean Jewry Marc Turkow, which was based in the AMIA building. Anita Weinstein herself pointed this out in a conversation I had with her.

9. Lury, *The Child in Film: Tears, Fears, and Fairy Tales*, 150.
10. Holmes, "Playing Woman in María Novaro's *Lola*," 70.
11. Aizenberg, "Argentine Space, Jewish Memory," 117.
12. Leen, "City of Fear," 480.
13. For a thorough discussion of the family in Argentina, see Amado and Domínguez, *Lazos de familia*. For an analysis of the role of cinematic men in the family, see Rocha's *Masculinities in Contemporary Argentine Popular Cinema*.
14. Rocha, *Masculinities*, 1–18.
15. Rocha and Seminet, *Representing History, Class, and Gender in Spain and Latin America*, 16.
16. LaCapra, *Writing History, Writing Trauma*, 22.

Works Cited

Films

Bechis, Marco, dir. *Garage Olimpo*. Perf. Antonella Costa, Carlos Echeverría, Enrique Piñyeiro. SBP. 1999.
Burman, Daniel, dir. "Untitled short." *18-J*. Distribution Company. 2004.
Carnevale, Marcos, dir. *Anita*. Perf. Alejandra Manzo, Norma Aleandro, Luis Luque. AVH. 2009.
Meerapfel, Jeanine, dir. *La amiga* (*The Girlfriend*). Perf. Cipe Lincovsky, Federico Luppi, Liv Ullmann. Neue Visionen. 1988.
Puenzo, Luis, dir. *La historia oficial* (*The Official Story*). Perf. Héctor Alterio, Norma Aleandro, Hugo Arana. Arrow Films. 1985.

Articles and Books

Aizenberg, Edna. "Argentine Space, Jewish Memory: Memorials to the Blown Apart and Disappeared in Buenos Aires." *Mortality* 12 (2007): 109–123.
———. *Books and Bombs in Buenos Aires: Borges, Gerchunoff, and Argentine-Jewish Writing*. Hanover, NH: University of New England Press, 2002.
Amado, Ana, and Nora Domínguez, eds. *Lazos de familia: Herencias, cuerpos y ficciones*. Buenos Aires: Paidós, 2004.
DEISICA (Departamento de Estudio e Investigación del Sindicato de la Industria Cinematográfica Argentina). *Informe sobre los aspectos económico-culturales*. Buenos Aires: DEISICA, 2009.
Feierstein, Ricardo. *Historia de los judíos argentinos*. Buenos Aires: Galerna, 2006.
Holmes, Amanda. "Playing Woman in María Novaro's *Lola*." In *Screening Minors in Latin American Cinema*, ed. Carolina Rocha and Georgia Seminet, 69–86. Maryland: Lexington Books, 2014.
LaCapra, Dominick. *Writing History, Writing Trauma*. Baltimore: Johns Hopkins University Press, 2001.

Leen, Catherine. "City of Fear: Reimagining Buenos Aires in Contemporary Argentine Cinema." *Bulletin of Latin American Research* 27 (2008): 465–482.
Lerer, Diego. "'Anita': Perdida en la ciudad." *Clarín*, 27 August 2009. http://edant.clarin.com/diario/2009/08/27/um/m-01986692.htm (accessed 9 February 2013).
Lury, Karen. *The Child in Film: Tears, Fears, and Fairy Tales*. London: Tauris, 2010.
Martínez, Adolfo. "Una emotiva historia de dolor y soledad." *La Nación*, 27 August 2009. http://www.lanacion.com.ar/1167248-una-emotiva-historia-de-dolor-y-soledad (accessed 9 February 2013).
Robson, Dave. "*Anita* a Unique Look at Tragedy." *Sound on Sight*, 9 April 2011. http://www.soundonsight.org/anita (accessed 24 March 2015).
Rocha, Carolina. *Masculinities in Contemporary Argentine Popular Cinema*. New York: Palgrave Macmillan, 2012.
Rocha, Carolina, and Georgia Seminet, eds. *Representing History, Class, and Gender in Spain and Latin America: Children and Adolescents in Film*. New York: Palgrave Macmillan, 2012.

PART III
NEW THEMES

CHAPTER 7

The Year My Parents Went on Vacation:
A Jewish Journey in the Land of Soccer

ALEJANDRO METER

After many years in which the world has afforded me many experiences, what I know most surely in the long run about morality and obligations, I owe to football.
ALBERT CAMUS, "WHAT I OWE TO FOOTBALL"

Official history ignores soccer. Contemporary history texts fail to mention it, even in passing, in countries where it has been and continues to be a primordial symbol of collective identity.
EDUARDO GALEANO, SOCCER IN SUN AND SHADOW

The Year My Parents Went on Vacation (*O ano em que meus pais saíram de férias*, 2006), by director Cao Hamburger, is a Brazilian film that serves as a vehicle for problematizing Jewishness in a Latin American context. In the film, soccer[1] becomes a transformative experience that helps shape the protagonist's identity and self-conception. Through his journey of self-discovery, the film's young protagonist, Mauro Stein (Michel Joelsas), learns what it means to be both Jewish and Brazilian. In this paper, I contend that soccer plays a pivotal role in Mauro's life and, more important, in his transformation into a Brazilian Jew. Soccer sets in motion a series of events that will compel Mauro to come to terms with his Jewishness as he is suddenly and unexpectedly required to examine his identity by learning to negotiate the expectations placed upon him by both Jewish and Brazilian traditions. Soccer and Jewishness thus become the guiding principles of the film.

Set in the year 1970, during the last few weeks before the start of the World Cup finals, *The Year My Parents Went on Vacation* tells the story of Mauro Stein, a twelve-year-old boy whose parents are obligated to leave in the care of his grandfather, a Jewish immigrant to Brazil, as they are forced into hiding by political persecution. They promise young Mauro that they will return from "vacation" in time for the games. In the hours that it takes Mauro's parents, Bia and Daniel Stein (Simone Spoladore and Eduardo Moreira), to travel from Belo Horizonte to São Paulo, the boy's grandfather unexpectedly passes away from a heart attack, thus creating a key twist in the plot that will introduce Mauro to his granddad's neighbor, a solitary and religious Jew named Shlomo (Germano Haiut), who ends up looking after him, albeit reluctantly, at least at first. While his parents are "away on vacation," Mauro pieces together a resourceful existence, learning to navigate the murky waters of a country torn apart by an authoritarian regime and a society gripped by World Cup fever.

In the movie's very first scene, in which we see young Mauro playing with his table soccer game as his parents scramble to leave the house in a hurry, we learn that unlike other boys his age, who usually fantasize of becoming strikers or stellar mid-fielders, Mauro wants to be a goalie because, we are told by the narrator, "goalies are different . . . they spend their time standing there, alone, waiting for the worst." This bit of wisdom, and a kind of premonition, passed down to him by his own father, becomes the film's main narrative thread.

Adrift in a new environment, Mauro becomes a stranger in his own land, a foreigner upon arrival, unintentionally left alone by the adults in his life to fend for himself in the highly diverse, multiethnic, and multilingual neighborhood of Bom Retiro, in São Paulo, Brazil's largest city. As he waits for his grandfather outside his apartment door, passing the time playing his game of "button football"—a popular game (and toy) in Brazil known as *futebol de botão*—feelings of loneliness and displacement overcome young Mauro. The sense of alienation intensifies when he suddenly meets Shlomo, his grandfather's next-door neighbor, who greets him sternly, not in Portuguese but in Yiddish: "Dus ist nicht kain platz tzu shpilen, farshteist? [This is not the place to play, you know?]," and informs him of his grandfather's passing as a result of a heart attack. In the next scene, Mauro attends his grandfather's Jewish burial during which Shlomo places a *kippa* (or yarmulke) on Mauro's head, a pivotal moment in the movie that symbolizes the beginning of Mauro's crash course in Judaism. In an act of kindness, and at the insistence of his rabbi, who compares Mauro's accidental abandonment by his parents with the story of Moses, Shlomo reluctantly agrees to let the boy stay at his place and look after him.

As the film progresses, Mauro becomes closer to his newly adopted extended family. This family is composed of other neighbors in the building, members of the synagogue, and especially Hannah (Daniela Piepszyk), a girl his age whom he befriends. As a result of all this he begins a process of identification with his Jewish origins. The parallel with the story of Moses is used as a kind of leitmotif throughout the movie, at times providing comic relief, as when the older, Yiddish-speaking neighbors confuse the name "Mauro" with "Moishe." Over the course of the film, Mauro learns about his Jewish background in a variety of ways: as he searches through his grandfather's papers and old photographs, when he watches Shlomo recite the morning prayers, and when he attends religious services at the synagogue and listens to music sung in Yiddish. In the episode where he is invited to his friend's bar mitzvah—a scene from which one can infer that he, too, will go through that rite of passage in the future—Mauro finally feels "at home."

The recovery of his Jewish roots and his (perhaps unconscious) affirmation of his Jewishness are directly linked to his passion for football. Mauro's Jewish journey in the land of soccer may thus be read on three different levels, each linked to a type of soccer play identified in the film: the game played at the professional level, represented in the movie by the Brazilian national team at the World Cup held in Mexico; amateur competition played at the neighborhood level, where "weekend warriors" come out to compete while representing their ethnic or religious community; and a more informal and casual kind of play, characterized by improvised games of street soccer among children. These three planes of interpretation are key to reading the transformation of Mauro's sense of self as both Jewish and Brazilian in the absence of his parents, who have gone underground.

For the first level, the context in which the film takes place is crucial. In 1970, Brazil, like many of its neighbors in Latin America, found itself at the epicenter of Cold War era tactics and was subject to a brutal military dictatorship aimed at suppressing leftist ideology and violent opposition. Any form of resistance to the regime was stifled through prison, torture, assassination, and exile. Accompanying this authoritarian and suppressive regime was an elaborate political machine used as an instrument for institutional propaganda created to manipulate public opinion and censure any form of dissent. The World Cup of 1970, though held in Mexico, was seen by the regime as the perfect opportunity to create a smoke screen that would give it the freedom to operate in the streets with greater impunity. It was a source of great national tension and anxiety: Brazil, having already won two World Cups at the time, was tied with Uruguay and Italy. If they could win this time as well, they would be crowned supreme and undisputed world champions, achieving what only a few years prior would have seemed unimaginable.[2] Regarded even today as the best Brazilian squad ever assembled—an all-star team made up of Pelé, Carlos Alberto, Tostao, Gerson, Jairzinho, and Rivelino, among others—Brazil's team was the favorite to win what came to be known as the most exciting World Cup Championship ever.

The expectation and high spirits generated throughout Brazil by the dream of conquering the third World Cup were quickly turned to the purposes of political propaganda in the hands of the military government. In this sense, the Brazilian dictatorship was intent on manipulating public opinion as the fascists and Nazis had done before them.[3] By the time the Brazilian national team took to the field in the 1970 World Cup game, the military government had already arranged for widespread, almost total, television coverage of the games. Brazilians would, for the very first time, have television access from north to south, all across the nation. As David Goldblatt has suggested, during the 1970 World Cup, "Brazil existed in a more complete way than at any other moment."[4] Many Brazilians were keenly aware of their government's intentions to manipulate the results. Early in the film, the young narrator offers proof of this when he explains that up until that time, "the national government had never really cared so much about the World Cup, but this year it was different," calling attention to the nervousness and anxiety that had taken over society as a result of the country's governmental policies.

In a very telling scene about the relationship between politics, football, and national identity, Marxist university students sit around the TV set to cheer for Czechoslovakia, hoping it will defeat Brazil as it makes its World Cup debut: "A triumph by Czechoslovakia will mean a victory for socialism!" proclaims Italo (Caio Blat), a student activist who develops a special bond with Mauro in the film. As the ever-increasing number of Brazilian goals points to the inevitability of victory, the fans find themselves jumping in uncontrollable ecstasy, chanting in unison: "Brazil, Brazil, Brazil!" proving soccer's capacity to mobilize the nation. The camera shifts back and forth between private and public spaces to show how the goals are celebrated at the Greek-owned restaurant down the street and at the homes of Hasidic Jews, and finally the camera turns to Mauro, proudly wearing his Brazilian jersey and watching the game as he celebrates and yells at the TV in the company of an apparently disinterested Shlomo. Fandom has thus become the true test of loyalty to the nation in spite of ethnic, political, or religious differences.

In the words of Pierre Bourdieu, the popularization of sport was a very successful means of controlling adolescents, and useful in "the mobilization and symbolic conquest of the masses."[5] As explained by Roberto DaMatta:

> Todas essas emoções retornam vivas e fortes, porque torcemos. Esse torcer que é para todos nos um ato que envolve muita magia e que é maior que o amor. Gesto que nos confere plena indentidade e garante que fazemos mesmo parte de um conjunto que pode atuar de forma armoniosa, forte e

honesta. Torcendo pelo Brasil, finalmente juntamos o Brasil, um país que tem bandeira, hino e um lado oficial, com o Brasil sociedade que apesar de suas imensas desigualdades, tem uma inesgotável alegria de viver.[6]

[All those emotions come alive and grow strong because of our support. Our fandom is for us an act filled with magic that is greater than love. This gesture gives us an identity and guarantees that we can all be part of a group that can act in a strong, honest, and harmonious way. By supporting our national team, we bring the country together, its flag, its national anthem, and its official story with a Brazilian society that, in spite of its enormous inequality, enjoys an immense lust for life.][7]

It is precisely within this type of international competition that one may come to see over time "an overlap of practical and symbolic constructions of national characteristics, national values, and national pride and sorrow."[8]

In his film Cao Hamburger shows the contradictions and complexities of a dictatorial Brazilian government that glosses over difference (racial, ethnic, religious, sexual, class), pretending that it does not exist, in contrast to the lives of ordinary Brazilians who must negotiate their multiple, dynamic, and diverse identities. The generals, however, understood soccer only as a cultural practice that could bridge the nation's complex social and racial hierarchies by generating a collective ritual and a historical narrative open to all Brazilians.[9] Thus, as shown by Harry Walker, organized team sports can be instrumental in promoting a new moral and political order: "As a vehicle of national sentiment, highly amenable to ritualization and bureaucratization, sport is central to the process by which the state expands its territory and influence."[10] Football, consequently, could be manipulated to *create* the nation.

In one of the last scenes of the film, images of Pelé and his teammates raising the Jules Rimet Trophy are juxtaposed with that of Mauro's mother, lying in the fetal position, alone in her bed. This suggestive scene, a metaphor for a nation violated by its own rulers, a family broken by a government whose purpose, among others, was to protect the family, closes the film on a somber, melancholy note. Writing about the celebration ceremonies held by the government following Brazil's third World Cup victory, Eduardo Galeano states:

At the victory carnival in 1970, General Médici, dictator of Brazil, handed out cash to the players, posed for photographers with the trophy in his arms, and even headed a ball for the cameras. The march composed for the team, "Forward Brazil," became the government's anthem, while the image of Pelé soaring above the field was used in TV ads that proclaimed: "No one can stop Brazil."[11]

The nation, accordingly, rather than deriving its strength from "purity," seeks to portray an image of an inclusive entity that is greater that the sum of its parts, and is thus able to include black and white, male and female, Jewish and Christian, Italian, Greek, and Polish. The achievements of members of minority groups act as a kind of utopian reframing of the nation as a more inclusive entity than the realities of its political, social, and economic policies would otherwise suggest.

In the second level that provides a key to reading this film, we move from the national stage to a more immediate scenario concentrated in the neighborhood of Bom Retiro, in the city of São Paulo, well known for its diversity—a space shared by Jewish, Greek, and Italian immigrants and their descendants during the 1960s and 1970s. In contrast with the pressures and expectations placed on the national team, the neighborhood is home to a more informal rivalry between "Jews" and "Italians." Divided along ethnic and religious lines, the teams come to represent the opposite of the homogenizing narrative espoused by the regime, thus unmasking the illusion of an inclusive, utopian nation constructed around soccer. They are not just Brazilian, but also Jewish, Italian, African, and Greek. As Mauro's voice-over explains:

> São Paulo is so big that it has all kinds of people and teams from all over the world. Shlomo was born in Poland and now spends all his time speaking with Italo, whose parents are Italian. Irene is the daughter of a Greek family but her boyfriend, I believe, had African grandparents.

According to Mauro, the Jewish team, while not as talented as the Italian, had a secret weapon: Edgar (Rodrigo dos Santos), the black goalkeeper, who from this point onward in the film becomes Mauro's hero. The narrator, upon seeing Edgar ruin the Italian team's chances of scoring a penalty shot, confesses: "And suddenly I knew what I wanted to be when I grew up: I wanted to be black and be able to fly." Playing in a position defined by both solitude and solidarity, the goalie is always seen as an eccentric and an outsider, a role with which Mauro feels a strong sense of identification. Galeano's thoughts on the fragility of the goalkeeper are quite illustrative of this particular player's unique condition:

> They also call him doorman, keeper, goalie, bouncer or net-minder, but he could just as well be called martyr, pay-all, penitent or punching bag. They

Mauro speaking with Edgar. *O ano que meus pais saíram das féiras* (*The Year My Parents Went on Vacation*) (2007), directed by Cao Hamburger.

say where he walks, the grass never grows. He's alone, condemned to watch the game from afar. Never leaving the goal, his only company, the three posts; he waits his own execution by firing squad. . . . It's always the keeper's fault. And if it isn't, he still gets blamed. . . . They leave him there in the immensity of the empty net, abandoned to face his executioner alone. . . . The rest of the players can blow it once in a while, or often, then redeem themselves with a spectacular dribble, a masterful pass, a well-placed volley. Not him. The crowd never forgives the keeper. . . . With a single slip up the goalie can ruin a game or lose a championship, and the fans suddenly forget all his feats and condemn him to eternal disgrace. Damnation will follow him to the end of his days.[12]

The metaphor of the goalkeeper as an outcast, a stranger, and a foreigner resonates heavily in the character of Mauro and helps illustrate the delicate balance he is required to navigate in his journey to adulthood. Given that he is a child, Mauro's view of the world presents to the viewer a fresh, uncontaminated perspective on difference and otherness that makes it possible and fully acceptable for his hero to be black. Ultimately, it is through soccer that Mauro is able to dream of becoming a strong, muscular goalkeeper, in the image of his black hero. At the same time, this shows a fluid and dynamic interpretation of identity, as Mauro voluntarily chooses to be "black" as much as he chooses to be "Jewish."

As explained by Julio Frydemberg in his groundbreaking book on the social history of football, soccer can play an essential role in neighborhood and individual identity formation. The neighborhood game constitutes a sort of ritual that provides a spectacle that is at the same time modern, profane, and peculiar.[13] Thus, a group cannot be understood without its territory, in the sense that their sociocultural identity is irretrievably linked to attributes of concrete space such as nature, architectural patrimony, and landscape. That territory has defined limits that distinguish the "us" from "them": group members are "insiders" while rivals are "outsiders."[14] Mauro, now a member of his newly adopted *bairro*[15] of Bom Retiro, effortlessly identifies with the Jewish team as a direct result of his own connection with Jewish tradition. The game played by these amateurs, divided along ethnic affiliations and based on group cohesion, resists the homogenizing project of a dictatorial government for whom Brazil could only speak with once voice.

In stark contrast to the World Cup games being televised from Mexico or the neighborhood rivalry between adult "Jews" and "Italians" is the game played in the *baldio*,[16] wherein lie the origins of Latin American football. In this third level, or interpretative paradigm, offering another approach to this filmic text, the movie shows a game played by Mauro and friends on an improvised soccer field in the streets of Bom Retiro, where Mauro's understanding of his Jewish condition is further heightened. The importance of this informal type of play is at the center of Mauro's transformation into a Brazilian Jew.

Johan Huizinga, for whom play is the primary formative element in human culture, discusses in his book *Homo Ludens* the important role of play in the development of a child's identity. For Huizinga, play is defined as "a voluntary activity or occupation executed within certain fixed limits of time and place, according to rules freely accepted but absolutely binding, having its aim in itself and accompanied by a feeling of tension, joy and the consciousness that it is 'different' from 'ordinary life.'"[17] Play, in addition, creates order in the midst of the chaos and confusion of life by bringing about a temporary and limited perfection.[18] In the backstreets and alleyways of Bom Retiro, soccer play allows for the formation of social groupings that tend to stress their differences from the common world.[19]

Unlike the game played on the international stage, where national identity, pride, and honor are at stake, the game in the *baldio* is a freer, unconstrained type of play that allows children to be themselves. As noted by Roger Caillois, play becomes "an occasion of pure waste of time, energy, ingenuity [and] skill."[20] For Mauro, Hannah, and the rest of the gang, play becomes a way to escape reality.[21] Play lets them feel free; play "is in fact, freedom."[22] But the game of street soccer is also a cultural phenomenon, "an aid to communion and collective recreation."[23] For Mauro, play becomes an essential way to endure and negotiate his parent's absence, if only temporarily.

In the scene in which Mauro is playing keeper for Hannah's team, a passing car that resembles his parents' momentarily distracts him. Thinking his parents may have returned, Mauro abandons the goal post, allowing the opposing team to score a goal. His distraction ultimately leads to a brawl between rivals in which Mauro and his friends are singled out and derided for being Jewish. Soccer in the streets of São Paulo is at once anarchic and capricious, allowing the children to express their identities, their desires, and their beliefs openly. For Mauro, playing in the *baldio* constitutes a rite of initiation not only into adulthood but also into being Jewish.[24] Through this type of play Mauro assumes his role as a Jew, an identity he does not dispute or put into question even when provoked by an anti-Semitic slur. It is precisely through play that Mauro is able to explain the world, both to others and to himself. Soccer play, whether make-believe or on television, with friends or adults, is what sustains the plot of this film. In the words of Sicart, "Play is not isolated in our eventful lives; in fact it is a string with which we tie our memories and our friendships together. Play is a trace of the character that defines us."[25]

As explained by Eduardo Archetti, the *baldio* is a place for improvisation, unconstrained by the strict rules of the game; here boys and girls learn the art of the dribble that contrasts with the more strategic, calculated game brought to the Americas by the British.[26] This is football in its most primitive form. For Mauro and his friends, this improvised soccer field, or *baldio*, in the city streets is a place that builds community, that teaches them how to relate to others, how to navigate, and how to negotiate difference. The *baldio* is a place that generates a sense of belonging that transcends ethnic, racial, and religious lines and allows blacks, Greeks, Jews, and Italians to become Brazilian. For Mauro the *baldio* is an authentic rite of passage through which he is able to symbolically acquire not only his Jewishness but also his Brazilianness. The importance the *baldio* has as an institution, very much like school, cannot be undermined. An amateur goalie from Algeria who would later become one of the most relevant figures of twentieth-century French thought, Albert Camus, wrote, "What I know most surely in the long run about morality and obligations, I owe to football."

The Year My Parents Went on Vacation offers a cinematic reflection on the dynamics of national, ethnic, and religious identity inherent in the processes of nation formation. This clever, impeccably structured film soundly rejects the usual stereotypes associated with Brazilian culture—those of a nation where music and carnival adorn a life of tropical hedonism—allowing the viewer to revisit and rethink the trauma of dictatorial Brazil in new ways. In the land of soccer, the "beautiful game" becomes a metaphor for the protagonist's coming of age into adulthood that occurs on multiple levels. It is through soccer that Mauro is able to reintegrate his fragmented self, becoming at once Jewish and Brazilian.

Notes

1. I use the terms "football" and "soccer," as it is known in the United States, interchangeably throughout the article.
2. In spite of having attained two World Cup victories up until that time (Brazil won in 1958 and in 1962), the loss at home to Uruguay in 1950, referred to as the "Maracanazo," remains to this day a source of national trauma. As explained by Roberto DaMatta: "até hoje somos assombrados pela derrota que, para nós, representa mais do que perder partidas, pois confirma uma inferioridade que nos persegue como povo e nação" (*A bola corre mais que os homens*, 42–43).
3. Held in Italy, the 1934 World Cup event was carefully orchestrated by Benito Mussolini and brought the hosts a much-coveted victory. Four years later, in 1938, when the championship series was being held in France, Mussolini sent a telegram to the Italian players before the final game requiring of them "Victory or Death" (see Sebreli, *La era del fútbol*, 156–159). In Germany, the Berlin Olympics of 1938 were made a showcase for Hitler's plans for a racially pure Reich. Joseph Goebbels, Hitler's minister of propaganda, who understood the massive importance of football to the spirit of the nation, observed in 1936 that "a victory in the football stadium is more important for the people than the conquest of a city or enemy territory" (as quoted in Oliven and Damo, *Fútbol y cultura*, 42).
4. Goldblatt, *Futebol Nation*, 14.
5. Bourdieu, "How Can One Be a Sports Fan?," 348.
6. DaMatta, *A bola corre mais que os homens*, 43.
7. All translations are mine.
8. Archetti, "Masculinity and Football," 236.
9. Goldblatt, *Futebol Nation*, xix.
10. Walker, "State of Play," 382.
11. Galeano, *Soccer in Sun and Shadow*, 138.
12. Ibid., 5.
13. Frydenberg, *Historia social del fútbol*, 125.
14. See Alabarces, *Fútbol y patria*, 170, quoting Lopes de Souza.
15. Meaning "neighborhood" in Portuguese; "barrio" is the Spanish term.
16. "Baldio" (Portuguese)/"baldío" (Spanish): an empty urban or suburban space used as improvised soccer field, throughout Latin America.
17. Huizinga, *Homo Ludens*, 28.
18. Ibid., 10.
19. Ibid., 13.
20. Caillois, *Man, Play, and Games*, 5–6.

21. Miguel Sicart explains that all types of play are contextual, meaning that it happens "in a tangled world of people, things, spaces, and cultures" (*Play Matters*, 6).
22. Huizinga, *Homo Ludens*, 8.
23. Caillois, *Man, Play, and Games*, 39.
24. Drawing on the work of both Huizinga and Caillois, Sicart suggests that "play is a cultural tool for being. Hence, ... play is a fundamental part of our moral well being, of the healthy and mature and complete human life. Through play we experience the world, we construct it and we destroy it, and we explore who we are and what we can say. Play frees us from moral conventions but makes them still present, so we are aware of their weight, presence, and importance" (*Play Matters*, 2, 5).
25. Sicart, *Play Matters*, 18.
26. Archetti explains, in an Argentinean context, the myth of two foundational styles of play: one Latin American, or *criollo*, and the other European, or more traditional; both have served to create a national soccer narrative in countries like Argentina, Brazil, and Uruguay (Archetti, "Masculinity and Football").

Works Cited

Film

Hamburger, Cao, dir. *O ano em que meus pais saíram de férias* (*The Year My Parents Went on Vacation*). City Lights Pictures. 2006.

Articles and Books

Alabarces, Pablo. *Fútbol y patria: El fútbol y las narrativas de la nación en la Argentina*. Buenos Aires: Prometeo, 2008.
Archetti, Eduardo. "Masculinity and Football: The Formation of National Identity in Argentina." In *Game without Frontiers: Football, Identity, and Modernity*, ed. Richard Giulianotti and John Williams, 225–243. Vermont: Ashgate, 1994.
Bourdieu, Pierre. "How Can One Be a Sports Fan?" In *The Cultural Studies Reader*, ed. Simon During, 427–441. New York: Routledge, 1993.
Bromberger, Christian. "Football as World View and Ritual." *French Cultural Studies* 6 (1995): 293–311.
———. *Significaciones de la pasión popular por los clubes de fútbol*. Buenos Aires: Libros del Rojas (UBA), 2001.
Caillois, Roger. *Man, Play, and Games*. Urbana: University of Illinois Press, 2001.
Camus, Albert. "What I Owe to Football." *France Football*, 1957.
DaMatta, Roberto. *A bola corre mais que os homens*. Rio de Janeiro: Rocco, 2006.
Frydenberg, Julio. *Historia social del fútbol: Del amateurismo a la profesionalización*. Buenos Aires: Siglo Veintiuno, 2011.
Galeano, Eduardo. *Soccer in Sun and Shadow*. London: Verso, 1999.
Goldblatt, David. *Futebol Nation: The Story of Brazil through Soccer*. New York: Nation Books, 2014.
Huizinga, Johan. *Homo Ludens: A Study of the Play-Element in Culture*. New York: Roy, 1950.
Oliven, Ruben, and Arlei Damo. *Fútbol y cultura*. Buenos Aires: Norma, 2001.

Sebreli, Juan José. *La era del fútbol*. Buenos Aires: Delbolsillo, 2005.
Sicart, Miguel. *Play Matters*. Boston: MIT Press, 2014.
Walker, Harry. "State of Play: The Political Ontology of Sport in Amazonian Peru." *American Ethnologist* 40, no. 2 (2013): 382–398.
White, Jim. *A Matter of Life and Death*. London: Head of Zeus, 2015.

CHAPTER 8

Coming of Age in Two Films from Argentina and Uruguay

CAROLINA ROCHA

The cinematic representation of Jews in films from around the globe has traditionally revolved around male and female adults struggling with their diasporic identity. As a result, certain stereotypes have dominated the portrayal of Jews in film: the *schlemiel* for insecure, passive Jewish men; the Jewish mother, for controlling mothers; and the Jewish Princess, for alluring, exotic young females.[1] Until recently this has also been the case in Latin American cinema.

Daniel Burman's first films—*Esperando al Mesías* (*Waiting for the Messiah*, 2000), *El abrazo partido* (*Lost Embrace*, 2004), and *Derecho de familia* (*Family Law*, 2006)—and Juan Pablo Rebella and Pablo Stoll's *Whisky* (2004) treat one of these types. Burman adapted the *schlemiel* to twenty-first-century Argentina, where the hapless character must grapple with the aftermath of a financial meltdown and the search for a male identity, and Rebella and Stoll look at a *schlemiel* leading a seemingly boring life in twenty-first-century Uruguay.[2] In recent years, however, a new generation of Jewish–Latin American film directors has started to represent younger characters: children, in the case of Cao Hamburger's *O ano em que meus pais saíram de férias* (*The Year My Parents Went on Vacation*, 2006), and youth, particularly in Gabriel Lichtmann's *Judíos en el espacio* (*Jews in Space*, 2005). While children and youth in these films are still part of a larger Jewish community composed of adults, it is through their eyes and actions that these plots are structured. Unlike the situations faced by their elders—adaptation to a new country, learning a new language—these young characters confront the issue of being hyphenated Jews.[3]

In this chapter, I analyze two films, Ariel Winograd's *Cara de queso: Mi primer ghetto* (*Cheesehead, My First Ghetto*, 2006) and *Acné* (*Acne*) (dir. Federico Veiroj, 2008), whose main characters are Jewish male adolescents.

I contend that these films depict what it means to come of age as a Jewish Argentine and a Jewish Uruguayan, respectively.[4] Amid close-knit Jewish communities in Argentina and Uruguay, Ariel and Rafael resolve moral and personal identity crises by finding their own voice. In defining their identity, these adolescents rebel against their elders, a move that directly influences their relationship to Jewishness. Here it is important to take into account Nancy Lesko's argument that "since adolescence has been defined as not adults, this opposition to adults, or at least the assumption that adolescents are distinctive from adults, will influence all cultural and class groups, although these ideas may have different implications and interpretations in particular moments and localities."[5] Indeed, the universality of adolescence makes Ariel's and Rafael's quests for self-determination an issue that expands and challenges the notion of Jewishness, which has traditionally been characterized, in Raanan Rein's words, by cultural superiority and communal cohesion.[6]

In exploring the coming-of-age narrative of two Jewish–Latin American adolescents, my analysis takes as its points of departure the assertions of film scholar Tzvi Tal, who notes that "las narrativas cinematográficas de la infancia o de la iniciación del adolescente han sido frecuentemente utilizadas como alegorías que reflejan procesos de la identidad nacional [the cinematic narratives of childhood and coming-of-age have frequently been used as allegories that reflect processes of national identity]."[7]

In the case of *Cheesehead* and *Acne*, the young characters are first and foremost alter egos of the directors themselves. This identification between director and protagonist is essential because both share a fresh view of contemporary Argentine and Uruguayan Jewish communities.[8] In addition, these young directors rely on their own experiences to create teenaged characters who feel inadequate and struggle with self-esteem issues. Through the lenses of these young males, the directors scrutinize the adult world, which stands for tradition, particularly in questions of Judaism and Jewishness. These young characters also engage in a process of reflection that signifies finding their roles as part of a third generation of Jews in Latin America. Therefore, what these films portray is an individual-specific and highly nuanced search for personal identity which constitutes a negotiation between their Jewish heritage on one hand and their Latin American upbringing on the other. Before analyzing these films, I will introduce their directors.

Cheesehead and *Acne* were written and directed by two young Jewish–Latin American directors. Ariel Winograd was born in Buenos Aires in 1977. He graduated from the University of Cinema and began his career making short films. His first feature-length film was *Cheesehead*, whose script was entered in the competition "Works in Progress" sponsored by Casa de las Américas and Fundación Carolina. Despite the fact that *Cheesehead* was an *opera prima*, the cast is first class, as it includes Federico Luppi, Mercedes Morán, Susú Pecoraro, and María Vaner, all well-established Argentine actors. In 2011, Winograd directed *Mi primera boda* (*My First Wedding*), also with Jewish characters, and more recently, *Vino para robar* (*He Came to Steal*, 2013). For his part, Federico Veiroj was born in Montevideo in 1976. He studied media at the Catholic University of Montevideo. Since 1996, he has been working on films, primarily making shorts. Of special interest is his short *Bregman, el siguiente* (released in English as *As Follows*, 2004), which has been well received at numerous film festivals around the world. Although *Acne* is his debut film, the film still received awards and nominations at several film festivals and is a Spanish-Mexican-Uruguayan-Argentinean co-production which was supported by the prestigious Ibermedia program. Veiroj's most recent film is *La vida útil* (*A Useful Life*, 2010), which received awards at the Havana, Lima, Warsaw, and Istanbul film festivals.

Both Winograd and Veiroj have acknowledged the autobiographical quality of their films. Winograd asserts, "Sentí que necesitaba contar otra cosa del Judaísmo que no se plasmaba en el cine actual [I felt I needed to tell something different about Judaism that was not being depicted in contemporary cinema]."[9] Thus Winograd's film provides an insider's point of view of a country club populated by Jewish families, that is to say, it shows communal life among Jewish Argentines across different generations. To develop this privileged point of view, Winograd uses an opening voice-over that stresses the personal nature of the film's perspective, which is also emphasized by the fact that the film's young protagonist has the same name as the director. Unlike the situation in *Cheesehead*, the young protagonist of *Acne* is not exclusively modeled upon Veiroj, though the filmmaker acknowledges that he included elements from his life as well as the lives of his brothers and friends for this "retrato de un chico adolescente en Montevideo [portrait of a male adolescent in Montevideo]."[10]

Both films mark the young characters as Jewish and place an emphasis on the marginal and uncomfortable stage these male protagonists endure during adolescence, much like the marginality and discomfort that often comes with being a Jew in Latin America. *Cheesehead* and *Acne* depict these teenaged characters as Jewish by having opening scenes take place in bathrooms, a technique that according to Nathan Abrams "is often used as a visual means of establishing Jewish characters."[11] In the case of Winograd's film, *Cheesehead* is young Ariel's nickname, but one he does not dislike. In

Veiroj's film, the suffering nature of adolescence—one meaning of the Latin verb *adolescere* is "to suffer"—as a transition period is highlighted by reference to the acne that affects some teenagers and especially defines Rafael Bregman's teenaged identity.

Ariel and Rafael's peripheral standing even within their families—both characters are middle children, having an older brother and a younger sister—is contradicted by their centrality in these films. In Ariel's case, he is an ideal example of the "eye among the blind." This is an expression used by German literature scholar Debbie Pinfold, who identifies disparate views between adults and children. Pinfold ascribes to young protagonists the special power to see what adults do not observe or prefer to ignore; thus, young characters usually offer a de-familiarizing view.[12] The de-familiarizing point of view constitutes an effective way to present an original take on Jewish life. Nonetheless, *Acne* provides a less critical examination of the Jewish community as a whole, since the critique appears limited to Rafael's family. Therefore, as I discuss adolescents in *Cheesehead* and *Acne*, I will also be contrasting the ways in which the adults are represented, usually as the object of the young characters' gaze.

Self and the Ghetto in *Cheesehead*

Cheesehead takes place during one summer in the life of a group of teenagers who spend their vacations in a country club populated by "more than one hundred Jewish families." The country club as a modern ghetto has been explained by scholar Tzvi Tal with reference to a dynamic of neoliberalism that was in place in the 1990s: "Los desplazamientos territoriales a otros barrios o a los country cerrados son la búsqueda de un ambiente de 'pares' en la capacidad de consumir y de un espacio seguro, donde no pueden irrumpir los 'otros' que representan lo que no se quiere ser [the territorial displacement to other neighborhoods or gated country clubs are part of a search for a group of peers regarding their capacity to consume goods and a space to be safe, where the 'other' cannot enter]."[13]

While all its member families share a religious background—alluding to the homogeneous composition of this community's population—life in this country club is not without problems. One day, Ariel (Sebastián Montagna) accidentally witnesses his best friend Coper (Nicolás Torcanowsky), who is somewhat chubby, being bullied by Alma (Tomás Kuselman), who urinates on him. Ariel is so overcome by shame and disgust by this action that he cannot defend his friend but watches the aggression while silently crying. In a voice-over, he confesses: "Soy un tarado. En vez de hacer algo me quedé como un tarado llorando [I am an idiot. Instead of reacting, I stayed there like an idiot, crying]." Even though Alma, the abuser, threatens both the victim and the witness so that they keep quiet about what happened, a well-respected adult member of the country club, Mr. Garchuni (Federico Luppi), overhears the commotion and appears ready to act. Ariel and Coper decide to ignore peer pressure and denounce the act of abuse, but when they do, they encounter resistance from country club employees. This disavowal of the teenagers' rights prompts Mr. Garchuni to request an investigation, but when this good Samaritan suffers a heart attack, Ariel and Coper find themselves back where they started: all alone.

Despite the fact that teenaged characters dominate the story line of the film, mixing klezmer music and Jewish humor, *Cheesehead* is more than a simple comedy dealing with awkward teenagers. I disagree with Adolfo Martínez, the reviewer for the Argentine daily *La Nación*, who characterizes the film as "comedia que habla del despertar de la adultez con elementos siempre dispuestos al permanente entretenimiento [comedy that speaks of the awakening of adulthood with elements always deployed for continuing entertainment]." For his part, Miguel Frías, Argentine film critic for *Clarín*, notes, "Su levedad es sólo aparente: la historia, narrada en clave satírica, nos lleva hasta las puertas de un mundo adulto que promete ser asfixiante, intolerante, injusto [Its lightness is only apparent: the story, narrated in a satiric form, takes us to the doors of an adult world that promises to be asphyxiating, intolerant, and unfair]." Indeed, what is highly innovative in this film is the fact that the suffocating universe belongs to the Jewish community and that the satirical view is presented by young Ariel, a thirteen-year-old who scrutinizes his family, friends, and community. Here it is important to take into account Pinfold's thoughts on "the intuitive wisdom of the child above the acquired knowledge of the adults; the child's state might best be described as an aesthetic innocence that has moral implications."[14] In addition to embodying aesthetic innocence, Ariel's scrutiny also involves the urge to define his place as part of, and different from, his Jewish family and the Jewish community.

The film begins with an aerial view of the country club El Ciervo, accompanied by Ariel's ironic voice-over: "Este es mi country. Aquí pasamos el verano más de cien familias judías felices, alejados de todo [This is my country. Here more than a hundred Jewish families happily spend the summer, far away from it all]." The manicured lawns, pristine water of the swimming pools, and well-kept golf course convey the idea of an idyllic environment, but this is also a setting for de-personalization, as residents are known by the numbers of the lots they occupy. Numbers replace names and are frequently referenced by the country club's management when pushing for more consumption of goods. This system forces members to conform and makes them anonymous. Corresponding to the prevailing type of socialization in Argentina in the 1990s—the time in which *Cheesehead* takes place—numbers prevail, making relationships superficial and based on competition instead of cooperation. The neoliberal mindset also encourages the power of the most affluent, where wealth buys prestige and influence.[15]

Ariel next introduces the members of his family, who belong to three different generations. Instead of showing love and respect for his family, however, Ariel gives a keen assessment of their weaknesses. The grandparents, Mollo (Juan Manuel Tenuta) and Chona (María Vaner), are depicted using the traditional stereotypes of the *schlemiel* and the Jewish mother. Mollo carries a walkie-talkie that Chona uses to control him from a distance, and thus, in the eyes of Ariel, he is a man dominated by his wife. As the domineering Jewish mother, Chona frequently gives money to her grandchildren, causing their parents, Lilli (Mercedes Morán) and Raúl (Carlos Kaspar), to constantly argue about it. For her part, Lilli is the country club's unofficial queen of the Israeli dance Rikudim. Ariel admits that she dances well, and her need to stand out is stressed as a flaw. Ariel's father is an absent figure who participates neither in the country club's soccer team nor in his family's life. Finally, Ariel introduces his older brother, David (Martín Piroyanski), and younger sister, Natalia (Martina Juncadella), who are both interested in sports. The seventeen-year-old David is "seriously" engaged with Romina (Julieta Zylberberg).

Although the film seems to concentrate on common adolescent experiences such as sexual awakenings and rites of passage, *Cheesehead* is actually a piercing critique of adults. The film's central axis—Alma's bullying of Coper, witnessed by Ariel—ultimately serves to condemn adults. This act of violence has important ramifications as it forces Ariel—and Coper, albeit indirectly—to make an ethical decision in a community that does not recognize the significance of his dilemma as a witness of bullying. With the exception of Mr. Garchuni, the only adult who is positively depicted, all others appear divided into those who ignore the event, such as Ariel's parents; those who divert their attention, such as Ariel's grandfather; and those who deny that the incident took place, such as the country club's management and Alma's father.

Moreover, as Ariel starts focusing more on adults, he also discovers other events that do not cast them in a positive light. One of these involves the manipulation of the mother of one of the boys in the country club, who uses

Poster. *Cheesehead, My First Ghetto* (2006), directed by Ariel Winograd.

her sexuality to increase her son's acceptance among the teenagers. Another involves Mrs. Garchuni and her adulterous relationship with the country club's president. Yet another involves Ariel's mother and his paternal grandmother, who compete over who gets more attention from a musician hired to perform at the club. These anecdotes portray the adults as self-centered and, ironically, childish.

In *Cheesehead* adults are represented as unfit role models, and their negative actions influence and are replicated by the adolescents. Female teen Ruthi (Inés Efrón) is shown as a mercenary in complete control, charging boys a fee for the opportunity to kiss her. But perhaps the most prominent mirroring of adult bad behavior occurs in Ariel's own family, where the grandmother, mother, and young Romina, David's girlfriend, "conspire" to control the men of the family. As Ariel's grandfather tells his grandson, the Jewish mother and the Jewish girlfriend become friends so that the mother passes the control over her Jewish son onto a female of a younger generation. Issues of control and domination render Jewish men powerless, as when the men of three different generations, Ariel's grandfather, father, and older brother, passively watch their respective wives and girlfriends perform onstage at a concert.

Within this community riddled with problems, Ariel and Coper face a huge moral dilemma: what will be the cost of rejecting violence, and can this be done without disrupting the close ties and emotional support among the members of this intimate ethnic community? By taking a public stand against violence, Ariel comes of age. After the incident of abuse, Alma alternates between unsuccessfully trying to co-opt Ariel and Coper and harassing them. He calls Ariel "Cara de queso" (Cheesehead), a pejorative name that stresses his powerlessness and awkwardness. But in a crucial scene, Ariel faces a mirror, a cinematic technique linked to the definition of one's identity, and repeats his nickname several times as if to internalize and appropriate the influence of the external word and, at the same time, to gather courage for the meeting in which he will testify about Coper's abuse. Once he accepts his identity—his "cara de queso"—the worst is over, and he can bear witness to the bullying of his friend. By choosing the ethically correct side, Ariel stands in stark opposition to the silence and indifference encouraged by the members of this country club. Consequently, *Cheesehead* is a film that focuses on the initiation into adulthood and the maturation of the male Jewish protagonist.[16]

Cheesehead has an open ending. The last scenes show the faces of the country club's board members to whom Ariel has to provide his version of the abuse that he has witnessed. There is a final attempt on the part of the country club's manager to dissuade him, but Ariel appears determined to unmask Alma's unacceptable behavior. His decision undoubtedly transcends the usual disputes among peers, given that it also involves adults who appear willing simply to restore the lost order and forget about the incident. As Frías notes, then, the film "muestra la marginación y la intolerancia impuestas, de un modo infinitamente menos brutal, pero desde adentro [shows the marginalization and imposed intolerance, in a much less brutal way but within the inside]." When Ariel crosses the threshold of the room in which he will present his testimony, he is also separating himself from the conformity and superficiality of life in the country club, El ciervo. It remains to be seen, however, if the older members of the board will, literally and figuratively, follow suit and discipline the aggressor.

The Marked Self: *Acne*

Acne takes place over several months and follows a thirteen-year-old boy named Rafael Bregman (Alejandro Tocar), who suffers from acne. The first scene shows him in front of a large mirror, meticulously examining the spots on his face. Rafael's inspection is interrupted by his brother, who announces that the family's housekeeper is ready to sexually initiate him. The teenager replies with a cautious "No sé si quiero [I don't know if I want to]," to which the brother replies "Claro que querés [Of course you want to]." Rafa then answers, "No sé si estoy preparado [I don't know if I'm ready]." This brief exchange encapsulates the whole range of emotions that Rafa is experiencing as a teenager: self-doubt, desire for independence, peer pressure, and sexual curiosity. To face these issues, *Acne* focuses on the comfort that Rafael finds in his friends and on his silent relationship with his father.

Like *Cheesehead*, *Acne* has an atmosphere redolent with Jewish stereotypes: the Bregman family is seen at dinnertime sitting around the table in a small and cramped dining room. The father's casual conversation with the housekeeper is quickly censored by his wife, Eva (Ana Julia Catalá). A question from Rafa's sister, Naty (Natalia Pipermo), about the family's summer vacation is also deflected by the mother. The communal sharing of their meal does not provide an opportunity for open and frank exchanges; rather, it is a time full of tension in which the young Bregmans strive not to cross either parent. As the film progresses, Rafael's parents, Eva and Simón (Gustavo Melnik), separate, a dramatic point suggesting a long period of strain between the two. The young Bregmans are never directly informed of their parents' decision: they eavesdrop while their parents make arrangements for their separation. Later, as Rafael watches a video of the joyous occasion of his bar mitzvah, it is possible to observe Eva's awkward body language as she stands apart from her husband, indicating that the parental estrangement developed over several months.

While the Bregman home is depicted as suffocating, multiple takes of Rafael show him in different, more liberating places. One of them is the classroom at his Jewish school. The well-lit schoolroom is the ideal background for Rafael to express the creativity and freedom that he cannot display at home: whether in English, Yiddish, or history class, he draws pictures of himself and his ever-present acne. Another setting for autonomy is the club, where he plays tennis and takes swimming lessons; the decision for him to take part in such activities was probably made by his parents but is sabotaged by his own pursuits, as Rafael appears more interested in his swimming instructor's body than in the swimming techniques themselves. Rafael's preoccupation with sex and pornographic films leads him to frequent the local brothel and a movie theater. Locations of socialization with his peers are also important: the streets in which he tries smoking, the dance club in which he gazes at his classmate, Nicole (Belén Pouchan), and the training camp that is attended by his Jewish Uruguayan peers. Finally,

Rafael also visits his father's wholesale appliance business, where he alternates between waiting for a ride and lending his father a hand in the work.

As in *Cheesehead*, in *Acne* Rafael has a tense relationship with his family's traditions and his Jewish heritage. In the video recording of his bar mitzvah, he acknowledges his parents: "Sin ellos no sería la persona que soy, no sería nada [Without them, I would not be the person I am. I would be nothing]." This spoken expression of gratitude, however, contradicts Rafael's quest throughout the film to define who he is—independent from his parents. For instance, if on the one hand, he capitulates to his brother Martín's pressure to be sexually initiated by their maid, on the other he resists conforming to and following in his older brother's footsteps. This resistance is evident when a month-long trip to Israel is advertised at school and he mentions it at home.[17] While Martín asserts that there is nothing to debate about this trip, full of opportunities to party and try new experiences, Rafa withstands his older brother's pressure by saying "Yo soy yo [I am myself]." This declaration of individuality shows him on the path to self-determination, separating himself from his family's traditions.

Other examples of Rafael's process of self-definition take place at school. One day his English teacher asks the class about their fathers' professions. While two of Rafael's classmates reply to this question—albeit in Spanish—Rafael states that he does not have a father. When the teacher tries his mother's profession, he also denies having a mother. These statements land him in the principal's office, where Rafael is lectured (in front of his mother) for his transgression. Once mother and son exit the office, however, Mrs. Bregman does not seek to engage her son in the motives behind the denial of his parents. Rather, she admonishes Rafael for tarnishing her image with a call to the principal's office and warns him to avoid these types of disruption to her life. When Rafael visits the principal's office a second time, he receives sad news about what he considers his "true" family: he learns that his friend Andy has decided to remain in Israel and will not be returning to school. The loss of a member of his inner circle of friends—that is to say, his family during adolescence—momentarily devastates Rafael.

Rafael's coming-of-age process also takes place in a protective environment. While there is not much communication between Rafael and his parents, the film stresses Rafael's family's upper-middle-class status as displayed in the brand new BMW that his father drives, the elegant apartment where they live, the live-in maid they employ, their vacations in the exclusive ocean city of Punta del Este, the private school that Rafael attends, and his extracurricular activities, tennis, swimming, and piano lessons. But perhaps the most noticeable marker of his family's high income and high standing in society is Rafael's acne treatments, which involve appointments with a specialized professional and with a doctor who prescribes an expensive ointment, which becomes a fetish for one of Rafael's less well-to-do friends. The standard of living of Rafael's family clearly provides him with comfort and security during adolescence.

Acne chronicles two of Rafael's obsessions: after losing his virginity to the maid, he longs for a real kiss that cannot be bought, and he also hopes to win the affection of Nicole, his classmate. Much of the film concerns Rafael's silent admiration of Nicole and his reluctance to approach her. In the last minutes of the film, he not only dances with her but also has a few minutes alone with her. After gathering his courage, he praises Nicole and compliments her on her hair, a sign both that he does not objectify her and that he tries to build her self-confidence. Coming from someone who is so concerned with his acne, Rafael's gesture shows empathy and respect. He also confesses his love for her. These statements are met with an awkward silence on Nicole's part. Her discomfort is evident when she says that she has to leave because her parents are picking her up, but Rafael follows her and discovers that she leaves with some other friends. Curiously, Nicole's rejection does not leave Rafael heartbroken, but rather more resilient and able to face the challenges of his teenage universe. It is in his own action—not in Nicole's response—that Rafael gains a new sense of confidence.

Indeed, Rafael's coming-of-age process amounts to finding his own voice both inside and outside the Jewish community. The first event that indicates his independence takes place after Nicole's rebuff. Instead of internalizing her rejection, he appears liberated, willing to explore other opportunities. With a newfound self-confidence, he approaches a girl who works at a convenience store and accepts her invitation to go for a walk. This scene mirrors Rafael's encounter with Nicole, but this time Rafael is the receiver of compliments about his hair. Unlike Nicole, who remained silent while he praised her, Rafael thanks the girl and, without anticipating it, shares a long kiss with her. This moment not only marks the end of Rafael's quest for a kiss, but also illustrates his growth as he accepts the gift of the girl's spontaneous affection. Even though his face is still marred by acne, he can be as desirable as any other adolescent.

The final event in Rafael's pursuit of his own voice also involves acceptance, this time of his friend Andy's decision to migrate to Israel. Rafael prepares a package for Andy that he takes to his friend's house, where he asks Andy's father the time difference between Uruguay and Israel. The final scene captures Rafael calling Andy's *kibbutz* in Israel and leaving a message for his friend. In this act, Rafael shows that he has found his voice and is able to respect and live with his friend's choice of relocating to Israel. In both instances, Rafael has to problem-solve on his own and ultimately deals in a positive way with issues that involve attachment and separation.

Cheesehead and *Acne* stage the coming of age of a Jewish Argentine boy and a Jewish Uruguayan boy, respectively. Both films portray these painful processes of growing up, and both Ariel and Rafael have to figure out what they can adapt from their Jewish heritage and make relevant to their twentieth- and twenty-first century lives. As they do so, they are represented as "orphans" in dysfunctional families and without any paternal influence that could strengthen their links and emotional ties with Judaism. The effacement of their fathers is, however, offset by their close friendships with other boys of the Jewish community, with whom they share joys and moments of crisis as they slowly leave behind the protected and innocent milieu of childhood. The negative portrayal of the Jewish adults, however, has to be taken with a grain of salt, as tension-filled clashes are a hallmark of the adolescent movement of separating from elders and signaling self-determination.

Through their debut films, Winograd and Veiroj represent their young Jewish protagonists as both different from—because of their Jewish backgrounds—and also similar to other middle-class boys. These filmmakers concentrate on universal themes of bullying and sexual awakening that are experienced by all boys in contemporary cultures. Thus, their films show the lives of secular Jewish boys whose Jewishness is a mark of both otherness and belonging—belonging to a distinct community that is the object of their own scrutiny and even criticism.

Notes

Throughout this essay, all translations are my own.

1. For more on these stereotypes, see Desser and Friedman, *American Jewish Filmmakers*; Abrams, *The New Jew in Film*; and Antler, *You Never Call! You Never Write!*.
2. See Rocha, "Identidad masculina y judía en la trilogía de Daniel Burman" for a more detailed analysis of Jewish characters in Burman's cinematography.
3. For an interesting discussion of this topic, see Rein's *Argentine Jews or Jewish Argentines?*, 2–3.
4. Here I am following Jeffrey Lesser and Ranaan Rein's suggestion of using the term "Latin American–Jewish" instead of "Latin American Jews."
5. Lesko, *Act Your Age*, 12.
6. Rein, *Argentine Jews or Jewish Argentines?*, 5.
7. Tal, "Alegorías de la memoria y del olvido en películas de iniciación," 134.
8. The film scholar Tamara Falicov asserts that the film, along with the ones di-

rected by Burman and Lichtmann, "explores questions of Jewish identity in a largely Catholic country" (*The Cinematic Tango*, 134).
9. Silvert, "Entrevista con Ariel Winograd."
10. In an interview with the film scholar Marina Moguillansky, Veiroj also explains that "la idea de hacer *Acné* surgió de un guión muy ambicioso que escribimos con mi hermano mayor en 2001, en donde se retrataba una familia a lo largo de 15 años. Dicho guión que llevaba por título 'Imperio cerámico' estaba inspirado en mi familia y en mis amigos [The idea of shooting *Acne* came from a very ambitious plot that I wrote with my older brother in 2011, in which we depicted a family and followed it for 15 years. That script that was entitled "Ceramic Empire" was inspired by my family and my friends]" (Moguillansky n/p).
11. Abrams, *The New Jew in Film*, 186.
12. Pinfold, *The Child's View of the Third Reich in German Literature*, 4.
13. Tal, "Terror, etnicidad y la imagen del judío en el cine contemporáneo argentino." Ricardo Feierstein mentions, in *Historia de los judíos argentinos*, the different neighborhoods that Jewish Argentines have favored: from Lavalle at the turn of the twentieth century, to Plaza Once in the first decades of the twentieth century, to Villa Crespo in the 1950s and other areas such as Palermo, Barrio Norte, and country clubs since the 1970s.
14. Pinfold, *The Child's View of the Third Reich in German Literature*, 5.
15. I develop this idea in "Post-Menem Argentina and Systemic Violence in Claudia Piñeyro's *Las viudas de los jueves*."
16. For more on this film as a bildungsroman, see my article "Jewish Cinematic Self-Representations in Contemporary Argentine and Brazilian Films."
17. Here it is worth taking into account the words of Jewish Argentine critic Tzvi Tal, who explains that during neoliberalism, "el estímulo a la visita de adolescentes y jóvenes a Israel dejó de estar orientado a la realización sionista para transformarse en la comercialización de un producto turístico enfocado en la conservación de la identidad [the emphasis on adolescents' and youths' visits to Israel stopped being associated with the Zionist realization to turn into a commercialization of a touristic product focused on preserving identity]" ("Terror, etnicidad y la imagen del judío en el cine contemporáneo argentino").

Works Cited

Films

Burman, Daniel, dir. *Derecho de familia*. Perf. Daniel Hendler, Julieta Díaz, Adriana Aizemberg. BD Cine/INCAA/Classic Film. 2006.
———. *El abrazo partido*. Perf. Daniel Hendler, Adriana Aizemberg, Jorge D'Elía. BD Cine/Classic Film/CinemART. 2004.
———. *Esperando al Mesías*. Perf. Daniel Hendler, Héctor Alterio, Enrique Piñeiro, Imanol Arias. Astrolabio Producciones/BD Cine. 2000.
Hamburger, Cao, dir. *O ano em que meus pais saíram de férias*. Perf. Michel Joelsas, Germano Haiut, Daniela Piepszyk. Gullane/Coa Produções Cinematográficas/Miravista. 2006.
Lichtmann, Gabriel, dir. *Judíos en el espacio*. Perf. Gabriela Andermann, Axel Anderson, Gerardo Chendo. INCAA/Primer Plano Film Group. 2005.

Rebella, Juan Pablo, and Pablo Stoll, dir. *Whisky*. Perf. Andrés Pazos, Mireilla Pascula, Jorge Bolani. Pandora Filmproduktion/Rizoma Films/Control Z Film. 2004.
Veiroj, Federico, dir. *Acné*. Perf. Alejandro Tocar, Ana Julia Catalá, Gustavo Melnik. Control Z/Federico Veiroj/Rizoma Films. 2008.
Winograd, Ariel, dir. *Cara de queso: Mi primer ghetto*. Perf. Felipe Colombo, Nicolás Condito, Sergio Denis, Inés Efron. Haddock Films/Tresplanos Cine. 2006.

Articles and Books

Abrams, Nathan. *The New Jew in Film: Exploring Jewishness and Judaism in Contemporary Cinema*. New Brunswick, NJ: Rutgers University Press, 2012.
Antler, Joyce. *You Never Call! You Never Write!: A History of the Jewish Mother*. New York: Oxford University Press, 2007.
Desser, David, and Lester D. Friedman. *American Jewish Filmmakers*. 2nd ed. Urbana: University of Illinois Press, 2004.
Falicov, Tamara. *The Cinematic Tango: Contemporary Argentine Film*. London: Wallflower, 2007.
Feierstein, Ricardo. *Historia de los judíos argentinos*. Buenos Aires: Ameghino, 1999.
Frías, Miguel. "En el gueto interno." *Clarín*, 12 October 2006.
Lesko, Nancy. *Act Your Age: A Cultural Construction of Adolescence*. New York: Routledge, 2001.
Lesser, Jeffrey, and Raanan Rein, eds. *Rethinking Jewish–Latin Americans*. Albuquerque: University of New Mexico Press, 2008.
Martínez, Adolfo. "Despertar a la adultez." *La Nación*, 12 October 2006.
Moguillansky, Marina. "Entrevista a Federico Veiroj, director de *Acné*." *Tierra en Trance*, 10 October 2013.
Pinfold, Debbie. *The Child's View of the Third Reich in German Literature: The Eye among the Blind*. Oxford: Clarendon, 2001.
Rein, Raanan. *Argentine Jews or Jewish Argentines? Essays on Ethnicity, Identity, and Diaspora*. Leiden: Brill, 2010.
Rocha, Carolina. "Identidad masculina y judía en la trilogía de Daniel Burman." *Letras Hispanas* 4, no. 2 (2007): 26–37.
———. "Jewish Cinematic Self-Representations in Contemporary Argentine and Brazilian Films." *Journal of Modern Jewish Studies* 9, no. 1 (2010): 37–48.
———. "Unpublished interview with Ariel Winograd." Buenos Aires, 30 June 2011.
———. "Post-Menem Argentina and Systemic Violence in Claudia Piñeyro's *Las viudas de los jueves*." *Arizona Journal of Hispanic Cultural Studies* (2011): 123–128.
Silvert, Nicolás. "Entrevista con Ariel Winograd." 19 September 2012.
Tal, Tzvi. "Alegorías de la memoria y del olvido en películas de iniciación: *Machuca* y *Kamchatka*." *Aisthesis* (2005): 134–140.
———. "Terror, etnicidad y la imagen del judío en el cine contemporáneo argentino." *Nuevo Mundo Mundos Nuevos*, January 2010.

CHAPTER 9

Waiting for the Messiah: The Super 8mm Films of Alberto Salomón

ERNESTO LIVON-GROSMAN

I had a subscription to Cahiers du cinéma *and* Sight & Sound, *which were the two leading cinema magazines. And an American one,* Film Comment. . . . *I received them every month, counting the days until their arrival as if they were the Messiah's return.*
ALBERTO SALOMÓN IN *INTERVIEW* (2014)

Film has the unique capability of making us imagine that we can think our stories in a cinematographic way. That allure has been around since the earliest days of cinema, but it took on a new meaning with the industrial production of 8mm and Super 8mm cameras, which opened the door to home movies. In this essay I intend to look at the particular case of Alberto Salomón (1933–2015), an Argentine Jewish director of amateur films, and observe what his films tell us about being Jewish in Argentina during the second half of the twentieth century.

Noncommercial, amateur films and home movies are a port of entry into an underground historiography that could provide an insight to a vast registry of private and public events that are not accessible to conventional industrial cinema. These small-gauge films are capable of providing answers to what it meant to be an immigrant, a Jew, and a transgressor of social conventions in a time of censorship. By so doing they unveil to us an unknown dimension. To what extent is the director's gaze determined by the medium?[1]

I begin by outlining what became Alberto Salomón's Super 8mm films project. Three years ago, while working in Buenos Aires at the Film Museum for an ongoing project on the visual representation of the Argentine family during the 1960s and early 1970s, I expanded my archival sources from advertising and orphan 35mm film to home movies. To include home movies was a decision that followed the idea that the project would benefit from finding the intersection of the private and the public spheres. It was my desire to catch those fleeting images at a point where we might see a revealing moment that provides a unique insight on the way that those decades were represented within the intimate environment of the home movie. It was less the impulse of reading the personal as political than the intuition that those home movies might provide a glimpse of the public sphere recorded from an intimate point of view. The 1960s and 1970s were decades deeply transformative for Argentina as a country, and they influenced social structures as well as the political life for many years to come. In working with home movies of that period I was also looking for that particular moment in which those recorded images from the past might provide a preview of the public sphere as we experience it today.

In the process of viewing and transferring to digital format friends' family films in Super 8mm I found, like so many people before me, that home movies can be thematically repetitive—birthdays, weddings, sweet sixteen parties, bar mitzvahs, vacation trips—which tends to make for a very restrictive selection of the everyday. In addition to a limited repertoire of themes, they have in common unstable camera takes and more often than not a consistent absence of montage: in fact for the most part the images we see in those films are in the order in which the camera captured them, and almost always without editing. I found images of family scenes in private settings that disclosed a candid view of everyday life, short films about nothing in particular, that tended to avoid references to political and media events. These were films that made a registry of domestic habits, gestures, and consumption on camera, and that in many cases were not meant to be shown outside the family circle. At this point in my search for home movies I was centered on the formal qualities of those films as much as on their narratives.

In spite of what at first seemed to be the constrained range of themes, I decided to continue screening my friends' Super 8mm and 16mm family reels and even some footage found on the street, because in most cases I did not know what I would find in those reels. When I thought that a reel could be interesting for the project, I digitized it before returning the original films to their owners, together with a copy of the digital version. In the process of searching out and digitizing home movies I came across a collection of fiction films produced and edited by Alberto Salomón, the grandfather of one of the collaborators in my archival project.

Salomón's films brought up new questions and expectations not contemplated at the outset of the original project. In fact they were at the opposite end of the spectrum from a conventional home movie. There were eleven short Super 8mm silent narrative films, scripted, directed, and produced by Alberto Salomón with the help of his immediate family. They were all extensively edited and in some cases produced very carefully. Although shot in Super 8mm, the most accessible format in Argentina during those decades—16mm was much more expensive and therefore less popular—his films were nonetheless intensively choreographed and edited. Salomón's collection also contained many hours of home movies, on Super 8mm and 8mm, shot between 1960 and 1990, produced and edited by him as well. The films include family members as well as many close friends who acted for him.

The son of a Jewish immigrant from Greece, Salomón was brought to Argentina in 1934, when he was only one year old and his family was fleeing from Europe's spreading fascism. Salomón's father founded and developed Argentina's largest family-owned textile company, La Bernaleza, textiles being one of the most popular trades among immigrant Jews during the first half of the twentieth century. The future of the factory was intimately linked to the financial ups and downs of the country, and from the late 1950s on, Salomón's family business entered a long downfall toward bankruptcy.

Traditionalist that he was, his father expected Alberto to follow in his steps and take over the business. This expectation became the source of much anguish for the son. In fact, as I later discovered, the pressure from his father was also one of the forces behind his film work. This paternal pressure to lead the family business against his will and the fall of the company as the result of multiple national financial crises turned the son into an alcoholic. As he told me in an interview: "I'm a recovered alcoholic. Some films I did as a kind of therapy, to unload in a sense. Alcohol is present in every one of them, as you must have noticed."[2] This confluence, where his personal crisis became indistinguishable from business and national financial disasters, is what motivated Salomón to turn to filmmaking as a way of processing, at least on a personal level, what was not possible to solve at a collective one. It was only later that I perceived the connection between the critique of certain social institutions one could find in his films and Alberto's relationship with his father and his position as a Jewish immigrant.[3]

Amateur filmmaking became for the son what the factory had been for the father—an important source of personal satisfaction—and from Alberto's point of view it allowed the creation of a symbolic space where he was able to examine some of his sexual, political, and social concerns. His films have all the attributes that in Liz Czach's view define amateur films: "They are serious leisure, aesthetically ambitious, carefully constructed, have an identifiable genre, and are clearly authored."[4] These characteristics are shared by and expected from a dedicated amateur film practice such as his. Less usual is that Salomón's film narratives are often a commentary on social norms, telling stories that end up blurring the distinction between private and public spheres. His films work as ethnographical personal diaries because at the time they were made they remained private, intimate productions, and because having such a small public made it possible for his films to raise questions that would have been less likely had they been part of a larger, public circuit.[5]

Once these eleven films were digitized and color corrected, I uploaded them to Vimeo, with title cards indicating that the films were processed by me in collaboration with his grandson, not by the director.[6] During the process of screening and transferring his films I met with Alberto Salomón several times and recorded a short interview with him that became an integral part of my project.[7] During the process of transferring the films to digital format it became clear in my critical reading that Salomón's narrative film and his home movies were often blurring dividing lines, not only between the private and the public but also between the amateur and the experimental.

Besides the already mentioned recurrent theme of alcoholism, his films are melodramatic fictions where religion, sex, crime, and dreaming play key roles. Although most of Salomón's films are critical of social normatives, that criticism is embedded in a rabbi's social transgressions and in the exaggerated portrayals of the hypocrisy of the bourgeois lifestyle of secular Jews. The recurrent narrative of these films is that dramatic development involves a break from normative behavior: as when a wife kills her husband to run away with another woman or the presence of an incestuous brother-in-law. Sexuality linked to pornography and the ever-present alcoholism are the backbone of some of the stories in his films. The narratives are always somehow opposed to middle-class mores yet they come with a twist: the plots always have a touch of humor, a grotesque quality that keeps them from becoming kitsch while allowing them to retain a transgressive tone.

All the actors in Salomón's fictional films were close friends or family members, and through the twelve films the cast remained almost the same, with little variation. Screenings were private events at his home, and since they were silent films, he played music from records, adjusting the volume and the musical selection while the films were shown.[8] These live screenings were important social events that included family members, friends, and acquaintances as well as the actors, creating an environment that resembled more an *expanded cinema* event than a traditional family reunion.[9] I find the performativity of the screenings, the almost open quality of these gatherings, consistent with the experimental aesthetics of his films.

One thing that intrigues me is the hybridity of his aesthetic project: the multiple sources that he brought together in his films to construct their narratives. In addition to the performative component of the screenings, Salomón's shorts move across genre boundaries by interspersing his narrative films with documentary clips from televised newscasts as well as from his own home movies. Some of those home movies were staged performances and others were candid family takes, but in any case they were shot independently of the master narrative that his editing ultimately brought together. The deliberate mixing of visual materials from different and sometimes unrelated sources is at the root of Salomón's fictions and underlines the experimental practice of taking fragments and resignifying them in a different context as if it were a compilation film. In this process of resemantization, Salomón consistently includes in his film fragments of archival materials, home movies, television shows, and clips from rented films, and by doing so he creates a gap between what is shown and the social critique that is suggested, leaving it up to the viewer to bridge the divide. His films often rely on the notion of transgression, whether incest, parricide, or pornography, and the results point consistently to a breaking away from bourgeois social conventions. The strategy is particularly striking where his films intersperse images taken from television newscasts, which provide a temporal contextualization while upsetting genre distinctions such as fiction and documentary—a trend that was extensively explored by the films that he watched and that clearly influenced him.[10]

These combined images are integrated into his films to add an additional narrative layer, as when the main female character asks for advice from a rabbi after killing her husband and running off with her husband's lover. The confessional retelling of the murder is interspersed with porn clips taken from rented VHS tapes, suggesting lust as one of the motives for the murder and bringing to the plot a visual representation of her confession. In some films, he includes news clips that provide a historical anchoring. He uses materials taken from television: a World Cup soccer final, a clearly identifiable politician, or a well-known television host. The way he uses these clips highlights how the private sphere is constantly connected to a network of social and political references in his films.[11]

Salomón's films interweave two separate concepts: the family archive and the notion of memory as the interpretation of history. The extensive practice of recording and collecting private family images year in and year out—a vacation, a family reunion, a birthday party—is what Salomón describes as a record of change: "Y también el paso del tiempo porque muchas son películas viejas, metidas ahí, donde se ve el crecimiento de algunos chicos, mis nietos."[12] The second, more hidden concept in his work is his perception of memory as a kind of retelling of history, as when he records a family member at a political demonstration or brings into his films a snippet of a television broadcast to anchor the film in a precise historical moment. In *Sans soleil* (1983), Chris Marker rigorously describes this tension between history and representation: "I will have spent my life trying to understand the function of remembering, which is not the opposite of forgetting, but rather its lining. We do not remember, we rewrite memory much as history is rewritten."

Salomón's films actively reframe events by integrating clips from multiple sources as a structural component of family reels in a fictional plot. In so doing he constructs a personal view of history that becomes larger than his immediate family narrative. By fictionalizing his home movies and then connecting them with the public sphere, he effectively inserts these films into Argentina's amateur and experimental film tradition. The three aspects that characterize Salomón's films are the performatic, the fragmentary, and the political. These traits put Salomón on a par with other Argentine experimental filmmakers working at the same time as him, but who did not know of each other's existence.

Argentina's experimental film practice developed in the early 1970s thanks to the arrival of Super 8mm cameras. Unlike what happened in the United States, where filmmakers have been using 16mm from early on, Argentina would have to wait for Super 8mm film to arrive before a community of amateur filmmakers could arise. It was not until 1972 that a small but very active group of filmmakers founded UNCIPAR (Unión de Cineastas de Paso Reducido [Association of Small-Gauge Filmmakers]), one of the first Super 8mm organizations in Latin America. The big attraction of Super 8mm, besides its price, was the format's flexibility, granting the filmmaker the potential to think outside the box without having to follow the much more structured rules of industrial cinema. Another main attraction was the ease of screening.[13]

The persuasive work of critics and artists such as Roger Odin, Efrén Cuevas, Péter Forgács, and Patricia Zimmermann, among others, has shown the importance of home movies as primary sources for cultural and historical research. Salomón's films also reveal that home movies and amateur films are able to create a cultural register that is not easily available in other forms of cultural production, and they do so while staying aligned with an experimental tradition. Within this experimental tradition, Salomón's films are a good example of how experimentation and political commentary could work together to create a critical record of social norms. One case particular to Buenos Aires involves the popular reception of art films during the

Director Alberto Salomón during the shooting of *Interview* in 2014.

1960s and 1970s, decades during which directors such as Michelangelo Antonioni, Luis Buñuel, and Jean-Luc Godard reached levels of vast popularity. Salomón's films consistently make reference to those directors through the inclusion of film posters in indoor scenes as well as street shots announcing film screenings. For Salomón, the French New Wave was as much a personal point of reference as it was for the middle-class moviegoer. Although he had a highly trained filmic eye, his references were widely accessible. In my interview with Salomón he describes how important these foreign films were for him and how much he looked forward to receiving the film journals that analyzed them:

> Yo estaba suscrito a *Cahiers du cinéma* y a *Sight & Sound*, que eran las dos revistas más importantes de cine, y a una americana, *Film Comment*, que creo que todavía sigue saliendo, ¿no? Las recibía mensualmente y las esperaba como la bajada del mesías, eran para mí la lectura más fascinante.[14]

I would like to suggest that small-gauge film and Salomón's experimental aesthetics have a place of their own within Argentina's film history and should be considered on an equal footing with any other cultural product. Returning to my first interest in the intersection of the public and the private, it is key to see how this intersection is articulated in Salomón's films. The narratives of his films are always transgressive of bourgeois manners, and they seem to expose a profound discomfort about moral conventions.

In order to explore what I mean by Salomón's films being at odds with social norms, I would like to focus on one of his most memorable films: *Neró*, from 1987. For the most part the 1970s and the beginning of the 1980s were decades marked by military dictatorships, brutal repression, and a very effective censorship that eventually affected the national film industry as well as the distribution of certain foreign films. These political conditions permeated every possible public institution. In that environment formal experimentation became a form of resistance. It was never a one-on-one relationship where any one avant-garde gesture was a critique of a particular issue, but rather avant-garde artistic expressions became a way of questioning social values, able to escape censorship because of their marginal position, limited exposure, and formal difficulty. In this sense I find Salomón's films political for the consistent way in which they criticize conventional family values and the advertising industry as well as larger political issues.

In *Neró*, Salomón exposes a twofold morality by which a religious figure, in this case a rabbi, can be a source of spiritual authority while he drinks himself to death during a consultation with the female character. In Salomón's films social critique goes much further than it first appears. An example of this is the constant recurrence of alcohol and advertising as destructive forces that stand as the ultimate allegory of capitalism's consumerism. Salomón's critique builds on the hypocrisy of social conventions. Through *Neró* he chooses to highlight the gap between what is expected and what the rabbi really does; it is a frontal critique of Judaism in particular and of religion in general. His more or less standard secularism—"I am Jewish but I do not believe in God" (in conversation with the author), which could pass for indifference—can be viewed as more of a critical stance when we take into account the details of the rabbi's character in this film.

In what becomes *Neró*'s establishing shot, we see a rabbi, his back to the camera, wearing a prayer shawl. At first it looks as if he is praying. Standing in front of a bookshelf, the rabbi turns around with a glass of whiskey and walks away from the shelves to play a record. What the shot made us believe was a religious ritual turns out to be what we cannot see at first: his compulsive drinking. Hard of hearing, the rabbi uses an oversized funnel to listen to the music; eventually, the funnel will also become a drinking device. This opening shot with its devotional fervor for the bottle sets the tone of the first sequence dedicated to building and defining the character of the rabbi. Everything is hyperbolic in this scene: the funnel he uses to drink, the bucket of ice that implies a large amount of liquor, even the number of bottles that are present in that sequence. In a way, exaggeration frames the rabbi and his actions, echoing the dramatic strategies of early silent films. Salomón's representational strategies are less a nostalgic gesture than the reuse of a an older narrative technique in a new narrative context. Every move, even the excessive speedy gestures of the maid working in the kitchen, points in the direction of the anti-naturalist portrait of a religious man; the absurd humor of the scene becomes the dividing line between a realist and an experimental aesthetic. Salomón's critical portrait brackets the rituals of the rabbi's role by displacing his authority and emptying the devotional meaning of his actions.

The rabbi frames the narrative of this moral film by showing the ultimate failure of religion through the unsustainable ethical predicament by which the Judeo-Christian tradition pretends to hold a higher moral ground. In *Neró* two social pillars are broken: neither family nor religion can keep together a structure that in this particular film ends in two deaths, first the husband's at his wife's hands and then the rabbi's by his own lust. Salomón does not leave much room for the recuperation of the religious man. It is not just drunkenness that can be seen as an illness but a general sense of decadence, something that seems suggested by the idea that the woman dressed as a maid is also his lover. Kinkiness is a constant in the suggested relationship between the maid and the rabbi as well as in the narrative of the woman at the moment of describing her husband's lust and later on her own desire for the maid after the rabbi dies. Salomón shows a propensity for staging sexually transgressive scenes, incest, double crossings, and pornography to suggest a sense of dubious institutional moral ground for religion, marriage, and even, in other films, the medical establishment.

In Salomón's films, the gaze belongs to the outsider or at the very least to someone who resists conformity: the son who refuses to keep the family business alive; the adult who portrays himself as more than anything else an alcoholic with an expansive libido, always crossing the limits of morality; and, on one particular occasion, the Jew who turns religion into a mix of kitsch and ridicule. Traditional Jewish law demands that a meeting between a rabbi and a woman take place in the presence of a third person. In *Neró* the third person is the maid, who seems to perceive the excitement of the rabbi as he listens to the confession of the adulterous woman. Eventually his excitement leads him to more drinking, and that in turn precipitates a quick succession of events that end up killing him. The story could be a cautionary one if it were not for the fact that once the rabbi is dead, the main female character and the maid seem to initiate a romance, creating a new ripple of sexual attraction and death.[15]

Repetition is a key structural element in Salomón's fictions, an anti-absorbent device that points to the actual artificiality of film as a medium and to its oneiric qualities. Repetition is the formal device, and transgression its content. A woman dreams of her husband, the man she killed, and in her dream she repeats three times an anecdote from her husband's childhood. A boy drinks from a glass, gets up, and vomits the liquid that he just drank. That boy, who becomes her husband, drinks, and she kills him, when he is an adult, by giving him a drink. The rabbi who is the audience for her confession drinks himself to death. Repetition in her dreams as much as when she is awake seems to confirm the irrelevance of any prescribed norm, whether secular or religious. The main female character moves from one situation to the next, from the vacation during which her husband will die to the dream sequence where she reconstructs her husband's childhood to the encounter with the rabbi. For Salomón's female character, it seems that the only way to freedom is to break with the institutions—marriage and religion—that keep her connected to these men, which is accomplished by the killing of her husband and the suicide of the rabbi. In another of Salomón's films all the children of a large family gang up against the adults and kill them one by one, and in still one more film, adultery ends in multiple deaths. It is not family, religion, or a particular social institution that Salomón's films target, but a composite of all of them.

To the critique of religion, a trademark of the leftist political discourse that permeated the public sphere during the 1960s and 1970s, one should also add the secularism of a large segment of Argentina's Jewish community. In this sense Salomón's critical view of religion is fairly representative of that particular moment. More striking still is his abrasive depiction of family as an institution, in particular when one recalls that most of the characters in his films are portrayed either by his own family members or by very close friends and their family members. Although a psychoanalytical reading of his portrayal of family as dysfunctional and the relationship of Alberto Salomón with his father is very much called for here, in his insistence on targeting a variety of other institutions and the inclusion of references to contemporary public and political life, it is clear that Salomón's critical perspective extended well beyond the personal. In *Neró* there is an element of displacement and also of condensation: the first death takes place in a foreign country, Greece, where Salomón was born, and the second one on the woman's visit to the rabbi in Argentina. They both stand for otherness, and one could argue, they also suggest a connection between death and otherness. After all, in Salomón's case, Jewishness and foreignness are inseparable ways of being in the world.

In closing, I would argue that amateur films and home movies, usually associated with a lack of resources and a lack of distribution, possess an often overlooked richness that comes from their freedom from expectation, from their not being the product of an industrial circuit, and from their potential to bear witness to domesticity in a manner and degree that before the arrival of the Internet were nowhere to be found. They are the potential platform in which to investigate a historiography that would be hard to find in any museum of the much more institutionalized commercial cinema.[16] Working with Alberto Salomón's films, and creating an archival project that will eventually bring together his fiction and home movies, opened up for me a unique point of access to a type of representation that is inseparable from the films' own material restrictions. Home movies are, after all, an integral part of a cinema without which we are condemned to watch the endless repetition of spectacle. Films like Salomón's are the tip of an iceberg of that minor cinema that is waiting to be seen in the larger critical landscape of Latin American cinema. It is up to us to find those home movies and look at them, perhaps for the first time, in order to gain a new and expanded understanding of Latin American film as a field study.

Notes

1. The expression "small-gauge film" refers to the smaller formats that made possible massive consumption and production of homemade films. All of them are smaller than the 35mm, which is the most widely used commercial format. Some of the most popular small-gauge formats are 16mm, Super 8mm, 8mm, and 9.5mm. In most instances these formats require a specific camera and its own projection system.

2. *Interview* (2014).

3. Even at eighty years old, Salomón had a slight Greek accent. His connection with his birthplace was very much present in his mind and his films. His wife, Annie, a Jewish immigrant from Albania, was the leading female actress of most of his films.

4. Czach, "Home Movies and Amateur Film as National Cinema," 30.

5. Some of his home movies can be seen as silent, long-distance relatives of Jonas Mekas's films.

6. Salomón's films can be accessed at the Salomón Project, https://vimeo.com/album/2724742.

7. *Interview* (2014), a short documentary in conversation with Alberto Salomón and the author, can be accessed at https://vimeo.com/surynorth/salomonen.

8. Salomón's films made use of a very well defined repertoire of symphonic rock and contemporary tango. There were three major musical sources for his films: the Alan Parsons Project, the Electric Light Orchestra, and Rodolfo Mederos.

9. "Expanded cinema" refers to the widening of the conventional screening space to create a performatic environment and event. In Salomón's case these events took place at his home, giving new meaning to the term "home movie."

10. For a detailed description of his cinematographic influences, please see *In-*

terview, where Salomón describes in depth the impact of the French New Wave in his own work.

11. Salomón's films have an echo of Osvaldo Lamborghini's short stories, in which perversion becomes the best, if not the only, possible form of political and social commentary.

12. "Some of those movies are rather old and they show the passage of time, my children and grandchildren growing up" (*Interview*, 2014; my translation).

13. One of the reasons for the creation of UNCIPAR was the desire of these small-gauge filmmakers to erase the difference between amateur and experimental. This is in contrast to what happened in the United States, where filmmakers managed to create their own institutions (such as the Film Makers' Cooperative in 1962 and later on the Anthology Film Archives in 1970). Some of Argentina's Super 8mm experimental filmmakers were loosely organized around the Goethe-Institut through Marie Louise Alemann, one of the members of the group and film curator at the Goethe. The other filmmakers associated with this circle—Narcisa Hirsch, Claudio Caldini, Jorge Honik, Horacio Vallerregio—were in part connected through Alemann. The rich and complex history of this foundational moment in Argentina's experimental film is waiting to be written. For a compilation of critical articles on avant-garde film see Sitney, *The Avant-Garde Film: A Reader on Theory and Criticism*. Special thanks to Ricardo Parody, who very generously shared with me his own research on the history of Argentina's experimental film.

14. "I had a subscription to *Cahiers du cinéma* and to *Sight & Sound*, which were the two leading cinema magazines. And an American one, *Film Comment*, which I think is still in print, no? I received them every month, counting the days until their arrival as if it were the Messiah's return. I was fascinated by what I read about the different directors and movies, which gave me ideas for things I was working on" (*Interview*, 2014).

15. Salomón's narratives resemble the delirious fictions of Argentine novelist César Aira.

16. One of the most striking cases of historiography based on home movies is the work of Hungarian filmmaker Péter Forgács, who used family films from the 1920s and 1930s to reconstruct the deportation of Hungarian and Dutch Jews to extermination camps. For an extensive critical analysis of his films, see Nichols and Renov's edited volume on his films, *Cinema's Alchemist*.

Works Cited

Films

Livon-Grosman, Ernesto, dir. *Interview*. Surynorth Productions. 2014.
Marker, Chris, dir. *Sans Soleil*. Argos Films. 1983.
Salomón, Alberto, dir. *Neró*. Arghellas Producciones. 1987.

Books and Articles

Czach, Liz. "Home Movies and Amateur Film as National Cinema." In *Amateur Filmmaking: The Home Movie, the Archive, the Web*, ed. Laura Rascaroli, Gwenda Young, and Monahan, 27–37. New York: Bloomsbury, 2014.

Lshizuka, Karen L., and Patricia R. Zimmermann. *Mining the Home Movie: Excavations in Histories and Memories*. Berkeley: University of California Press, 2008.

Nichols, Bill, and Michael Renov, eds. *Cinema's Alchemist: The Films of Péter Forgács*. Minneapolis: Minnesota University Press, 2011.

Odin, Roger. "El cine doméstico en la institución familiar." In *La casa abierta*, ed. Efrén Cuevas Álvarez, 39–60. Madrid: Ocho y Medio, 2010.

Rascaroli, Laura, Gwenda Young, and Barry Monahan, eds. *Amateur Filmmaking: The Home Movie, the Archive, the Web*. New York: Bloomsbury, 2014.

Sitney, Adams, ed. *The Avant-Garde Film: A Reader on Theory and Criticism*. New York: New York University Press, 1978.

PART IV

DIASPORAS AND DISPLACEMENTS

CHAPTER 10

Geographic Isolation and Jewish Religious Revival in Two Contemporary Latin American Documentaries

ARIANA HUBERMAN

El fuego eterno (*The Fire Within*, 2008), by photographer and filmmaker Lorry Salcedo Mitrani, and *Adio Kerida* (*Goodbye Dear Love*, 2002), by anthropologist and filmmaker Ruth Behar, portray two fascinating cases of religious and cultural survival and a renaissance of Judaism in geographically and politically isolated areas of Latin America. *Adio Kerida* centers on Behar's personal journey back to the Cuba of her childhood. In her documentary Behar reveals the current state of the Jewish community in Cuba,[1] including the lives of the Jews and their descendants who stayed behind after Castro's rise to power, many of mixed religious and ethnic backgrounds. Of the prosperous twenty thousand Jews who lived in Cuba before Castro, only about a thousand remain today.[2] Salcedo's film, *El fuego eterno*, tells the story of a community of Jewish mestizos in the Amazonian town of Iquitos, Peru.[3] They are offspring of indigenous women and Jewish men from Morocco and several other countries in Europe who went to the Amazonian jungle at the end of the nineteenth century, attracted by the rubber boom. Most of the original members of this community left when the boom was over at the beginning of the twentieth century. Roughly two hundred Jews live in Iquitos at the present time.

Victor Edery Sr. was responsible for bringing the Jewish community in Iquitos back to life, and Dr. José Miller did the same in Cuba.[4] Their stories follow a similar pattern: each man started inviting fellow Jews and their descendants to join them in Shabbat services and holiday celebrations, and the communities grew larger over time. Both documentaries tell the story of these communities' survival and their religious revival. They also feature how, in recent years, many of their members have been officially converting to Judaism in order to make aliyah (emigration to Israel). While this represents a happy ending, the new phase also assures their disappearance from

Cuba and Iquitos. The experience of the Jews of Iquitos who have made aliyah has been a success.[5] Of the three hundred community members who left after the first round of conversions in 2002, only two came back, in spite of the environmental, linguistic, and cultural challenges of adapting to life in Israel. Salcedo's film explores the problems these mestizo Jews have encountered in seeking recognition of their Jewish identity, but it also celebrates how their tenacity bore fruit. In fact, the level of geographic and political isolation in both communities has fluctuated over the years as their respective populations have established stronger connections to Jewish organizations in Israel, the United States, Canada, and Argentina. This essay will address links between isolation, religious enthusiasm, construction of memory, and exoticism.

Both films show photographs, books, Torah scrolls, menorahs, and other objects left behind by the original members of each community. These objects and photographs have become relics of a Jewish past, but they have also helped Jews in Cuba and Iquitos build a sense of community. They are used in the practice of daily rituals and holidays, and they are essential tools to validate their members' Jewishness when they choose to go through the formal process of conversion in order to be recognized as Jews in Israel. In the context of the documentary, these relics serve in the film as key props that authenticate narratives of identity and elicit nostalgia.

Objects taken from Europe, Morocco, and Turkey to Cuba and Iquitos, and from there to the United States and Israel, are so predominant in both films that they may be perceived as collections of exotic souvenirs. In fact, exoticism is a major overarching issue in both cases. Susan Stewart explains that "to have a souvenir of the exotic is to possess both a specimen and a trophy; on the one hand, the object must be marked as exterior and foreign, on the other it must be marked as arising directly out of an immediate experience of its possessor."[6] A critical review of the way these objects and photographs are featured in the films is crucial for explaining the bridges they build between individuals and their Judaism, and from the Jews of Iquitos and Cuba to Jews in the rest of the world.

Salcedo's film *El fuego eterno* is organized around a series of interviews with numerous members of the Iquitos community and those who have emigrated to Israel, as well as with some of the rabbis involved in their mass conversions and several historians who conducted research on the group's history. The interviews overlap in montage fashion and include images of Iquitos in Israel, indigenous peoples going about their daily lives in the Amazonian jungle, depictions of the poverty of Iquitos in the present, the Amazon River, abandoned ships, horizons, black-and-white photographs of prosperous Jews in Iquitos at the end of the nineteenth century, and current footage of tombstones in Iquitos in the old Jewish cemetery.[7] The documentary also shows people praying in modest buildings, old Jewish books, and other objects used for religious practices.

The conflict the Iquitos Jews have endured due to rejection by Lima's conservative and Orthodox Jewish communities has a prominent place both in the film and in Ariel Segal's book *Jews of the Amazon* (1999).[8] Recognizing the Jews of Iquitos as such is at the center of this tension. Formal recognition became particularly important for them when a large part of the group decided to make aliyah. Since most of them are offspring of Jewish fathers—and members of fourth and fifth generations—they needed to convert in order to be considered Israeli citizens (the right of return admits up to the third generation).[9]

The interweaving of old photographs and the footage of those people's descendants in Iquitos and in Israel today reveals the changes the group has gone through. This cinematic choice creates a narrative that emphasizes the connection between the Jews who arrived in Iquitos in the nineteenth century and their current descendants who are making a case for their own Jewish identity.[10] Moreover, the interviews, photos, and film footage appearing in the documentary represent an effort to assert an "objective" historical authority through the film narrative.

Religious Enthusiasm and Exoticism

In *El fuego eterno*, the rabbis who presided over the large group conversions talk about the contagious enthusiasm and religious conviction of the Jews of Iquitos. In fact, Salcedo's documentary makes a case for their Jewish identity by contrasting their excitement and tenacity during the conversion process with the seemingly less enthusiastic religious practices of the conservative and Orthodox Jews of Lima who appear in the film. There is visible discomfort and skepticism among the leaders of the Lima Jewish community regarding the Salcedo interviews, with the exception of Guillermo Bronstein, the conservative rabbi in charge of the Asociación Judía de Beneficencia y Culto in Lima since 1985 who has supported the group from the moment he was contacted to help with the conversions.[11]

When watching this film and reading about this group one wonders how Judaism could thrive generation after generation in such an isolated place with such a high level of intermarriage and without any formal instruction or organization. Geographic isolation could be one of the reasons they chose to practice the Judaism of their ancestors. The choice to emigrate could be motivated by a desire to extend connections to Jews outside their country.[12] But the hope for a more prosperous future in Israel also represents a big part of the motivation for the Jews of Cuba and Iquitos who make aliyah.

This religious enthusiasm can also be explained by religious hybridity.[13] The other cultural and religious heritages of the Jews of Iquitos influenced the way they practiced Judaism at first. In *Jews of the Amazon*, Segal says that their religious practices include elements of Jewish, Catholic, and Protestant traditions brought by the many immigrants who have come to Iquitos throughout its history. They also incorporated elements from Amazonian indigenous beliefs and traditions (65). Segal's description of the syncretism in this group's initial approach to the practice of Judaism includes, among other examples, the story of a leader of the community raising a pig for a feast and a girl lighting a candle to a saint to make her wish for aliyah come true (2). He concludes: "In this culturally homogeneous city, the descendants of Jews share a syncretic cosmology, fluidly intertwining Christian, Jewish, and Amazonian cultural references, to arrive at a perfectly coherent system of beliefs."[14] Segal describes their perception of Judaism as "something mysterious and mystical to them" that might be related to how the Amazonian jungle has historically inspired people's imagination.[15] According to him the prevalence of magical beliefs is a result of the strong connection between man and nature in the jungle (65). An example of Amazonian mystical beliefs comes up in an interview with Father Joaquín Ramos, who claims not to believe in forest spirits and yet talks about having heard a *Tunchi*, or spirit, while walking in the jungle (69). Such beliefs are not foreign to Jews, as Segal reminds us, and they also exist in Jewish folklore (75).

The racial makeup of Iquitos Jews needs to be addressed because it might explain the interest this group has sparked among Jews of the diaspora and in Israel.[16] The image used for the film poster is a good example of the problem of perception this documentary creates. While many of the members of the Iquitos Jewish community are partly indigenous, there is another group, named Bet Jacob, of roughly two hundred people that is entirely indigenous (like the person in the poster). While these groups maintain a good relationship with each other, they have ideological differences. The members of Bet Jacob are not descendants of Jews and for the most part were not included in the aforementioned conversion processes (Bronstein interview). Therefore, the poster for *El fuego eterno* does not represent the group it features, but speaks loud and clear to the fact that the indigenous side of the group and their Amazonian location is a big part of the appeal the group holds among Jews of the diaspora and in Israel who know about them. The fact that this image was chosen to publicize a film that is mostly about the legitimate claim of a mestizo group to the Judaism of their paternal ancestors seems difficult to understand, until we step out of academia and recognize that marketing operates with a completely different set of rules. Accuracy tends to take a back seat to the purposes of advertising.

The documentary ends with interviews and images of Jews from Iquitos who now live in Israel and of one of the community leaders who returned to Iquitos for personal reasons. The montage of changing images is accompanied by Jewish music that is nostalgically evocative for the viewer. The music has a bittersweet effect. On the one hand it celebrates this group's success in making aliyah, which is suggested, for example, by footage of one of their young members praying at the Wailing Wall. On the other hand the music recalls sadness for the loss of their "untouched paradise" in the Amazonian jungle.

Building Bridges with Personal and Religious Objects

Adio Kerida opens with Ruth Behar arriving by boat in Cuba. Filmically, the harbor appears juxtaposed with the images of postcards (e.g., one reads "La Cuba que dejamos"—"The Cuba that we left behind"), black-and-white pictures from Behar's childhood in Cuba, photographs of her parents when they were young there, a map of *Sepharad*, all with the highly nostalgic Ladino folksong "Adio Kerida"[17] playing in the background.

The storyline explores Behar's personal relationship with the island as well as her family history.[18] Like most members of the Jewish community in Cuba, her family left after Castro came to power.[19] In the film we follow Behar as she interviews members of the community, including some who knew her and her family. Some are elders and others are Jews of mixed religious and racial backgrounds. One of the people she visits is Danayda Levy, who was eleven years old at the time the film was shot.[20] Her father, who had a Catholic mother, is a practicing Jew. Danayda's mother is not Jewish; she is a Jehovah's Witness. Her half-sister practices Santería. Behar interviews the three women in their apartment. There is a scene where Danayda's sister explains some basic concepts of the Santería religion and sings a Yoruba song. The music in this scene and the references to the three religions celebrate the successful coexistence of religious diversity in Cuba. Danayda's mother talks about religious tolerance.

Danayda Levy's strong Jewish identity is remarkable not only because she grew up in a diverse household but also because both Danayda and her fa-

Danayda and her father at the synagogue. (Adio Kerida, still courtesy of Ruth Behar.)

ther inherited their Judaism from the paternal side.[21] How does the film explain her strong affiliation? Everybody has their own complex combination of reasons for personal identification, but the film addresses this question by explaining that Judaism is rare on the island and that the community receives help from American Jews, the Joint, the Canadian Jewish Congress, and the Argentine Lubavitch organization. Being Jewish also offers a safe passage out of Cuba, which eventually Danayda and her father chose to take.[22]

Behar pieces together an explanation for the survival and renaissance of Judaism in Cuba by showcasing the traces of Jewish life in Cuba. Objects and photographs brought by Jews from the Old World to Cuba and from there to the United States punctuate the rhythm of the film and books. They play a big role in this group's strong connection to their Jewish identity. The objects shown, or mentioned, were left behind by Jews who moved to the United States in the 1950s and '60s. We see Torah scrolls brought from Turkey that are still housed in the Sephardic Center in Havana as well as old siddurs and tallises left behind. Sometimes the objects are mentioned but are not shown, as when Behar searches for the oud, a stringed instrument similar to a lute, that belonged to her grandmother—she used to play Sephardic songs with it[23]—and the reference to the house keys that Jewish Cubans took with them when they emigrated to the United States, in the hope of returning one day (like the Jews of Toledo in the fifteenth century).[24] Other objects seen in the film are newer, like the notebook that contains the names of members of the Centro Sefaradí in Havana. The names of those who have made aliyah are crossed out in red pencil.[25] This notebook is one of the newer additions to the collection of vestiges and traces Behar documents, and it is one to which every new Jewish immigrant from Cuba to Israel can relate. Their crossed-out names stand out on the white paper as phantasmagoric remnants of their lives in Cuba.

Behar's book *An Island Called Home* (2007), published five years after the film was released, can be read as an updated, written version of *Adio Kerida*. It includes Humberto Mayol's photographs of many of the people she interviews in the film. The book opens with a brief history of the lives of Jews in Cuba. Each succeeding chapter features a different community member. She writes about their lives before and after the revolution and about their descendants, who joined the community after the government amended its constitution in 1992 to change the status of Cuba from atheist to secular.[26] A chapter entitled "Traces" includes pictures of community members displaying furniture with Jewish stars, wine cups, candleholders, documents and letters, passports and ketubahs, and pictures of tombstones.[27] Behar refers to the people who look after these items as "memory keepers" because they preserve the remaining physical fragments of Jewish life in Cuba. Some of these objects have become national treasures and cannot leave the island while others are not subject to this restriction. She interviews Cuban Jewish women in the United States who cook Sephardic food while wearing evil eye pendants brought by their ancestors from Turkey. Some of these women show the camera photographs of themselves as young Jews in Cuba.

I wonder about the capacity of these objects to retain memories over time, across nations and generations. In this case, the evil eye pendants, the personal photographs, and the worn-out kippahs are authentic reminders of a distant experience in a not-so-distant land. But can they be considered souvenirs? Susan Stewart defines souvenirs as "traces of authentic experience."[28] If their intrinsic value lies in producing nostalgia, as time passes and objects travel and are inherited by younger generations, they may lose personal value, because objects cannot retain memories if they are taken out of context. Stewart explains, "The souvenir is not simply an object appearing out of context, an object from the past incongruously surviving in the present; rather, its function is to envelop the present within the past." Once the object loses context, it can become part of a collection, and subsequently "the collection replaces history with classification."[29] In order to prevent the portraits, the evil eye pendants, and other objects lovingly brought by Cuban Jews to the United States from simply being considered part of an exotic collection, they must be presented as part of a personal life, which is exactly what Behar does, possibly because she shares this concern. When she describes Jewish American tourists, journalists, and scholars fascinated by their story of survival and renaissance, she wonders if they perceive them as exotic. Behar writes: "As a student of anthropology, I read many books about exotic people, but I never thought that 'my people,' the Jews of Cuba, would come to be considered exotic."[30] The more we learn about these groups and

Iquitos girl with an Israeli flag. *The Fire Within* (2008), directed by Larry Salcedo Mitrani

the objects that link them to the Old World and Jewish Cuba from their own perspective, the more the objects and photographs hold their value as traces of an amazing story of religious and cultural survival.[31]

Many of the photographs in Behar's book show the people holding an object, a document, or a photograph that links them to their Jewish ancestry or religious practice. We learn about the objects, the photographs, and their owners in these essays. The people photographed in the book, as in the documentary, invite the reader to become what Behar has coined a "vulnerable observer," because the reader is expected to engage with their story. They look directly into the camera inviting us to get involved. The invitation is very compelling. The photographs also reveal the level of comfort they feel with their observers (Behar and Mayol), and their active choice to participate in the project. These photographs build bridges.

Salcedo's book, *El eterno retorno: Retrato de la comunidad judío-peruana* (2002), is very different. It is a compilation of portraits of the Jewish community in Lima found in archives. It includes two introductory essays, one by Isaac Goldemberg and another by Fortuna Calvo-Roth, and at the beginning of each section, there are brief descriptive texts written by Salcedo's cousin Henry Mitrani Reaño. The photographs in these texts stand as evidence of the affluence and achievements of the Jewish community in Lima, and in the interior of the country, between the years 1870 and 1950. These mostly professional and staged photographs document the commercial success, the cultivated European lifestyles, and the social activities of this community. Even though Salcedo is a renowned photographer, because of the historical period that Salcedo chose to cover, there are no contemporary images like the ones in Behar's book. In both photography and film, Salcedo and Behar differ in the level of engagement that they elicit from their viewers and readers. Salcedo, for the most part, presents "evidence" of the legitimacy of the Jews of Iquitos in the documentary, and of the early presence and success of the Jewish community in Peru. But, unless you have a personal connection to the people the images portray, it is difficult to engage with them because a large portion of the photos are formal and staged, and many people in the photographs do not look into the camera.

Behar's *Adio Kerida* and Salcedo's *El fuego eterno* profile Jewish communities that at some point in history were abandoned, eventually prospered, and are now dwindling because many of their community members are moving to Israel. Both films juxtapose black-and-white pictures of these communities in the past with interviews of current members, and they include background music that evokes nostalgia in the viewer. But Behar's film is extremely personal and her narrative does not attempt the objective tone of Salcedo's film. This is not to say that Behar's narrative lacks authority. Her sources are the people who knew her as a child growing up in Cuba and became repositories of her memories. Her informers are Cuban Jews on the island and in the United States, some family members, friends, and many of the community members she interviews in Cuba.[32]

Because *El fuego eterno* is structured by the conflict between Iquitos and Lima Jewish communities, the story is told mainly by the scholars and rabbis who help validate the Jewish identity of this group. In *Adio Kerida*, Behar does not need to interview historians or rabbis to confirm the group's Jewish identity. While ethnic and religious hybridity are central in *Adio Kerida*, and the question of "Who is a Jew?" is addressed by celebrating the diversity of the Jewish people in Cuba, Behar's film does not have to deal with the problem of acceptance. This is probably because of the support the group has received from organizations abroad.

It is important to note, however, that in Miami there has been tension between the Jewish Cubans that left in the late '50s and early '60s and those more newly arrived in the '70s, '80s and '90s. The Cuban Jewish community of Miami has given the newer arrivals a cold reception, mostly because of suspicion that those who had stayed behind supported Castro. Issues related to the process of integration into the United States explain this reception. I wonder if the mixed ethnic and religious background of the newer arrivals may have something to do with this as well, resembling the situation in Peru that Salcedo features in his film.[33]

While Behar's film seeks to elicit more nostalgia than Salcedo's, both documentaries build their narratives through music, photos, objects, and edited juxtapositions. This technique produces in each a similar effect: they invite the viewer to witness firsthand the fragmented experience and memory of these unique communities. In contrast with Behar's film, Salcedo does not ask questions while the camera is running, probably because his documentary seeks an objective tone.

Behar is well known for her controversial practice of a type of anthropological field work that highlights the personal. She connects with the people she observes in order to secure an understanding based on mutual engagement. Her "anthropology that breaks your heart" shapes the books and film addressed here. She believes that the anthropologist as "vulnerable observer" acquires a "situated knowledge" that is more useful than that attained by an anthropologist who relies more heavily on science,[34] and yet many people may prefer Salcedo's more rigorous and less personal approach. Her "anthropology that breaks your heart" shapes the perspective in her book and documentary in that both texts speak from the perspective of the observed as well as of the observer. Nevertheless, the predominant use of the dissolve technique on both old and more recent images in these two films imbues the lives of Jews in Iquitos and Cuba at the present time with a compelling bittersweetness.

In sum, because of the geographical and political significance of the locations where these groups reside, as well as the ethnic, cultural, and religious hybridity of their members, both films succeed in their aim of creating a combination of fascination, nostalgia, and exoticism. They appeal to the viewer's emotions and feature the community members as the main informants.

The portrayal of Jews of mixed backgrounds in both films and the emphasis they place on the objects and photographs that connect the subjects to their Jewishness raise the concern that exoticism taints the filmmakers' lenses. In spite of this, both documentaries are at once convincing and compelling.[35] While they render their subjects exotic at times, they also have the valuable potential of connecting these communities with viewers abroad who might be inspired by their unique story of religious survival even in the face of political and geographic isolation.

Notes

1. Behar confirms that many people, including Cuban Jews in the United States, were surprised that the community survived (*An Island Called Home*, 22). Even US Cubans thought that whoever was left would not be able to practice Judaism under Castro. The history of the community's renaissance started in 1992, when José Miller, the president of the Jewish community in Cuba, decided to contact the American Jewish Joint Distribution Committee (JDC). Referred to as "El Joint," the JDC started sending money to help repair the Patronato, the main temple in Ha-

vana, and sponsored Argentine teachers to teach in Havana. The Canadian Jewish Congress was already sending Passover packages when the JDC got involved. In addition, since that time there has been a constant influx of American Jewish tourists wanting to help what they see as a miracle of Jewish survival. Behar reports that the Castro government has been very respectful of the Jewish community. She believes that it has something to do with a feeling of solidarity with Israel in the fight for survival because both countries are surrounded by enemies. In regards to the Middle East conflict, however, they are officially pro-Palestinian (*An Island Called Home*, 32). The film is so centered on Behar's relationship with Cuba and her past there that we do not hear much about Cuban Jews in Miami and their perceptions of the Jews in Cuba today (*An Island Called Home*, 22–23). Margalit Bejarano says that there were ten to twelve thousand Jews in Cuba before the revolution. The minority of the Jews that stayed behind were granted special privileges, like access to kosher beef and Passover goods. They were also allowed to keep their institutions and their Jewish schools. In 1975, two years after Castro broke relations with Israel following the Six-Day War, the government decided to close the schools (*An Island Called Home*, 126–128).

2. But only roughly twenty-five of them are Jewish from both the mother and the father (*An Island Called Home*, 27).

3. Isaac Goldemberg ("El eterno retorno," in Salcedo, *El eterno retorno*, 13–18) mentions that the journalists from Lima took an interest in the Jews of Iquitos in the mid-1960s, during a time the government was encouraging expansion into the Amazonian territories (*El eterno retorno*, 15).

4. *An Island Called Home*, 24.

5. *El fuego eterno* includes interviews with Iquitos emigrants living in Israel, who talk about the process of immersing themselves in Israeli culture. The people interviewed discuss their search for work and good housing and also about the difficulties involved in making friends.

6. Stewart, *On Longing*, 147.

7. In fact, pictures of the tombstones were at times the only documentation some of these descendants had with which to claim their Jewish identities in order to make aliyah. Like the photographs, the objects used for Jewish daily life give their descendants an authentic claim to their heritage.

8. The reality that the community originated from Jewish fathers and indigenous mothers and the religious hybridity of their practices were obstacles to their recognition as Jews. In *Jews of the Amazon*, Segal frames the group's circumstances within the debate of "Who is a Jew?" with a focus on the gulf between the Ashkenazi Jews of Lima and the mestizo Jews of Iquitos. Segal explains his book's subtitle as a reference to Iquiteños holding on to their particularism to distinguish themselves from Lima's Jews.

9. The film includes footage of the conversion process and detailed explanations by the rabbis who helped them achieve their dream. At one point the film shows men and women getting into a lake (used as a mikveh) outside Iquitos and submerging themselves three times to end the conversion process. This experience seems "foreign" because of the size of the group conversion and the natural environment of the jungle. This footage is moving not only because of the size of the group but also because many of them endured serious hardships in order to be able to become

Jewish. One example is the story rabbi Guillermo Bronstein tells about a woman who failed to pass the exam for her conversion. He had to tell her that she needed to study more and try again in the future, knowing that there may not be another opportunity to do this. She waited five hours to be able to talk to him again. When he finished reviewing the cases they had scheduled for that day, she told him that it had taken her several days to travel by canoe to get to Iquitos, and that even though she knew she had to study more, she wanted another chance. At that point, Bronstein recalled a comment by Shimon Peres: "If someone shows their conviction and their desire to be Jewish, who am I, and who is anybody, to say no?" This story goes to the core question of "Who is a Jew?" Given the absence of maternal lineage or enough study, is conviction enough to allow one to become a Jew? Bronstein admits that the rabbis involved in the conversion process knew that by converting individuals who were not as well prepared as they would hope, they were getting out of their comfort zone, but he then gives the reason they moved forward: "We knew we were witnessing the miracle of the survival of the Jewish people."

10. In his book, Segal summarizes the history of the arrival in the Amazonian region of Peru of Jews who were seeking their fortunes in the exploitation of rubber and its related industries. Many Jews ended up opening department stores to provide tools and other goods to tap the rubber trees. Segal himself became deeply involved with the community, acting as a religious mentor and a representative of the group. His account of their story is personal and compelling.

11. This contrast may also reflect cultural differences between the two regions of Peru. In the film Ronald Reátegui Levi, ex-president of the Jewish community of Iquitos, says that in Lima they don't consider the Iquitos Jewish. George Gruenberg, president of the Jewish community in Lima, refers to the Jews of Iquitos as a "pseudo-Jewish community . . . [with] very little knowledge of what Judaism is all about," and later on in the interview he says "they are not Jewish" because their heritage is patrilineal. Elias Szczytnicki, a historian and member of the Orthodox Jewish community of Lima, alludes to a possible inherent racism in the Jews of Lima derived from the fact that the Jews of Iquitos do not display the typical cultural, ethnic, and racial characteristics of their group. The rejection has touched a nerve in the Iquitos community. Reátegui openly says that his community experiences effects of the racism of the Lima community. Luckily it seems that these tensions have dissipated over time, and Rabbi Guillermo Bronstein says that today friendships are well established between members of the two communities, even if formal connections between their institutions have still not been made.

12. This is also true for the Jews in Cuba.

13. This point was brought up in my interviews with Rabbi Ruben Saferstein of Argentina and Guillermo Bronstein. Bronstein confirms that religious hybridity among the first group of converts was in evidence at the time of Segal's book publication, when the first group conversion took place to make aliyah, but it is no longer a factor for the current Jewish community of Iquitos.

14. Segal adds: "I utilize the term 'syncretism' as a neutral concept referring to any kind of synthesis of different religious traditions and cosmologies that borrow from each other" (*Jews of the Amazon*, 5). He also talks about their experience as a new kind of Marrano category that results from the natural assimilation of a religious system that coexists with, without eclipsing, a group's original Jewish heritage (145).

15. Segal summarizes the history of mythical quests such as the search for El Dorado. Over the centuries, the Amazonian jungle has inspired the imagination of conquerors and travel writers (*Jews of the Amazon*, 20–25).

16. Segal notes that the *Jerusalem Post* has discussed another group of mestizos from Peru who were not descendants of Jews but chose the Jewish religion following a religious leader who wanted to study the Hebrew bible in the following articles: "Extraordinary New Jews" and "Amazon Jungle Community May Come: More Peruvian Olim Arrive in Eilon Moreh" (*Jews of the Amazon*, 29).

17. The canonical Ladino song "Adio Kerida" was based on a melody from Verdi's *La Traviata*, but has evolved and changed over the years; Cohen Serrano, "*Adio Kerida* Julie."

18. Among Behar's family members were Ashkenazi and Sephardic Jews who spoke Yiddish, and Ladino Jews who arrived in Cuba after escaping growing anti-Semitism in Poland and having served in the military in Turkey at the end of the nineteenth century. At that time, Jews were admitted to Cuba in order to "whiten" society (*An Island Called Home*, 5–6).

19. For an illuminating study of the Jews who stayed behind and those who chose to participate in the revolution, see Levine, *Tropical Diaspora*. In this book, Levine also talks about normalization of religious tolerance under Castro in the '70s and '80s (249).

20. Behar, *Traveling Heavy*, 163.

21. Danayda Levy's father became the president of the center and prepared her for her bat mitzvah (*An Island Called Home*, 116).

22. In addition to a profound spiritual connection to her Jewish identity, leaving Cuba was part of Danayda's motivation to practice Judaism. Her father decided to make aliyah as well (Behar, *Traveling Heavy*, 165–167).

23. In *An Island Called Home* (165), Behar includes a picture of a family holding the only oud left in Cuba. It is considered a national treasure that cannot be taken abroad.

24. Behar opens her documentary by saying: "I want to believe in the possibility of return, that's why I'm dedicating this journey, this film to my father."

25. Behar, *Traveling Heavy*, 166. This image from Cuba complements the images in *El fuego eterno* of the young Iquitos, Oleh, in Jerusalem, praying at the Wailing Wall.

26. Behar, *An Island Called Home*, 20.

27. Some of these vestigial objects can serve a practical purpose when it comes time to make aliyah because they prove the person's Jewish lineage (Behar, *An Island Called Home*, 163–170).

28. They are the result of a process of estrangement: "for the invention of the exotic object to take place, there must first be separation. It must be clear that the object is estranged from the context in which it will be displayed as a souvenir" (Stewart, *On Longing*, 149).

29. Stewart, *On Longing*, 151.

30. Behar, *An Island Called Home*, 30–31.

31. Yet time and distance will inevitably turn these objects of memory into souvenirs, especially as the younger generations inherit them, and this is natural. See chapter "Departures" on this subject (Behar, *An Island Called Home*, 235–244).

32. In her documentary Behar does not interview people who have made aliyah

from Cuba in recent years like Salcedo does, although she follows some of their diasporic stories in "The Freedom to Travel" (Behar, *Traveling Heavy*, 157–187).

33. Caroline Bettinger-López documents some of the conflicts between '60s Cuban emigres and later arrivals, many of whom are professionals but need to take menial labor jobs in the United States. Beyond the political suspicions, there are reports of the established community being cold and distant because some expect the more recent Cuban Jews to go through difficulties in the process of establishing themselves as they had to in the past or for fear of alienating the anti-Castro Cuban establishment. For more on this topic, see Bettinger-López, "The 'Other' Cuban Jews: Émigrés of the 1970s, 1980s, and 1990s," in *Cuban-Jewish Journeys*, 190–213, and Sue Fishkoff's article "A Revolution in Faith," *Jerusalem Post Magazine*, 15 September 1993, 6–12, cited by Bettinger-Lopez.

34. Behar's approach has encountered resistance. She talks about her critics in *The Vulnerable Observer*, 25, 162–163.

35. Bill Nichols, *Introduction to Documentary*, 50.

Works Cited

Films

Behar, Ruth, dir. *Adio Kerida (Goodbye Dear Love)*. Women Make Movies. 2002.
Salcedo Mitrani, Lorry, dir. *El fuego eterno (The Fire Within)*. Ruth Diskin Films. 2008.

Interviews

Bronstein, Guillermo. Personal interview, 24 June 2014.
Saferstein, Ruben. Personal interview, 23 January 2014.

Articles and Books

Behar, Ruth. *An Island Called Home: Returning to Jewish Cuba*. New Brunswick, NJ: Rutgers University Press, 2007.
———. *Traveling Heavy: A Memoir in Between Journeys*. Durham, NC: Duke University Press, 2013.
———. *The Vulnerable Observer: Anthropology That Breaks Your Heart*. Boston: Beacon, 1996.
Bejarano, Margalit. "The Jewish Community of Cuba: Between Continuity and Extinction." *Jewish Political Studies Review* 3, nos. 1–2 (Spring 1991).
Bettinger-Lopez, Caroline. *Cuban-Jewish Journeys: Searching for Identity, Home, and History in Miami*. Knoxville: University of Tennessee Press, 2000.
Cohen Serrano, M. "Adio Kerida Julie." *Aki Yerusahalyim* 50 (1994): 48–49.
Fishkoff, Sue. "A Revolution in Faith." *Jerusalem Post Magazine*, 15 September 1993, 6–12.
Levine, Robert M. *Tropical Diaspora: The Jewish Experience in Cuba*. Gainesville: University Press of Florida, 1993.
Nichols, Bill. *Introduction to Documentary*. Bloomington: Indiana University Press, 2001.

Salcedo Mitrani, Lorry, and Henry Mitrani Reaño. *El eterno retorno: Retrato de la comunidad judío-peruana*. Lima: Fondo Editorial del Congreso del Perú, 2002.

Segal, Ariel. *Jews of the Amazon: Self-Exile in Paradise*. Philadelphia: Jewish Publication Society, 1999.

Stewart, Susan. *On Longing: Narratives of the Miniature, the Gigantic, the Souvenir, the Collection*. Durham, NC: Duke University Press, 1993.

CHAPTER 11

Negotiating Jewish and Palestinian Identities in Latin American Cinema

TZVI TAL

The appearance of Jewish and Palestinian themes in Latin American and Spanish films highlights the cultural transformation and demographical changes produced by migratory currents, the participation of minorities in the public sphere, and current cinematographical trends. I have worked with three films that deal with ethnic memories and migration: the Argentinean *Legado* (*Legacy*) (2004), the Chilean *La última luna* (*The Last Moon*) (2005), and the Spanish *Seres queridos* (*Only Human*) (2004). The first of these reconstructs the memories of the migration of Jews to Argentina, and the second deals with Palestinian immigration to Chile, in both cases by reproducing the hegemonic construction rhetoric of the past in each country. The Chilean movie politicizes ethnic memory by adopting the narrative of the Organización para la Liberación de la Palestina (OLP; in English, Palestine Liberation Organization) narrative, but infantilizes national history; in contrast, the Argentine film encourages Jewish integration by infantilizing ethnic memory and depoliticizing history.[1] The third film under consideration here deals with the encounter of Jews and a Palestinian in Madrid, and conveys the unease of the Spanish citizens' identity in the face of Islamic migration: the Jewish family is the included Other that must determine whether the Palestinian Other can be successfully integrated.

Globalization, Identities, and Cinema

Globalization and multiculturalism opened new opportunities for the expression of identities that were formerly marginal or repressed, and cinema was recognized as one of the platforms on which the past might be reconstructed in order to reassign it to current conflicts. The subaltern identity processes can clash with the imaginary frontiers of national identities, so that the tensions of the multicultural era become evident in the difference between the epic narratives of political and economical accomplishments and melodramatic accounts of the grief and violence suffered by the individual.[2]

With globalization, different cinematographical modes emerged, and their distinctiveness was attributed to the migration of moviemakers. Diasporic cinema highlights cultural pluralism, community issues, and the performative aspect of identities; ethnic cinema focuses on conflicts within the social and cultural context where the filmmakers dwell; cinema of exile preserves its identity and is rebellious toward its cultural context. In contrast, contemporary multicultural and transnational cinema places ethnic and migratory issues in the mainstream, where the cultural difference becomes a pleasant consumer object.[3]

Ethnicity and Memory

The Jewish immigration to the agricultural colonies in Argentina was organized toward the end of the nineteenth century, consonant with the demographic policies of an oligarchic State. The conquest of the interior coincided with a search for a solution to East European Jewish suffering undertaken by Baron Maurice Hirsch, a Jewish philanthropist. In order for the nation to be consolidated, ethnic memory had to be subordinated, so the Jewish culture was used as a vehicle for assimilation, and the memory of the Jewish agricultural colonization was built up around the tradition conveyed by the image of the Jewish gaucho.

For many years the Jewish Argentine identity was besieged by xenophobic and anti-Semitic tendencies, but the terrorist attacks on the Israeli embassy (1992) and against AMIA, the Jewish community center in Buenos Aires (1994), together with the consequences of the neoliberal reforms carried out in that period, opened the door to new forms of solidarity between Jews and non-Jews.[4]

In neighboring Chile, the Palestinian minority is calculated at 100,000 to 350,000 members, proportionately much larger than the Jewish minority in Argentina, estimated at something over 180,000. Until the beginning of the twentieth century many Palestinian Christians from the villages around Jerusalem and Bethlehem emigrated to Chile, with no support from state policies, which were aimed at European immigrants. From 1947 new waves of immigrants, mostly Muslim, began to arrive. The Palestinians became integrated into Chilean urban society, but following the second intifada in Israeli-occupied territories (2000), community institutions have advocated a reconstruction of identity based on identification with the Palestine Liberation Organization and the introduction of the Middle East conflict into the national agenda, while the younger generations renew their attachment to tradition.[5]

Legado: The "Gauchification" of Jews

The movies generated by the New Argentine Cinema (NAC), which emerged in the last years of the twentieth century, display their disappointment in the face of the social and cultural situation but refrain from proposing solutions, and limit themselves to putting forward the facts within the framework of personal narratives: the characters seem overwhelmed by the urban existence to which they are trying to adapt. Against this background, groups and identities that were formerly invisible in Argentine cinema begin to take shape. Jewish topics and characters, frequent in NAC, are part of the everyday experience of the urban middle class, members of which are usually ignorant of the Jewish past and the community's institutional life. Jewish cultural peculiarities are portrayed in a folkloric version that poses no threat to the Argentine identity. Compared with the unmistakable racial and cultural differences of Korean, Bolivian, and Paraguayan immigrants in the public space, the image of the Jew becomes a focus for identification rather than differentiation.[6]

In contrast with New Cinema's fictional representations of the Jewish experience, *Legado* (*Legacy*) is a full-length documentary film that reconstructs the memory of the Jewish migration to the agricultural colonies organized by Baron Maurice Hirsch. The documentary was commissioned and financed by an international NGO founded by Baruch Tenembaum, who was born in one of the settlements.[7]

Marcelo Trotta, one of its directors, declared that the film demonstrates that a different and better country is possible, thereby defining the documentary as a vehicle of integration that preserves ethnic identity rather than diluting it, and stating that the efforts of the Jewish immigrants to improve their situation is an example for all the Argentinians caught up in the crisis.[8] In contrast with New Cinema's experimental aesthetics, the conventional approach of *Legado* promotes empathy and integration with the Jews, commending their heroic conformism in the face of difficulties, without demanding a structural change in society.

The identity construction in *Legado* is built upon the past described by Alberto Gerchunoff in his book *Los gauchos judíos* (*Jewish Gauchos*), published in 1910 to celebrate Argentina's hundredth anniversary. The book conceives a Jewish gaucho identity that puts aside its European and diasporic roots and adopts Hispanic, *criollo*, and biblical characteristics in the new Promised Land.[9] The film version of *Los gauchos judíos* (dir. Juan José Jusid, 1975) took advantage of the existing appreciation for national and popular themes and conveyed an integrative attitude, backed by the massive participation of Jewish activists in the political effervescence of the period. In contrast, *Legado* supports integration by depoliticizing memory, focusing on the testimonies of elderly people who remember their childhood in the agricultural colonies. There is hardly any mention of the events in Europe preceding the migration, and no reference at all to the social or political conflicts that rocked Argentine society during the twentieth century; the Jews had to tackle the forces of nature, a lack of resources, and Baron Hirsch's bureaucrats. With the exception of a brief account from someone who immigrated to Israel, there are no references to the intense Zionist activity carried out in the colonies. It is a narrative in favor of integration, infantile and noncritical, that extols the Jewish immigrants' ability to surmount difficulties, presented as an example worthy of imitation by Argentinians.

La última luna: The Palestinization of Chileans

While the depiction of the Jewish experience is frequent in contemporary Argentine cinema, only one Chilean movie portrays the Palestinian Chilean identity. *La última luna* is a historical drama about the conflict in Palestine directed by Miguel Littin, one of the pioneers of Latin American political cinema; he embarks on the project in order to retrieve his family history. In 1990 Littin published a novel based on the migration of his Greek grandfather, who during the journey to Chile helps young Palestinian women to arrive safe and healthy. The storyline is based on the memories of relatives in Chile and in the village of Bet Sajur, near Bethlehem in Palestine. The movie, for which he obtained financial support from Chilean state organizations, was shot in authentic settings, with three professional Chilean actors and a number of Palestinian amateur performers; it was spoken in Arabic with a few lines in Hebrew.[10]

Combining fictional and documentary material, the film begins as a historical drama set in 1917, when the British army was fighting the Ottoman Empire, and then transforms into an epic narrative that describes the suffering of Palestinians at the hands of Zionism, starting in the past and continuing to the present. The film recycles a fundamental theme in Chilean post-dictatorship cinema: the configuration of identity rooted in treachery and confrontation. The conflicts between brothers, which in Chilean films represent the country's polarization before Pinochet's coup d'état in 1973, are transferred in this film to the friendship between a Palestinian Christian, Suleiman, and Yaakov, a Zionist Jew of Latin American origin. The disarticulation of chronological time and the prevalence of brownish hues, such as in the soil and stone that signal the Palestinian's connection with his homeland, create an atmosphere evoking magical realism, a form of representation that expresses the resistance of Latin American intellectuals to European rationalism, of which Zionism also partakes.[11]

La última luna narrates the events in Palestine from the childish viewpoint of someone who was sent by his parents to Chile in pursuit of an idyllic New Palestine where immigrants would be able to rebuild their life in peace and justice, in a manner analogous to the utopian vision that impelled the Jewish colonization in Argentina. Without referring to the integration process in the new country, the movie makes a case against the barriers that separate human beings, thus both criticizing the dividing wall that the Israelis were just then building in order to sever connections with the Palestinians, and also passing judgment on the social rift in Chile. Although there are some moments of violence, the main conflict in the movie is between the Palestinian's benign nature and the Zionists' evil nature: the Palestinian is subjected to oppression because his candor makes him easy prey.

The victimization of Suleiman, the Palestinian, in *La última luna* is carried out by Yaakov and Aline, played by two Chilean actors. The imprecise origin of these characters is an allusion to the Wandering Jew; they exert both an exotic and an erotic fascination for the Palestinian, reversing the terms of the Orientalist relationship. Yaakov is a Latin American who teaches Suleiman to dance the tango, and his ambiguous status is revealed in the first scene, when he is filmed via low-angle shots and a rising camera movement that makes him seem threatening despite his good-natured appearance. Alternate close-ups of Yaakov and Suleiman's feet emphasize their difference—the Jew's heavy military-style boots and the Palestinian's peasant sandals—and anticipate what their relationship will be at the end of the film.

Aline is a beautiful, mysterious woman whom the Palestinians sheltered when she was pursued by Ottoman police. She is an agent of Knowledge, equivalent to the serpent in Eden, and she shows Suleiman a modern, automated Israeli kibbutz, which is anachronistic in the time frame of the story—the 1910s—and serves to heighten the contrast with the Palestinians' primitive technology. In the scene of the ritual performed to frighten off a mythical menace that is stalking the village, the editing intercuts the image of Aline and the ritual dance, demonizing her. This is confirmed at the end of the movie when she arrives on the scene in command of Jewish militia and orders the expulsion of the Palestinians from their homes, showing neither gratitude nor compassion.

The Palestinian Chilean identity is negotiated by means of the portrait of Captain Arturo Prats, a Chilean hero who fell in the war against Peru in 1879. The portrait, sent by relatives in Chile, is framed and adorned with seashells and mother-of-pearl, a handicraft typical of the Bethlehem area, that the children of Suleiman will be taking back to Chile, as they are sent there looking for a better future. The memory of Prats references a constituent of national identity that does not cause dissension, as it would do in the case of the dictator, General Pinochet, or the legalist general, Carlos Prats, assassinated in exile in 1974 by Pinochet agents because of his support for the deposed government.[12] However, these "childhood memories" propagate the narrative of the Palestinian Liberation Organization, which was founded long after the events took place, overriding family memory, as it is adapted to the viewpoint of the Palestinian Christian minority and demonizes Zionism.

The memories in *Legado* reinforce the Jewish *ethos* of education and culture, which is in keeping with the self-image of the People of the Book. In contrast, *La última luna* does not mention either education or cultural projects; almost all the Palestinian characters are illiterate and superstitious, which is consistent with the self-image of victims.

Both films avoid references to the ideological, political, and historical conflicts that shook Argentine and Chilean society in the twentieth century, so they pose no threat to the hegemonic identity of these countries. Jews in Argentina and Palestinians in Chile hold prominent positions in cultural, economic, and political life, but these films portray them as simple, humble characters whose main ambition is to improve the situation of their family. In this way, the social, economic, political, and cultural ascent of the immigrants can be attributed to successful integration and not to the suspicious traits ascribed to them by xenophobic and anti-Semitic fantasies.

Immigration and European Ethnic Comedy

In contrast with the dramatic historical tone of the films discussed so far, the interethnic comedy *Seres queridos* proposes a romantic solution to the Israeli–Palestinian conflict, but the realistic style produces an ideological effect that naturalizes the subaltern character of the identities in regard to the hegemonic Spanish identity. The transnational cultural industry leaves little room for the expression of the minorities' authentic perspective and viewpoint. Cultural difference is represented by folklorizing idiosyncrasies that do not appear as a threat to the hegemonic identity: food, clothing, music, and sports are the favored domains in which hybridization can take place.[13]

Humor produces an attitude of narcissistic superiority in the adult viewer, who is allowed to appreciate reality from a critical distance, but these distancing resources are only effective when the recipient is aware of the cultural codes governing the discourse. Comedy breaks with the logic established by the hegemonic discourse but does not contradict it, though it lays bare some distortions or problematic facets in everyday life. Stereotypical characters and situations easily recognized by the spectator are among the most effective comical resources, so while laughing at an alien culture does not contribute to its understanding, laughing at one's own customs is a form of integration that gratifies the spectators, who perceive themselves as critical and aware.

Since the end of the twentieth century, European realist comedy has exhibited a change of direction in relation to hegemonic neoliberal discourse, suggesting that it is possible to change reality as long as the balance of power that sustains it is not affected.[14] The European neoliberal reforms have awakened resistance from citizens who blame the flow of Third World immigrants for the loss of rights formerly guaranteed by the welfare states.[15] This grievance focuses attention on identities that the hegemonic discourse addresses through films like *Seres queridos*.

Hispanization of the Conflict in the Middle East

The encounter between the Jewish Dalinski family and Palestinian academic Rafi in *Seres queridos* envisages the ethnic Others from the point of view of the Spanish hegemony. The Dalinskis, whose surname is evocative of the Spanish cultural hero Salvador Dali, represent Others who are already included in legitimate European Spanishness. On the other hand young Leni's boyfriend, Rafi, a Palestinian professor who lives in Barcelona, is the Muslim immigrant whose diversity must be put to the test. The name Lenina Dalinski represents the Spanish identity overcoming the historical division between pro- and anti-Franco supporters. Her first name recalls the Communist leader Lenin and the left defeated in the 1936–1939 civil war, and her surname foregrounds the sector of Spanish society that lived under Franco without rebelling. The Palestinian's lack of a surname suggests a liminal state, prior to integration. The humorous tone and happy ending of the film alleviate the anxiety induced by Muslim immigration and the worldwide escalation of Islamic terrorism.

Despite the cultural diversity in the Spanish population, hegemonic discourse envisions a homogeneous Hispanic identity, one that is clearly differentiated from that of immigrants. In *Seres queridos*, with the exception of the brief and discordant apparition of a Spaniard whose clothing characterizes him as symbolic of the European community, nearly all the action takes place in the Dalinski home, decorated with ornaments that are only partially Jewish but create an ethnic space; a few scenes take place in the empty offices of a large company, and in the darkness of the streets walked by immigrant prostitutes, signaling a space where "authentic" Spaniards do not meddle.[16]

The movie was completed in 2003, and it expresses the fear that spread through the West in 2001 after the September 11 attacks in the United States. Though the news from the Middle East during the production of the film laid emphasis on the violence and suicide terrorism during the second intifada, the dialogues between the characters provide a sequence of arguments that are antithetical, obsolete, and irrelevant to the understanding of the conflict after the Oslo Accords in 1992. They do not facilitate any understanding of the Islamic terrorist attacks in Madrid that took place on 11 March 2004, shortly after the film was completed.

The directors, Dominic Harari and Teresa Pelegri—an interethnic couple in real life—seek to contribute to a better coexistence between Israelis and Palestinians by countering violence with humor. They also take care to point out the existence of normative Jewish Spanish citizens, as a means of disqualifying anti-Semitic myths that have been rooted in Spanish culture ever since the expulsion of Jews in the fifteenth century.[17] Notwithstanding these aims, the Middle East conflict merely provides the background against which the comedy is played out, as in the scene in which Leni and Rafi vent their anxiety by arguing about the historical claims of Israelis and Palestinians. A similar role is played by the analogy between grandfather Dudu's reminiscences of when he was a volunteer in the Israeli army during the 1948 Arab-Israeli War, and Rafi's teenage recollections of throwing stones at Israeli soldiers during the first intifada (1989–1991).

The Dalinskis had lived in Israel and Argentina, and finally settled in Spain, where they raised their family. Unlike the mythological "Wandering Jew," they raise no xenophobic feelings in the viewer. The fear that the Palestinian awakens in the mother is offset by his appearance, his aca-

Seres queridos (*Only Human*) (2004), directed by Dominic Harari and Teresa Pelegri.

demic standing, and his good manners, recalling the image of Edward Said, the Palestinian American intellectual who chose to speak his mind about the Palestinian tragedy and demand a non-imperialist American policy.[18] In this way the film puts forward the image of a Palestinian who is integrated into Western culture and whose alterity is not menacing. However, the movie illustrates the conflict between Jews and Palestinians without restricting it to the Middle East, thus conveying the idea that the Palestinian and Jewish identities are at odds everywhere, in coincidence with the Islamist position that validates attacks on Jewish institutions outside Israel. The romantic denouement of the film is not the consequence of a complex, profound vision of the conflict, but a mise en scène of a parodic version of the Romeo and Juliet myth that has no tragic ending.

The movie is a transnational co-production by Spanish, Argentine, British, and Portuguese companies; Argentinian actors Norma Aleandro and Max Berliner enrich the production by portraying ethnic characters who are deeply entrenched in their country's culture and identity.[19] The younger generation is played by Spanish actors well known locally. One of them is the daughter of an Argentinian actor who disappeared in the hands of the military dictatorship. Rafi is played by Guillermo Toledo, a well-known Spanish television and movie actor who has openly criticized Spain's immigration laws as racist.

The Palestinian becomes an object of desire for Leni's mother and sisters and is pressed into performing an exotic, titillating belly dance. His undulating movements and subordination to the women suggest a feminization of the character, a habitual trope in Orientalist texts, but the dance—executed on the boardroom table of the great company where the father works—is also a sign that the Muslim presence is a burning issue on the public agenda.[20] His image is reminiscent of the noble savage, a colonial fantasy about alterity that served the interests of the Europeans. In 2003 the Spanish economy was flourishing and needed immigrant labor but could not tolerate an influx of Otherness that might destabilize the dominant identity. Hence, Rafi's explanation of the Muslim religion, given over dinner, is received with relief by the family, who recognize its universal values.[21]

Ethnic Space and National Home

Occidental culture recognizes the value of the home as a place of stability and refuge, but "home" is more of a changeable feeling than a stable situation. For many it is an unremitting displacement in search of the place where they will feel at home. The dialectics between place and displacement situate people on a cognitive map where history and culture are the background of the search for identity. The "inside/outside" dichotomy with which we refer to our home presupposes that inside we are members of a family or community, whereas the strangers are outside, and we ourselves are strangers out there. When we refer to our country as a home, a new area of imprecise relationships emerges: within the "national home" there are plenty of encounters with strangers, so being "home" no longer consistently ensures our identity.[22]

The Dalinskis' home is matriarchal and grotesque. The father, absent through most of the film, is emasculated psychologically by his wife and economically by the company he works for; the teenage son practices the Orthodox Jewish religion with the same fanaticism that he previously dedicated to Trotskyism; the senile grandfather plays with a rifle, which is a phallic relic of his virile past in the Israeli army; Leni's sister is a nymphomaniacal single parent, who performs Oriental belly dances and whose preschool daughter fantasizes about being pregnant. The family setting brings to mind Pedro Almodóvar's films, in which Spanish women voluptuously and grotesquely free themselves from traditional gender repression. The women in the family are engrossed in personal problems and need men to help solve them; on the other hand, they do not want to depend on men. In the same way that Almodóvar's films are a genuine component of Spanish cinema, the Jews in this film are a genuine part of Spanish culture.

In the Dalinskis' apartment there are many ornaments with brightly colored geometric motifs; they are ostentatiously ethnic but not rooted in Jewish aesthetic traditions. Outside the apartment the night is filled with unexpected menaces. The soundtrack blends the usual musical conventions with klezmer music, which many spectators might identify as "Jewish wedding music." The cozy image of the home, though overbearingly Spanish, allows the audience to identify with the Dalinskis and accept Rafi into the bosom of the national family.

The film projects Spanish fears about the loss of homogeneity in a time when the internal diversity sanctioned by the Constitution must harmonize with growing ethnic and religious diversification. Whereas in the past the Spanish Catholic culture demonized the image of the Jews, this movie represents them as go-betweens in the inclusion process of the Muslim identity, whose trail in Iberian history perturbs the Spanish identity. The happy ending, in which Rafi and Leni are finally consolidated as a couple, conveys the sense of a multicultural utopia inhabited by Jews without horns and Muslims who are not terrorists. *Seres queridos* offers an ethnic spectacle that encourages the adoption of a tolerant liberal posture, but the rhetorical strategies by which the images are constructed contain fragmented vestiges of colonial discourse.

Conclusion

La última luna tells a tale of the victimization of the Palestinians at the hands of Zionism, in keeping with the version divulged by the Palestinian community institutions in Chile. The national narrative instituted by the PLO is superimposed on childhood memories of events prior to migration, thus transforming it into an allegorical protest against the oppression of those who remained in Palestine. *Legado*, on the other hand, retrieves childhood memories of the Argentinian agricultural colonization project, though the number of people involved in the project was quite small in proportion to the sum total of Jewish immigration to that country. In this way the movie endorses a model of Argentine citizenship that does not give up in the face of obstacles but avoids any mention of social and political strife. By eliding references to the conflicts that shook both countries, these movies contribute to the construction of identities that have their place in the current multicultural mosaic. By means of the rhetorical strategies of infantilization, politicization, and depoliticization, analogous to the hegemonic approach in each country, the films transmit narratives that give meaning to the social and cultural presence of ethnic groups that do not renounce their distinctiveness. The Palestinian Chilean movie reasserts the Palestinian right to territory in the Middle East without proposing a return, as Zionism did in the past, while the film about Jewish Argentine memory emphasizes the community's entrenchment in the land, minimizing Zionism.

Los seres queridos provides a sketchy version of the historical arguments that play a part in the Israeli-Palestinian conflict, while focusing on the Spanish quandary in the face of the wave of Muslim immigration that threatens their imaginary homogeneity and transcends the constitutional limits of multiculturality. Jewish otherness becomes an element to mediate in the negotiation, which puts the Spanish identity's tolerance to the test, as well as the necessary flexibility of the newly arrived Muslims in a postcolonial Western society.

Notes

1. Tal, "Migración y memoria."
2. Hall, "Introduction: Who Needs Identity?"; García Canclini, *La globalización imaginada*, 31–36; Kellner, "Cultural Studies, Multiculturalism, and Media Culture."
3. Naficy, *An Accented Cinema*, 10–17; Higbee and Lim, "Concepts of Transnational Cinema."
4. Zablotzky, "Filantropía no asistencialista"; Humphrey, "Ethnic History, Nationalism, and Transnationalism in Argentine Arab and Jewish Cultures."
5. Olguín Tenorio and Peña González, *La inmigración árabe en Chile*; Abu Eid, "Comunidad palestina de Chile"; della Pérgola, *Jewish Demographic Policies—Population Trends and Options in Israel and the Diasporas*; Fagundes Jardim, "Os inmigrantes palestinos na América Latina," 178; Baeza, "Les Palestiniens du Chili."
6. Falicov, *The Cinematic Tango—Contemporary Argentine Film*, 115–119; Aguilar, *Otros mundos*, 135–142; Tal, "Jews in Cinema—The Other Becomes Mainstream."
7. The Raoul Wallenberg Foundation endorses the values of solidarity and civic courage that inspired the quest of the Saviors of the Holocaust. *Legado* was produced in 2001 with the support of the National Institute of Cinema and Visual Arts and premiered in 2004. In 2009 it was declared of national interest by the National Secretariat of Culture (http://www.raoulwallenberg.net [accessed 9 September 2006]; http://www.raoulwallenberg.net/es/destacados/film-documental-quot-legado [accessed 1 January 2014]).
8. Blejman, "Hoy estamos como cuando ellos vinieron a este país"; Fontana, "La Argentina como patria soñada."
9. Senkman, "*Los gauchos judíos*—una lectura desde Israel," 146–147.
10. "Encuentros digitales: Miguel Littin"; "Miguel Littin: '*La última luna* es mi modo de contribuir a la paz y al entimiento en oriente medio.'"
11. Jameson, "On Magic Realism in Film"; Ramírez, "Convertirse en forastero"; Chanady, "The Territorialization of the Imaginary in Latin America."
12. Sater, *La imagen heroica en Chile*; Zougbi, "Mother of Pearl: A Traditional Palestinian Craft."
13. Mistry, "Can Gramsci's Theory of Hegemony Help Us . . . ?"
14. Schmidt Noguera, "Realismo y humor en el cine actual."
15. Balibar, "Es gibt keinen Staat in Europa."
16. Richardson, *Postmodern Paletos*; Tal, "La prostitución de la imagen: Inmigrantes en *Princesas* (de Aranóa, España, 2005) y *En la puta vida* (Flores, Uruguay-España, 2001)"; Villar-Hernández, "El Otro: Conflictos de identidad en el cine español contemporáneo."
17. "'Seres queridos' o el conflicto árabe israelí visto con humor."

18. Fundación Príncipe de Asturias, http://www.fpa.es/es/premios-principe-de-asturias/premiados/2002-daniel-barenboim-y-edward-said.html?texto=discurso&especifica=0.

19. Aleandro starred in Puenzo's *La historia oficial* (*The Official Story*, 1985)—an allegory about Argentina waking up to the horrors of the military dictatorship—and has played some Jewish roles, including, in Mignona's *Sol de otoño* (*Autumn Sun*), a spinster who feigns a courtship with a man of Italian descent just to reduce family pressure. Berliner has been a star in Argentinian Jewish theater since 1923, when he was only five years old. He has performed in classic Yiddish plays spoken in Spanish as well as universal classics spoken in Yiddish. He acted in the films *Los gauchos judíos* (*Jewish Gauchos*) and *18-J*, a collective NAC creation in memory of the victims of the terrorist attack on the headquarters of the Jewish community in 1994. Teatralizarte, http://www.teatro.meti2.com.ar/historiaargentina/crisoles/teatrojudio/maxberliner/maxberliner.htm (accessed 1 April 2013); http://www.imdb.com/name/nm0001903 (accessed 1 April 2013).

20. Todorov, *On Human Diversity: Nationalism, Racism, and Exoticism in French Thought*; Bhabha, "The Other Question."

21. Solé and Parella, "The Labour Market and Racial Discrimination in Spain"; Instituto Nacional de Estadística, "Contabilidad nacional de España."

22. Ahmed, "Home and Away: Narratives of Migration and Estrangement"; Karaminas, "Review Essay: *Dispositions.*"

Works Cited

Films

Harari, Dominic, and Teresa Pelegri, dir. *Seres queridos* (*Only Human*). Tornasol Films/Greenpoint Productions/Madragoa Produçao des Filmes/Patagonik Film Group. 2004.

Imar, Vivian, and Marcelo Trotta, dir. *Legado* (*Legacy*). Centro de Investigación Cinematográfica (CIC). 2004.

Jusid, Juan José, dir. *Los gauchos judíos* (*The Jewish Gauchos*). Film Cuatro. 1975.

Littin, Manuel, dir. *La última luna* (*The Last Moon*). Latido Films. 2005.

Puenzo, Luis, dir. *La historia oficial* (*The Official Story*). Historias Cinematográficas Cinemanía/Progress Communications. 1985.

Articles and Books

Abu Eid, Xavier. "Comunidad palestina de Chile: Historia de un gigante dormido." http://www.jerusalemites.org/articles/ spanish/sept2003/9.htm (accessed 1 January 2006).

Aguilar, Gonzalo. *Otros mundos—Un ensayo sobre el nuevo cine argentino*. Buenos Aires: Santiago Arcos, 2006.

Ahmed, Sara. "Home and Away: Narratives of Migration and Estrangement." *International Journal of Cultural Studies* 2 (1999): 329–347.

Baeza, Cecilia. "Les Palestiniens du Chili: De la conscience diasporique à la mobilisation transnationale." *Revue d'Études Palestiniennes* 95 (2005): 51–87.

Balibar, Étienne. "Es gibt keinen Staat in Europa: Racism and Politics in Europe Today." *New Left Review* (March–April 1991): 5–19.
Bhabha, Homi K. "The Other Question: Difference, Discrimination, and the Discourse of Colonialism." In *Out There: Marginalization and Contemporary Cultures*, ed. Russell Ferguson, 18–36. New York: New Museum of Contemporary Art, 1990.
Blejman, Mariano. "Hoy estamos como cuando ellos vinieron a este país." *Página 12 digital*, 13 October 2004. http://www.raoulwallenberg.net:80/?es/filmlibros/acercade/1835.htm (accessed 9 September 2006).
Chanady, Amaryll. "The Territorialization of the Imaginary in Latin America: Self-Affirmation and Resistance to Metropolitan Paradigms." In *Magical Realism—Theory, History, Community*, ed. Lois Parkinson Zamora and Wendy Faris, 124–144. Durham, NC: Duke University Press, 1995.
Della Pérgola, Sergio. *Jewish Demographic Policies—Population Trends and Options in Israel and the Diasporas*. Jerusalem: Jewish People Policy Institute, 2011.
"Encuentros digitales: Miguel Littin." *El Mundo*, 30 November 2006. http://www.elmundo.es/encuentros/invitados/2006/11/2270/index.html.
Fagundes Jardim, Denise. "Os inmigrantes palestinos na América Latina." *Estudos Avançados* 20 (2006): 172–181.
Falicov, Tamara. *The Cinematic Tango—Contemporary Argentine Film*. New York: Wallflower Press, 2007.
Fontana, Juan Carlos. "La Argentina como patria soñada." *La Prensa*, 14 October 2004. http://www.raoulwallenberg.net:80/ ?es/filmlibros/ acercade/1843.htm.
Fundación Príncipe de Asturias. http://www.fpa.es/es/premios-principe-de-asturias/premiados/2002-daniel-barenboim-y-edward-said.html?texto=discurso&especifica=0 (accessed 1 July 2013).
García Canclini, Néstor. *La globalización imaginada*. Buenos Aires: Paidós, 2000.
Hall, Stuart. "Introduction: Who Needs Identity?" In *Questions of Cultural Identity*, ed. Stuart Hall and Paul Du Gay, 1–15. London: SAGE, 1996.
Higbee, Will, and Song Hwee Lim. "Concepts of Transnational Cinema: Towards a Critical Transnationalism in Film Studies." *Transnational Cinemas* 1 (2010): 7–21.
Humphrey, Michael. "Ethnic History, Nationalism, and Transnationalism in Argentine Arab and Jewish Cultures." *Immigrants and Minorities* 1 (1997): 167–188.
IMDB. http://www.imdb.com/name/nm0001903/. 1 April 2013.
Instituto Nacional de Estadística. "Contabilidad Nacional de España. Serie contable 2000–2003." http://www.ine.es/prensa/np342.pdf (accessed 13 March 2013).
International Raoul Wallenberg Foundation. http://www.raoulwallenberg.net (accessed 9 September 2006); http://www.raoulwallenberg.net/es/destacados/film-documental-quot-legado (accessed 1 January 2014).
Jameson, Frederick. "On Magic Realism in Film." *Critical Inquiry* 12 (1986): 301–326.
Karaminas, Vicki. "Review Essay: *Dispositions*." *Genders* 3, no. 2 (2004). http://www.borderlands.net.au/vol3no2_2004/karaminas_dispositions.htm (accessed 7 July 2010).
Kellner, Douglas. "Cultural Studies, Multiculturalism, and Media Culture." In *Gender, Race, and Class in Media—A Text Reader*, ed. Gail Dines and Jean M. Humez, 5–17. London: Sage, 1995.
"Miguel Littin: '*La última luna* es mi modo de contribuir a la paz y al entendimiento

en Oriente Medio.'" *La Casa América—Archivo.* http://www.casamerica.es/contenidoweb/miguel-littin-la-ultima-luna-es-mi-modo-de-contribuir-la-paz-y-al-entendimiento-en-orie (accessed 12 March 2012).

Mistry, Reena. "Can Gramsci's Theory of Hegemony Help Us to Understand the Representation of Ethnic Minorities in Western Television and Cinema?" http://www.theory.org.uk/ctr-rol6.htm (accessed 27 July 2011).

Naficy, Hamid. *An Accented Cinema: Exilic and Diasporic Filmmaking.* Princeton: Princeton University Press, 2001.

Olguín Tenorio, Myriam, and Patricia Peña González. *La inmigración árabe en Chile.* Santiago de Chile: Instituto Chileno-Arabe de Cultura, 1990.

Ramírez, Christian. "Convertirse en forastero." *El Mercurio,* 10 April 2005.

Richardson, Nathan. *Postmodern Paletos: Immigration, Democracy, and Globalization in Spanish Narrative and Film, 1950–2000.* London: Bucknell University Press, 2002.

Sater, William F. *La imagen heroica en Chile: Arturo Pratt, santo secular.* Santiago: Ediciones Centro de Estudio Bicentenenario, 2005.

Schmidt Noguera, Margarita. "Realismo y humor en el cine actual." *Area Abierta* 3 (2002). http://revistas.ucm.es/index.php/ARAB/article/view/ARAB0202230001A/4268 (accessed 11 March 2008).

Senkman, Leonardo. "*Los gauchos judíos*—una lectura desde Israel." *EIAL* 1 (1999): 141–152.

———. "'Seres queridos' o el conflicto árabe israelí visto con humor." *El Mundo,* 15 July 2003. http://www.elmundo.es/elmundo/2003/07/14/ cine/1058186208.html (accessed 1 August 2007).

Solé, Carlota, and Sonia Parella. "The Labour Market and Racial Discrimination in Spain." *Journal of Ethnic and Migration Studies* 1 (2003): 121–140.

Tal, Tzvi. "Migración y memoria: La reconstrucción de la identidad de judíos y palestinos en películas recientes de Chile y Argentina." In *Árabes y judíos en Iberoamérica/Similitudes, diferencias y tensiones,* ed. Raanán Rein, 417–437. Seville: Fundación Tres Culturas del Mediterráneo, 2008.

———. "Jews in Cinema—The Other Becomes Mainstream." In *Princesses, Petty Criminals, and Pariahs: Facets of Jewish Experiences in Argentina,* ed. Adriana Brodsky and Raanan Rein, 365–391. Leiden: Brill, 2012.

———. "La prostitución de la imagen: Inmigrantes en *Princesas* (de Aranóa, España, 2005) y *En la puta vida* (Flores Silva, Uruguay-España, 2001)." In *El otro en la España contemporánea: Prácticas, discursos y representaciones,* ed. Silvina Schamma Gesser and Raanan Rein, 337–360. Seville: Fundación Tres Culturas, 2011.

Teatralizarte. http://www.teatro.meti2.com.ar/historiaargentina/crisoles/teatrojudio/maxberliner/maxberliner.htm. 1 April 2013.

Todorov, Tzvetan. *On Human Diversity: Nationalism, Racism, and Exoticism in French Thought.* Cambridge, MA: Harvard University Press, 1993.

Villar-Hernández, Paz. "El Otro: Conflictos de identidad en el cine español contemporáneo." *Working Papers in Romance, Languages, and Literatures* 6 (2001). http://academia.edu/219812/El_Otro_conflictos_de_identidad_en_el_cine_espanol_contemporaneo (accessed 1 July 2013).

Zablotzky, Edgardo. "Filantropía no asistencialista: El caso del Barón Maurice de

Hirsch." Documento de trabajo 264, Universidad del Cema, Buenos Aires, 2004. http://coloniasjudiasarg.amia.org.ar/filantropia-no-asistencialista-el-caso-del-baron-maurice-de-hirsch/ (accessed 15 June 2013).

Zougbi, Saleem. "Mother of Pearl: A Traditional Palestinian Craft." *This Week in Palestine* 109 (2007). http://www.thisweekinpalestine.com/details.php?id=2130&edid=140 (accessed 1 July 2013).

CHAPTER 12

From a Dream to Reality: Representations of Israel in Contemporary Jewish Latin American Film

AMALIA RAN

Throughout the greater part of the twentieth century (at least until late 1960s and the aftermath of the Six-Day War), Israel embodied for Jews worldwide the millenary Jewish aspiration to return to the biblical homeland of their ancestors. In concrete fact, it represented the revitalization of a dream, brought about by the Zionist project and the establishment of the State of Israel in 1948.

Early-twentieth-century film and literature portrayed Israel as a legendary and mystical place, emblematic of Theodor Herzl's "If you will it, it is not a dream." Oftentimes Israel represented not only the Jewish cultural and spiritual homeland but also a place in which all dreams came true and miracles happened.[1] Nonetheless, other issues and concerns were invoked by mention of the Jewish state—Israeli militarism, violence, and terrorism; Israel's role in the Middle East crisis; and ultra-orthodoxy and secularism in Israel—and these are all themes that inform the various Jewish Latin American films of recent years, a rich tapestry offering a wealth of perspectives, which I will discuss in this paper. The films—*El brindis* (*To Life*, 2007), directed by Shai Agosín; *Cartas para Jenny* (*Letters for Jenny*, 2007), directed by Diego Musiak; *Morirse está en hebreo* (*My Mexican Shivah*, 2007), directed by Alejandro Springall; and *El nido vacío* (*Empty Nest*, 2008), directed by Daniel Burman—offer different representations emphasizing that Israel remains a natural destination for tourism and immigration despite its political context. Moreover, at times it also symbolizes a place of refuge as well as a space for escapism and fantasy.

Although some cinematic references to Israel still focus on its glorious past, on its efforts to create the "new" Jew who is rooted in his land, and on conflicts of faith and religion in the Jewish state, these films also portray Israel as a nation that is dealing with dilemmas common to places around

Graffiti in Israel: "Lo rotzim, lo tzarich . . ." ("If you don't want it, don't bother [or forget about it]), a parody of "If you will it, it's not a dream."

לא רוצים,
לא צריך...

the globe, from drug trafficking and delinquency to corruption and corresponding indifference to it. Jewish Latin American films emphasize the fact that Jewish visitors to the Jewish state feel at ease there. In spite of this, little importance (or none at all) is given to the significance of the relationship between Israel and the Jewish diaspora or to the meaning of Jewishness in Israel. The films highlight Israel's attractiveness and uniqueness, as seen through the eyes of foreigners who come to visit and/or explore. Yet these works of cinema hardly ever offer an analysis of the Jewish state's significance for these Jewish travelers and visitors.

One cannot ignore the wider context in which certain cinematic images emerge in these films. For instance, the impacts of the Israeli-Arab conflict on Jewish Latin American communities—which led to the terrorist attacks in Buenos Aires during the 1990s; the attacks against the Jewish community of Venezuela, supported by late president Hugo Chavez; violent demonstrations against Israeli president Shimon Peres during his 2009 visit to Argentina and Brazil;[2] as well as the open declaration by Argentina, Brazil, and Peru (among other Latin American countries) that they would recognize the future Palestinian state—are all indicative of a wider context in which regional conflicts, such as the one between the Arabs and Israelis, are never just a local matter. These events are televised and transmitted all over the globe, molding the image of Israel while dehistoricizing it from its political and social contexts. The result is a simplistic representation of what is caught in the eye of the camera, a cliché. I contend that such clichés have become the central cinematic representations in recent Jewish Latin American films.

Social, demographic, and economic changes shape cultural representations also. It seems that Israel has ceased to be the spiritual *patria* ("homeland") for many Jews around the world, including many Latin American Jews.[3] Furthermore, it is no longer the main destination for Jewish migration.[4] As other host countries come to hold even more appeal for Jewish immigrants from Latin America (for example, Spain, France, Canada, and the United States), the notions of Jewishness and *Judeo-latinoamericanidad* ("Judeo-Latin Americanness") are shifting to reflect a new paradigm. There are multiple "promised lands," which offer safety, economic success, and personal growth. As a result, more and more Jewish Latin American films speak of interfaith relationships, assimilation, and detachment as typical characteristics of contemporary Jewish selfhood. The image of Israel is associated more with personal crisis, soul searching, and mental transformation than either with a communitarian or national agenda that promotes aliyah (immigration to Israel) or with Zionist aspirations.

It seems almost naïve today to return to a minor scene taken from the Argentine film *Aquellos años locos* (*Those Crazy Years*, 1971, directed by Enrique Carreras), in which the actor Palito Ortega sings passionately, "Volveré a mi Tierra allá en Israel [I will return to my Land, my land of Israel]."[5] A lot has changed since that idealized musical representation of aliyah was filmed on the docks of Buenos Aires with Israeli folk dancing and Klezmer melodies.[6] Aliyah is hardly a central theme anymore. Has the Zionist dream been lost?

The first type of cinematographic representations that I wish to study in this framework does not involve audiovisual references to Israel—scenes filmed in Israeli locations, Israeli music in the soundtrack, voices speaking in Hebrew, written Hebrew texts in the setting—but rather textual remarks. These references are inserted in the dialogues and narrations of films as brief reflections, comments, and observations made by the characters and/or narrators about Israel. More important, in these references Israel is associated with other multiple and delicate issues relevant to Jewish memory and to Jewishness. For example, in the film *El brindis* (*To Life*, directed by Shai Agosín, 2007)[7]—a Chilean and Mexican co-production—Israel is mentioned very briefly by the community's rabbi in one of his Torah-reading ceremonies, while he recalls his rabbinical training in Jerusalem. I will return to this reference later on in my analysis, since it symbolizes the changes in the Israel/Jewry relationships mentioned previously.

This film focuses on a young Mexican photographer of Jewish origin who is invited to Chile after many years of separation to participate in her father's late bar mitzvah celebration: an unfulfilled dream of his not achieved until his late years. Upon her arrival in Valparaiso, Emilia (played by Ana Serradilla), the protagonist, not only discovers her roots and gains a relationship with her detached father, Isidoro, now old and sick, but also goes through an internal transformation as she investigates, and reconnects with, her Jewish roots.

As a photographer, Emilia distances herself from these new surroundings by using her camera as a shield against the pain of past abandonment, her fear of solitude, and her loneliness arising from the fact that she does not seem to belong. Nevertheless, as her visit continues, she realizes that she cannot escape her Jewishness and ignore the collective past, which is her past as well. During her first night in Valparaiso, she meets the community's rabbi, David (Francisco Melo), and soon becomes involved in a love affair with him. Emilia's first encounter with David occurs in a dark room at her half-brother's house during a Shabbat dinner. As she explores the room, she is suddenly startled by the rabbi's entrance and drops an expensive ceramic menorah to the floor, shattering it into pieces. The rabbi, instead of scolding her for this careless act, offers with amusement to cover for her, while she sneaks back into the main dining room. By offering Emilia his alliance as an accomplice covering up her role in this accident, the rabbi seemingly strips himself of his duties and oath, highlighting his juvenile masculine traits rather than his position as a man of God.

This innocent and playful encounter soon evolves into a physical relationship, hence violating religious, social, and familial norms. Desperate to maintain his status as a perfect family man and a devoted community leader, David is nothing less than a symbol of the "good" Jew. In this sense, the reference to his stay in Jerusalem, where he studied and was ordained as a rabbi, only strengthens his image as a devout and studious man. The encounter with Emilia seems to trigger a wish on his part to destroy this image of perfection, to ignore his faith, and, through one moment of lust, to "taste heaven" for a short while, as the character admits.

The film first explores the subject of interfaith relationships by following Emilia's affair with David, and then becomes an aspect of her renewed interest in her father, Isidoro (José Soriano). The plot shifts to narrate the story of Isidoro's true love—Emilia's mother, who is not Jewish either. As portrayed by this film, tradition is something fluid; it changes with time and with circumstances. Israel plays a minor role in a depiction of living according to this tradition. One scene in which David refers to his stay in Jerusalem highlights this attitude in particular. Emilia arrives at the synagogue, but her attempt to enter through the main gate is thwarted by a young security man in civil uniform, who requests to see her identification documents. This brief prelude to the scene filmed within the synagogue emphasizes the daily reality of many Jewish communities today: the fear of terrorism against Jewish targets (partially, as mentioned above, as a result of the Arab-Israeli conflict); the need for additional security measures; and the enclosure within gated buildings. Yet Israel's own responsibility for this complicated situation, while alluded to indirectly, is not mentioned explicitly in the film.

The next scene takes place in the dimly lit memorial room where Emilia has been told by the guard to wait. A close-up of Emilia's face reveals a faded sign behind her with the Hebrew/Spanish phrase "To remember and not to forget." A sad melody plays in the background, and the camera shifts to an exhibition of black-and-white photographs from the Holocaust. The camera travels down to a collection of Jewish memorabilia from the Holocaust and then travels around to another wall of the room on which additional photographs are hung, including the sign "Dictadura en Chile 1973–1990 [Chile's Dictatorship, 1973–1990]." The camera cuts to Emilia's face as she explores the collection and then switches away to a third sign, "Madres de Mayo, Argentina, 1976–1983 [Mothers of May, Argentina, 1976–1983]." The fade-out comes as another poster and additional photographs are shown: "Matanza de estudiantes, México, 2 de octubre 1968 [Massacre of Students, Mexico, 2 October 1968]," and finally the camera travels to another wall with photographs, accompanied by the label "Guerra de Bosnia y Herzegovina, 1992 a 1995 [Bosnia and Herzegovina War, 1992–1995]." Additional memorabilia from the Holocaust are exhibited in the middle of the room. After Emilia finishes looking around, the voice of the guard is heard in the background: "Excuse me, you can pass."

The two-minute scene described above affords multiple interpretations. Nevertheless, I wish to emphasize the interesting link, suggested by the film, between Jewish memory (the Holocaust) and Latin American collective memory (dictatorships, massacres) as well as universal memory of global events (wars and atrocities, the Holocaust included). As implied by the scene, the similarities among all these human tragedies impede the possibility of granting Jewish memory a sole place within Jewish consciousness. The film does not attempt to create any "hierarchy of evil," since all these atrocities are presented in the same room, in the same manner, and under the same roof. This cinematic statement informs the following scene, filmed in the synagogue, in which David mentions his stay in Jerusalem.

While Emilia enters and sits down, David is telling the congregants about something he learned from his *rav* ("rabbi" in Hebrew) in Israel. The *rav* asked his students where God is, and David recalls answering, "Everywhere!" like a good disciple. Surprisingly, admits David, the *rav* said that that was not the correct answer; rather, "*Hashem* [God] is where we let him enter." David concludes his sermon with these words, shifts his gaze, and looks directly at Emilia.

These moments illuminate another perspective concerning Jewishness today, one in which Israel occupies a still-vital yet smaller part of Jewish consciousness. According to this view, Jewish memory is inseparable from universal memory (regional, local, global), and the lessons from the past must be pulled forward so that compassion and understanding can flourish. In other words, this sequence of scenes implies that the mandate for Jewish memory does not derive from events in Jewish history alone. The recognized necessity of remembering eventually led to the creation of the Jewish state as a safe haven for every Jew around the world. It is a model for commemorating other traumas and atrocities; hence, there is a universal and human lesson to be learned from it.

Humanism and universalism explain many situations in this film. Isidoro is able to celebrate his bar mitzvah despite his age because everyone around him forgives him for old mistakes. David manages to maintain his image as a devoted rabbi despite his immoral behavior, particularly because he is portrayed as an imperfect man. Emilia may convert to Judaism after her father passes away, because her Jewishness is something that goes beyond notions of religion or faith. The reference to Jerusalem is this context serves to create a setting to discuss interfaith relationships, the meaning of being a "good" Jew, and the borders defining the normative Jewish community. Jerusalem is not the holy place from which one truth emerges; it is linked to other important locations that are relevant to Jewish memory according to the film, such as Nazi Europe, or Argentina and Chile during the dictatorship years (in which many Jews suffered as well, and in greater numbers as compared with their percentage within the general population). As indicated by David's story, Israel seems less relevant to Jewishness and Jewish faith today than values of humanism and universalism, which appear to dominate the current state of mind, according to Agosín's film.

Israel informs part of the dialogues in the Mexican film *Morirse está en hebreo* (*My Mexican Shivah*) as well. As mentioned earlier, the issue of interfaith relationships and the subject of assimilation and estrangement within the Jewish community constitute inseparable elements of Jewishness today. Springall's film begins with the sudden death of the head of a family and the mourning services that follow: the seven-day mourning period, the shivah. Fantastic elements erupt in Springall's plot in the shape of two angels, which are sent to escort the soul to its trial in heaven, according to Jewish tradition. These two characters (unnoticed by the mourning family) are dressed as old religious men; they speak Yiddish and are named "Aleph" and "Beit." The angels' presence at the shivah produces a comic effect, particularly when the viewer discovers that the only one who can actually see them is the granddaughter, Galia (Sharon Zundel), when under the influence of marijuana.

In this film Israel is mentioned rather matter-of-factly within the unfolding of the family's dysfunction, in which generation gaps play a role as well. Galia's problematic relationships with her mother (the daughter of the deceased) is analogous to Nicolas's—her cousin—with his father (the son of the deceased). Drug use is also related to this character, who became an ultra-Orthodox Jew in Israel but is constantly reminded of his past as a drug dealer. Yet, as indicated in the first scene in this film, the deceased grandfather, Moishe (Sergio Kleiner), is no saint. His is portrayed as a serial sinner who liked to drink, who abandoned his family for a non-Jewish lover, and who lived a flamboyant lifestyle as a womanizer and a squanderer, further suggesting that dysfunction runs in the veins of this family.

The film presents each family member as suffering from certain personal crises: drug abuse, coming-of-age challenges, midlife crisis, adultery, and crime, which in turn distance the Jewish family from the idyllic image of what Jewishness is all about. The shivah participants ignore (some on purpose and some accidentally) the mourning rituals, which provides comic effect, and everything that can go wrong happens during these days (unexpected pregnancy, a broken tooth, surprising confessions, and secrets exposed). In this context, Israel is mentioned in an allusion to Nicholas's drug problems.

As the truth about Moishe reveals itself, the family discovers that he was the one who sent Nicholas to Israel as a way to escape Mexican law enforcement officials. While in Israel Nicholas became observant, yet the film does not clarify whether this is an assumed identity used as a means of disguise or a real transformation. In any case, Israel is a refuge, a shelter from disgrace, and a place where Nicolas becomes a repentant Jew, at least in his physical appearance. The film does not confer moral judgment on any of the characters. Instead, it uses the construct of shivah to shed light on different conflicts within the Jewish family: faith and secularism, loyalty and betrayal, decency and deception. In this framework of time existing outside chronology—while time stands still for mourning and reflection—each one of the characters finds refuge from unpleasant circumstances and from truth (by religion, drugs, women, or food). Hence, Israel is understood as just one more option for escapism and oblivion. It enables Moishe to hide the truth about Nicholas from the rest of the family by using the pretense of religion as a legitimate explanation for Nicholas's stay in Israel. Israel also enabled Nicholas to distance himself from the family and the troubles in Mexico, while waiting for everything to relax back home.

Another group of films is more overt in its treatment of Israel. Some are set on location, in Tel Aviv, Jerusalem, or the Dead Sea, and others feature closeups and soundtracks foregrounding images and voices of the Jewish country. This second set of cinematographic examples tends to represent Israel as a colorful and unique place, holding a touristic allure and mystery.

The Argentinean film *Cartas para Jenny* (*Letters for Jenny*, directed by Diego Musiak, 2007) narrates the story of Jenny (Gimena Accardi), a Jewish girl from the province of San Luis who travels to Israel in unfortunate circumstances. The film relies on the bildungsroman genre in order to tell her story. Unlike the case for other Jewish Argentinean movies, Musiak's scenography is not Buenos Aires but the remote Argentine province. Moreover, Jewishness is marked only by Jenny's bat mitzvah, which opens the film, and by the golden *chai*[8] necklace that had been given to Jenny by her deceased mother.

The plot revolves around four letters dedicated to Jenny by her late mother, and the film moves back and forth from the writing process (by her mother, in flashbacks) to the decoding process (by Jenny, years later). The first letter is a gift for the day of her bat mitzvah, in which she reads her mother's reflections about puberty and femininity. Several years later, Jenny's father delivers the remaining three letters: intended for her first pregnancy, her wedding day, and a message entitled "for a day in which you feel there is no way out." The last letter speaks of Israel as a place for healing and meditation. A flashback reveals that Jenny's mother traveled to Israel when she became severely ill and found peace there with the help of two friends. The letter presents Israel as a place of refuge for those in dire need. Ironically, Jenny receives the three letters in a bunch after discovering that she is pregnant and abandoned by her boyfriend on the day of their wedding. Her mother's comforting words encourage Jenny to travel to Israel in order to heal and to consider her next steps in life.

The second part of the movie is filmed in Israel's two largest cities, where Jenny's search for answers begins: Jaffa, the ancient port of Tel Aviv, and the Old City of Jerusalem. Here we find her sitting in a narrow alley in the Arab market of the Old City under the sign "Via Dolorosa." Ironically, the film suggests that Jenny's path of suffering is similar to the path of other lost souls who have walked the same streets since ancient times. As suggested by the film, history, one of Israel's richest resources, offers comfort when the present is uncertain.

The stereotypical Israeli character in this film is a strong soldier, embodied by Eitan (Fabio Di Tomaso), the son of Jenny's mother's best friend, who immigrated to Israel and is mentioned in one of her letters. Dressed in military uniform, Eitan, an officer in the Israeli army, is a confident and attractive young man. His presence offers comfort and safety. And Jenny, who has just landed from Argentina in despair, discovers that her old friend is the complete opposite of her former lover. Unlike bohemian Kevin, who chooses to devote himself to music instead of marrying Jenny and raising their son, Eitan seems to be a stable man. At first he offers her honesty and tranquility, and then love and passion.

Nonetheless, Israel is also a place where secrets are revealed: from a sanctuary and safe haven, it transforms into a place where truth can be told openly. Jenny discovers that her mother was not killed in a car accident but committed suicide. This changes Jenny's opinion about raising her child as a single mother, and a decision is made in the scenic surroundings of the Dead Sea. While the streets of Jerusalem and Tel Aviv constitute spaces of refuge, the Judean desert and the Dead Sea are meditative and healing spaces, characterized by serenity and solitude. The distance from any urban center and from the city crowds allows Jenny to consider her options with clarity. Should she return to Argentina or stay in this newly discovered land? Should she chase after Kevin or allow Eitan to become part of her life? Should she have an abortion or raise her child as a single mother?

Lastly, Israel is also a place where dreams come true. The film ends with a closeup of the Wailing Wall in Jerusalem, where Jews have prayed and appealed to God for generations. As the camera zooms out, it focuses on Jenny, who is delivering an old wish from her mother and is hiding it between the stones of the wall, as is customary. The camera then follows Jenny as she walks away from the holy place, while a voiceover accompanies the scene. First it is the mother's voice asking God for happiness and for a dignified death. The audio then shifts to Jenny's voice, who is praying for a long and happy life with Eitan by her side and for healthy future children. With the Wailing Wall in the background, the film closes with her decision to stay in this place that is now, for her, "home."

Jewishness and Israel, along with urban, masculine, and middle-class experiences, are focal points in Daniel Burman's movies as well. The Argentinean director portrays his masculine characters as womanizers, cynical and self-centered anti-heroes who undergo some form of existential crisis. The film *El nido vacío* (*Empty Nest*, 2008) focuses on a middle-aged couple suffering from the "empty nest" syndrome after their daughter goes to Israel and settles there. Parody, fantasy, and imagination are at play in this work, particularly where Israel is concerned. Leonardo (Oscar Martínez) is an introverted writer struggling to face changes in his life. At the same time, his wife, Martha (Cecilia Roth), decides to return to school, seeking new meaning for her life as an aging woman. The film focuses on Leonardo's attempts to complete a new semi-autobiographical manuscript, but he is so confounded by reality that it is not clear whether his narrated memories are based on hallucinations or past events.

Burman's decision in *El nido vacío* to leave behind the Jewish neighborhood of Once in Buenos Aires and to disregard stereotypical Jewish themes led some Israeli film critics to dismiss this Hispanic and Argentinean coproduction, filmed partially by the Dead Sea and in the city of Arad, in Israel.[9] Yet I claim that this is a cinematographic representation of the neurotic *porteño*; a middle-aged man from middle-class Buenos Aires, who is terrified by the lack of sense in his life, is also an older version of Ariel, Burman's stereotypical Jewish man.[10] The film establishes clear delimitations between space "over there" and "over here": the urban surroundings of melancholy and feverish Buenos Aires, and the quiet and fantastic space of Israel, illuminated by the reflection of the waters of the Dead Sea.

Parody and absurdity play an important role in *El nido vacío* and highlight the characters' ongoing physical and mental perplexity in these two parallel spaces. For instance, the couple's arrival to Israel for a visit with their daughter begins with a routine security check at the airport. Leonardo's anxiety in facing his interrogators and his silence (since he is a Spanish-speaker who does not speak a word of Hebrew) transform into desperation, which leads his wife to lie to the customs officials. He then declares with bravado that his son-in-law is an Israeli Mossad agent, in the hope of gaining the sympathy of his interrogators. A fantasy scene commences at that moment: out of the blue Martha addresses the Israeli personnel in Hebrew and says: "Shalom, I have studied *rikudim* [Israeli folk dances], would you like to see?" This absurd and exaggerated situation ends in a vivid *hora* dance in the airport's arrivals hall, as passengers and staff dance hand-in-hand and sing together, mimicking old Zionist propaganda films. The camera zooms out to reveal a huge sign in the background, in which the Israeli national airline welcomes the new arrivals.

Interestingly, a scene in *Nido vacío*, filmed at the Dead Sea, echoes one from Musiak's *Cartas para Jenny*, in which Jenny and Eitan enjoy the serenity of the area and find peace in this touristic place that seems isolated and deserted. Since these films were released the same year, one can only assume that this cinematographic similarity is coincidental. The theme of the Dead Sea as a place for solitary meditation returns in Burman's film. The contrast between the dark scenes filmed in the couple's apartment in Buenos Aires and the bright images of Israel is significant, since it also highlights the distinction between reality (somber and confused) and imagination (fabulous and clear). In this scene, Israel belongs to the magical world created in the protagonist's mind. At the same time, it is also a destination for migration, in which the protagonist's daughter chooses to live, thus abandoning the couple in gloomy Buenos Aires. In Burman's films, living in Israel is simply a normative way of being Jewish.

Imaginary Israel is also a place to think about the protagonist's marriage and loyalty to his wife, as well as to discuss his fear of getting old and being alone. From his perspective, Israel is a virtual space, enclosed within the realm of fantasy, and a symbol of possible lives that offers calmness and safety far from the chaotic city. Whether this family reunion occurred or not is irrelevant; the serenity of the Dead Sea enables Leonardo to define himself again and to return to his writing. Was his trip to Israel pure fantasy or a memory to be told? Regardless of these possible interpretations, in Burman's film Israel is presented as a fantastic place because it disconnects the Jewish state from its historical and political background.

In the third category of cinematographic representations, Israel is implied only by the context of the films. There are no visual, auditory, or iconic references to the Jewish homeland, nor is it mentioned in the dialogues of the characters. This can be seen in a work by Lucía Cedrón, showcased in the film *18-J* (Argentina, 2004). In this short film, created to commemorate the AMIA bombing on July 18, 1994, a decade after the event, Cedrón returns to the day of the tragedy. Her film focuses on a middle-aged couple and their preparations to depart for Israel to visit their daughter. The camera in the couple's apartment centers in a medium shot on their conversations, which include their long-distance calls to Israel. Israel is thus represented first and foremost by the transatlantic communication with their daughter, and is responsible for her parents' concerns about her safety, due to its political situation. News about terrorist attacks overseas arrives daily in Argentina, provoking an anxiety which can be heard in the mother's voice. Tragically, a similar hellish scenario is about to break loose in Buenos Aires, although the couple is unaware of this. Therefore, the gap between the characters' knowledge of what is about to happen and the spectators' anticipation of the disaster provokes tension, which symbolically culminates in a black screen and a mute soundtrack. The camera follows the couple as they leave their apartment, still arguing about who is to blame for their daughter's decision to immigrate to Israel.

The next scene is filmed in a medium shot, and the camera focuses on a young woman who is traveling with an infant child in her lap. She looks very serious as she stares through the window of the bus. In the background, we hear a radio transmission in Spanish about the rubble produced by a terrorist attack. For a brief moment it is unclear where exactly this scene is filmed: is it Israel or Argentina? However, as we look at the view through the bus window, it becomes clear that a terrorist attack has occurred in Buenos Aires. Nothing is said about the identity of the bus passengers. It is only suggested by the radio transmission in the background that they are relatives of the victims (including the couple's daughter, who is never fully identified in the film) who are being brought straight from Ezeiza airport to the terror site. At this moment, the differences between one conflictive, remote, and insecure place (Israel) and another, up until this moment considered as a "safe home" (Argentina), are blurred or nonexistent. Terror has converted both countries into alienating, hostile, frightening places. Israel and Argentina can no longer be used to represent two distinctive experiences; both of them now are equated to a world dominated by violence, fear, and unknown laws.

Lastly, I wish to analyze briefly the image of Israel in Burman's *El abrazo partido* (*Lost Embrace*, 2004). Various critics have already studied this film, but its representation of Israel needs further analysis.[11] *El abrazo* presents the story of Ariel (Daniel Hendler), a Jewish adolescent who lives in the declining Once neighborhood and wishes to emigrate from Argentina in order to prosper somewhere else. In the background looms a financial disaster, the economic crisis of 2000–2001. The sudden appearance of Ariel's father, who has just returned from Israel, is surrounded by an aura of mystery, highlighted also by this character's amputated right arm. Once more, the representation of Israel is associated with imaginary elements and fantasy, here attached to the enigmatic character of the father.

Ariel's obsession with obtaining a foreign passport in order to emigrate begins with his efforts to receive one from a European country. As the grandchild of a Polish Holocaust survivor, he interrogates his grandmother concerning his right to Polish citizenship, but with no luck. The father's arrival opens a new possibility. As the son of an Israeli citizen and as a Jew, he is entitled to an Israeli passport, although the film never states this outright. As stated previously, Israel is not the only migratory destination explored by Ariel. His motives to depart are not ideological, political, or social but rather economic. Thus, in this film, Israel represents a destination offering economic relief.

The film also makes another reference to Israel. It ends with both characters (father and son) as they march in the crowded streets of Buenos Aires. The camera follows them from behind and focuses on their embrace as they both walk into the horizon. Its title, "The Lost Embrace," closes the film. I suggest an allegoric reading of this last image as another representation of Israel: as a "black hole" from which the past (embodied in the figure of the father) emerges—a void that "swallowed" the father for a long period of time and somehow makes him reappear in the turning point of the plot.

The various cinematographic representations of Israel studied here indicate that many Jewish Latin American filmmakers view Israel as an inseparable part of Jewishness. One can even assume that the lack of clear references to the Jewish state (when requested by the plot) is in itself an indication of this obvious relationship, accepted by many Jews in Latin America. Yet Israel is no longer the idealized place extolled in the first half of the twentieth century. Israeli militarism and the notion of violence acquire the shape of uniformed soldiers, armed guards, and remarks concerning fear of terrorist attacks. Nevertheless, Israel is also a sanctuary, a place for meditation, a shelter, and a soothing home. The Arab market in Jerusalem's Old City offers a unique experience and a travel back in time and history. Jaffa and the beach in Tel Aviv promote relaxation and oblivion. The Dead Sea incites escapism and calmness.

Perhaps the portrait of Israel as a reachable and concrete place that is also associated with imaginary realms points out, more than anything else, its predominance for Jewishness. In other words, despite the possible failure of Herzl's dream concerning the Jewish state's appeal for Jewish immigration and settlement, Israel nonetheless is inseparable from Jewish consciousness. In a paradoxical way, it is probably Israel's solid existence today as a normative country, despite the loss of this dream, that allows many Jewish Latin American films to incorporate it in a natural scenario for their plots or to ignore it all at once, simply because of its stagnant status as an obvious and secure place within Jewish conscience.

Notes

1. On this subject, see Amalia Ran, "'Israel': An Abstract Concept or Concrete Reality in Recent Judeo-Argentinean Narrative?"
2. The visit of the Israeli president to Argentina and Brazil in 2009 was marked by a series of protests in which photographs of Shimon Peres in Nazi uniforms were carried by protesters, who wished to condemn Israeli policy in the occupied territories.
3. Also, many Israeli citizens in Israel are disillusioned with the Zionist enterprise. Street graffiti art displayed in Tel Aviv and Jerusalem portrays Theodor Herzl, father of modern political Zionism, with the following title in Hebrew, "Lo rotzim, lo tzarich" (best translated here as: "If you will not will it, it is unnecessary"), paraphrasing his famous slogan and thus expressing disillusionment with the state apparatus and a sense of failure concerning Zionist aspirations.
4. For example, see the data provided by the Israeli Ministry of Immigrant Absorption: http://www.moia.gov.il/Hebrew/InformationAndAdvertising/Statistics/Pages/ImmigrationToIsraelCurrentYear.aspx.
5. My own translation.
6. For the full scene: http://www.youtube.com/watch?v=RthhR9mJpmY.
7. I wish to thank my colleague Tzvi Tal from Sapir College in Israel for granting me access to his film collection during my research in Israel.

8. The Hebrew letters "חי" ["Chai"] mean "alive" and symbolize happiness and luck, according to Jewish tradition.

9. See http://www.ynet.co.il/articles/0,7340,L-3635709,00.html.

10. A version of this character appears in previous films by Burman, including *El abrazo partido* (*Lost Embrace*, 2004) and *Derecho de familia* (*Family Law*, 2006), and he represents the alter egos of the director and screenplay writer, Marcelo Birmajer.

11. For example, Rocha, "Jewish Cinematic Self-Representations in Contemporary Argentine and Brazilian Films" and "Identidad masculina y judía en la trilogía de Daniel Burman." On Jewishness and contemporary Argentinean cinema see also Goldman, "To Be(come) Jewish and Argentine."

Works Cited

Films

Agosín, Shai, dir. *El brindis* (*To Life*). Agosín Films. 2007.
Burman, Daniel, dir. *El abrazo partido* (*Lost Embrace*). BD Cine et al. 2004.
———. *El nido vacío* (*Empty Nest*). BD Cine et al. 2008.
Cedrón, Lucía, dir. *18-J*. Aleph Producciones. 2004.
Musiak, Diego, dir. *Cartas para Jenny* (*Letters for Jenny*). INCAA. 2007.
Springall, Alejandro, dir. *Morirse está en hebreo* (*My Mexican Shivah*). Goliat Films. 2007.

Articles and Books

Goldman, Ilene. "To Be(come) Jewish and Argentine: Cinematic Views of a Changing Nation." *EIAL* 2 (1999): 151–157.
Ran, Amalia. "'Israel': An Abstract Concept or Concrete Reality in Recent Judeo-Argentinean Narrative?" In *Latin American Jewish Cultural Production*, ed. David William Foster, 24–40. Nashville, TN: Vanderbilt University Press, 2009.
Rocha, Carolina. "Identidad masculina y judía en la trilogía de Daniel Burman." *Letras Hispanas: Revista de Literatura y Cultura* 2 (2007). http://letrashispanas.unlv.edu/Vol4iss2/RochaF07.htm.
———. "Jewish Cinematic Self-Representations in Contemporary Argentine and Brazilian Films." *Journal of Modern Jewish Studies* 1 (2010): 37–48.

CHAPTER 13

On Becoming a Movie

ILAN STAVANS

Mirrors should think longer before they reflect.
JEAN COCTEAU

Filmmaking is the art of the twentieth century *par excellence*. What isn't found there isn't found anywhere; that is, the limit of our cinematic imagination is the limit of our universe. I wrote an essay called "I Found It at the Movies," included in my book *Singer's Typewriter and Mine* (2012), in which I describe—using the *New Yorker* critic Pauline Kael as a countervoice—my devotion to film, in particular the Jewish movies that have defined me. Here I want to expand on that discussion and maybe bring the arguments home even further.

At some point in my career as a movie fan the camera turned around on itself. Rather than consuming narratives, I became involved in a handful of them. Among various involvements, one is the movie *My Mexican Shivah* (2007), based on a short story of mine included in *The Disappearance: A Novella and Stories*, released in English the previous year. The film was directed by Alejandro Springall and produced by John Sayles. The plot is about the death of a patriarch, Moishe, in the Ashkenazi community in Mexico in 2000. Actually, the death is an excuse: it happens early on in the narrative and serves as a trigger to reunite a dysfunctional upper-middle-class Jewish family in the neighborhood of Polanco in the nation's capital. I based it on the shivah of a maternal uncle whose personality was larger than life. I wasn't able to attend services. The story was the way I fantasized about it.

Springall's adaptation used the basic premise but left out a crucial ingredient. The year 2000 marked the dramatic transition from the one-party rule of PRI (Partido Revolucionario Institucional) to an openly democratic Mexico. The advent of a new leader, Vicente Fox of the right-wing

PAN (Partido de Acción Nacional), led to the collapse of a political system based on favoritism. The story is called "Morirse está en hebreo ["To die" is in Hebrew]," a reference to a popular Mexican saying that refers to the inscrutable: "No entiendo nada, está en chino o en hebreo [I don't understand a thing. It's in Chinese or in Hebrew]." I wrote it at the end of Fox's six-year term.

It was clear already that his presidency had not changed Mexico as much and as deeply as people would have wished. Old mores were still in place. What did change, happily, was the new opportunity for the media. Whereas during the PRI's dictatorship the media was serviceably at the bidding of the government, democracy brought along an age of loud, boisterous, impatient journalism. Perhaps politicians were as corrupt as ever, but people were no longer silent about it. In my story, the microcosmos mirrors the macrocosmos and vice versa. The demise of the country's leader plays upon the sudden death of the Jewish patriarch.

I have already expressed my discomfort with the "cleansing" of the political aspects of the plot at the macro level.[1] My feeling is that Springall wanted to do a less ideologically charged and more intimate, domestic comedy. It seems to me that a more considered, probing approach, one that might have taken longer to wrap up, would have delivered a nuanced evaluation not only of the Jewish minority in Mexico but of the nation as a whole. I would like to delineate how previous movies about Mexican Jews inspired me to write "Morirse está en hebreo" and to collaborate with Springall. In addition, I want to meditate on films about Mexican Jewish experience that create a composite picture that, while fragmented, is refreshingly complex.

I remember the first time I saw Arturo Ripstein's *El santo oficio* (1974), titled in English *The Holy Inquisition*, about the religious ordeal of Luis de Carvajal the Younger, at the *filmotèque* CUC (Centro Universitario Cultural), when I was still living in Mexico City. After working as an assistant for Luis Buñuel, Ripstein had taken off on his own. This was, if my recollection is right, his second feature-length film; the first, *El castillo de la pureza* (*The Castle of Purity*, 1973), was about a mental asylum. My father, a prominent Mexican actor, had a small role in that one. Carvajal was a crypto-Jew in sixteenth-century colonial Mexico who was persecuted by the Inquisition because of heresy; namely, he believed himself a prophet whose mission was to reconvert other crypto-Jews as well as New Christians to the old Hebraic faith. The production attempted to re-create the life of Carvajal and his family, including his imprisonment and that of his mother and sister, as well as the auto-da-fé in which they all perished.

The ordeal is an extraordinary prism through which to view the crossroads where politics and individual freedom meet in Mexico. It would take until the war for independence in 1810, led by a Catholic priest, Padre Miguel Hidalgo y Costilla, in his secessionist drive from Spain, for a debate on civil liberties to be embraced nationwide. In Nueva España, as the colony was then known, persecution of dissidents, in this case a subversive "hidden" Jew with biblical aspirations, is an occasion to explore the survival of minorities in a tyrannical atmosphere. I didn't like the film when I first saw it and I don't like it now: it is slow-moving and needlessly obscure. But I applaud its treatment of the political and religious dilemma Carvajal faced. The movie left me with the sense that my own experience as a Jew in Mexico needed to be told on screen for a larger audience. There has been a plethora of plays, paintings, and biographies about him.

Years later, having immigrated to New York, I became close friends with the writer Hugo Hiriart, who had been close to my parents when I was an adolescent and who was Mexico's cultural attaché in the city.[2] His wife was Guita Schyfter, a Costa Rican filmmaker who a while back had come to the Distrito Federal from the Jewish community in her country's capital, San José. I remember my mother often talking about Schyfter's dream—and drama—of making a film in Mexico based on a novel that I had not read by an author my mother was excited about, Rosa Nissán. The novel was *Novia que te vea* (*Like a Bride*, 1989), about the friendship of two Jewish girlfriends in Mexico in the seventies, one a Ladino-speaking Sephardi, Oshinica, and the other, Rifke, an Ashkenazi descended from Yiddish-speaking immigrants from the Pale of Settlement. I eventually included the novel, translated by Dick Gerdes along with its sequel, *Hisho que te nazca* (*Like a Mother*, 1996), among the twenty-five titles in the Jewish Latin America series I edited under the aegis of the University of New Mexico Press. Schyfter and Hiriart had collaborated on the screenplay. The novel includes phrases in Ladino, and there are also some in the movie, which came out in 1994. I saw it for the first time on a videocassette from Schyfter. Schyfter gave the movie to my father because he was aware of my interest in cinema, especially Mexican, and about my curiosity about anything dealing with Jewish life in my own milieu. My impression of the movie was that while it didn't feel fully rounded, it had advanced the cause notably compared with Ripstein's effort.

Given how interested I had become in the way Jews in Latin America respond to the ideologies of the ecosystems they inhabit (one of the topics of my memoir about switching languages, *On Borrowed Words* [2002]), I especially admired its treatment of activism among the various protagonists. For instance, the Cuban Revolution, a cathartic event in the Hispanic world,

Novia que te vea (*Like a Bride*) (1989), directed by Guita Shyfter.

inspires students to march. Likewise, the character of Saavedra, a non-Jew in love with Rifke, is imprisoned for his political views during the visit to Mexico by John F. Kennedy to see President Adolfo López Mateos. There are significant moments in *Like a Bride* that are equally enlightening. At one point, Saavedra's mother movingly sings the "Internationale," alone and later on with Rifke, as an anthem for change. And a contrast between socialists and socialists at the youth organization Hashomer Hatzair—including the Hebrew-language slogan "Hazak Ve'ematz! [Be strong!]"—is emphasized. Overall, Jewish Mexican identity is at the center of heated discussion between Oshinica and Rifke, and between them and the friends in their immediate and larger milieus. At one point, Rifke tells a politician how many Mexican Jews there are, to which he responds: "¿Nada más? ¿Estás segura? Yo creía que había como dos millones. Parecen más; pero es que están en todas partes. Pero no se integran. [No more? Are you sure? I thought there were about two million . . . they are everywhere. But they don't mix]."

It was around then, I believe, that the Boston Jewish Film Festival invited me to introduce a documentary on Mexican Jews called *Un beso a esta tierra* (*A Kiss to This Land*, 1995), directed by Daniel Goldberg, about the generation of immigrants coming to Mexico, from the twenties onward, from Yiddish *shtetls* and from the Ottoman Empire. The festival organizers also sent me a copy by mail, asked me to write something for their catalogue,[3] and brought me into a large hall where there were at least a hundred in attendance. For about twenty minutes after the showing, I talked about the movie's assets and limitations. I was immediately struck by the interest—genuine, outflowing—I sensed in the audience. People were eager for cinematic representations of Latin American Jews, and of Mexican Jews in particular, since Mexicans at the time comprised approximately four-fifths of the total population of Latinos in the United States. They knew that population was overwhelmingly Catholic. What role did Jews play south of the border? What kinds of stories did they tell themselves and others? In retrospect, that moment, facing that audience, was indeed cathartic for me. I understood there not only that I was ready to pour my own experience into a story that I hoped would become a movie but also that an American Jewish public, already committed to attending festivals such as the one where I was speaking, was hungry for tales of this kind.

It would take another decade for my desire to coalesce. At some point, Alejandro Springall got hold of me and told me he had read a number of my books and was eager to collaborate. He wanted to know if he could come to visit. We made a date, which in turn became another and another. On several occasions, wherever we met, Springall would repeat to me that he wanted to do something about a close-knit Ashkenazi family in the Distrito Federal. I was writing stories for the BBC and several magazines at the time. Then my uncle, my mother's older brother, suddenly died of a heart attack while walking on the track of CDI (Centro Deportivo Israelita), the Jewish sports and community center in the northern part of the city. I was distraught after his death. Since I was traveling, I tried to make myself present through phone calls, correspondence, and other means. Every other day or so I also made a point of calling my mother, who would update me on all sorts of information. My mother is the first one to disclaim any attempt at being an objective observer; on the contrary, she enjoys all manners of editorializing, and so all the anecdotes she related to me arrived with a distinct dose of drama. The accrued effect of those telephone calls was enthralling, to the point that, as I look back, I realize that the story *My Mexican Shivah* almost wrote itself. I was merely *un escribidor*, a scribe.

As I consider the influence *Like a Bride* had on me, I do wish the story had incorporated an ideological dimension, although this is not to say that such an aspect is totally lacking. Nicolás, the young Orthodox Jew at the center of the plot, had left Mexico in a hurry years before after robbing a bank, painting this as "making aliyah," a subterfuge that tacitly views Israel as simultaneously the Promised Land of religious fervor and a refuge for crooks in the diaspora. At one point, Nicolás appears in a scene in prison, where he interacts with a bunch of delinquents. Anti-Semitism is never a factor in the exchanges because the cell's leader, a pimp who had recently been badly beaten by the prison guards, is a devout Catholic and appreciates religious fervor. A few minutes earlier in the film, the police come to arrest Nicolás in the apartment where the shivah is taking place. A subtle exchange between him and Ricardo, Nicolás's father, takes place that might be seen as xenophobic, but it is too brief to deliver a commentary on Jewish Mexican relations. The same thing happens, in my opinion, inside the prison, when the chief guard discusses the fate of Nicolás as a "prófugo," a runaway from the law.

The relationship between Nicolás and the *shiksa*, Julia Palafox, offers a window into Jewish-Gentile liaison, as does the portrait of the maids in Moishe's home. These episodes are endearing and they add detail to the plot, but they don't raise the narrative to a higher level on which the puzzle of Mexican Jewish identity might be explored with resolve and nuance. *My Mexican Shivah*, of course, is a comedy. It doesn't set out to solve that puzzle, I tell myself. It is designed as entertainment. Yet I am also aware of the capacity of sophisticated comedies to cut into the heart of a quagmire like a masterful surgeon, with stunning if unnoticed precision.

Still, the movie was a success in film festivals. I received many invitations for showings and interviews. The fact that my father was in the cast became a magnet. There were studies comparing the story to Springall's adaptation. In spite of my own reservations, audiences seem to be enraptured by it. At times I felt I was the only one wishing the political component of the plot hadn't been sidelined and that a more intricate portrait of Mexican power had been offered. I was in the process of making peace with all this when another Mexican Jewish movie came along, *Cinco días sin Nora* (2008), directed by Mariana Chenillo, who also wrote the screenplay. It was released in the United States a couple of years later as *Nora's Will*. Bizarrely, the plot is close to that of *My Mexican Shivah*: a death in a Jewish family in Mexico City, in this case an elderly woman, creates a space for all sorts of ruminations about the family, Mexican culture, and the afterlife. It felt like a coincidence that, with an inexhaustible treasure trove of material, two films from the same "foreign" country would be so similar. But to me Chenillo's *opera prima* was more reminiscent of another literary artifact: a stage adaptation of a one-woman show called *Cinco horas con Mario* (*Five Hours with Mario*, 1979), based on a novel released in 1966 by the Spanish writer Miguel Delibes. I saw the adaptation in Madrid in 1979 with the actress Lola Herrera and remember the play quite vividly.

In 2010 I wrote an essay, also titled "Nora's Will," exploring the points of contact between that movie and *My Mexican Shivah*. I want to push those links further here, discussing the narrative that films about Mexican Jews provide. I am thrilled that the colonial period, often ignored in historical, demographic, and sociological surveys, is part of it through Ripstein's bio-epic of Luis de Carvajal. Still, as a result of its subject and style, *The Holy Office* is different from the rest. *A Kiss to This Land*, in a nonfiction mode, gave voice to the immigrant generation. The other three movies, *Like a Bride*, *My Mexican Shivah*, and *Nora's Will*, form, in my eyes, a kind of triptych that depicts, in idiosyncratic fashion, the pluralistic conundrum that is Mexico in the last few decades. An array of themes is represented in them, at times humorously, more often seriously: the labyrinth of Mexican Jewish identity; the ideological need to get involved in national politics; religious rituals and liturgy; the subtle yet troublesome anti-Semitism present in the country since the colonial period, at times sponsored by the Catholic Church and at others more a popular manifestation based on ignorance and stereotypes; the role Israel plays as magnet and refuge; the relationship between Jews and non-Jews; the link between Ashkenazim and Sephardim. Indeed, as I consider their overall effect, in spite of their limitations, I believe they offer a trustworthy map of the intricacies of Mexican Jewish life.

In any case, these are the stops in my own voyage from outside the screen to its most luminous center. I see them as versions of myself, imperfect yet striving for precision. They prove to me, once again, that life itself occurs in parallel universes: the one revealed in the movies and everything else. I have been at the intersection.

Notes

1. I described my reaction to Springall's adaptation in an essay called "A South-of-the-Border Search for Identity" that was published originally in *The Forward* (26 December 2006) and was later collected in the volume *A Critic's Journey* (2010) under the title "My Mexican Shivah."

2. Hiriart was a lover of marionettes, as am I, and was drawn to chivalry novels. This fascination, through his recommendations, redefined my own interest in the Renaissance as the source of our concepts of heroism and romantic love.

3. I included the essay and one about *Like a Bride* in the first edition of my book *The Riddle of Cantinflas* (1998).

PART V

COMPARATIVE PERSPECTIVES:
NORTH AND SOUTH AMERICAN CINEMA

CHAPTER 14

Jewish Urban Space in the Films of Daniel Burman and Woody Allen

JERRY CARLSON

Michel de Certeau begins his classic essay "Walking in the City" (1984) with a description of the view from the 110th floor of the World Trade Center in New York. As he puts it, "To be lifted to the summit of the World Trade Center is to be lifted out of the city's grasp" (92). This represents a culminating modern image that has its origins in medieval and Renaissance paintings of cities that grant to the spectator "a celestial eye" looking down on the city as a panorama. Later this becomes the "rational city" of Enlightenment thought. Symbols of the panoptic vision range from the Eiffel Tower in Paris to the Taipei 101 building in Taiwan. Among these symbols, one must count the Obelisk of Buenos Aires, inaugurated on May 23, 1937, at the intersection of Avenue July 9th and Corrientes Avenue. In its symbolic logic, everything truly "porteño" (that is, of Buenos Aires) issues from this site just as the integrated modernity of New York City is best envisioned from the perch of its skyscrapers.

But Certeau is quick to observe that this "utopian discourse" of the city—this dream of a kind of national homogeneity—is always contradicted by daily experience. In his elegant phrasing, "The ordinary practitioners of the city live 'down below', below the thresholds at which visibility begins" (93). Walking in the city immerses one in "swarming activity" that allows one to see, feel, and live with "proliferating illegitimacy," that which exceeds, resists, or rejects imposed norms of nationality, ethnicity, religion, or sexuality (96).

For filmmaker Daniel Burman, to be one of the roughly 250,000 Jews among the 40 million citizens of Argentina is to be part of the "proliferating illegitimacy." His films—among them, *Waiting for the Messiah* (2000), *Family Law* (2006), and *The Tenth Man* (2015)—explore issues of Jewish identity through a heightened sense of daily experience within the urban spaces of

Buenos Aires. While each film follows a distinct path, commonalities bind them to a larger artistic project. Each film features a young *porteño* Jewish protagonist (always named Ariel) who undergoes a family crisis in which the issue of being Jewish in Argentina plays a significant role. Each film offers voiceover commentary by the protagonist about his situation. And in terms of cinematic style, each film is multitextured with diverse musical tracks, visual styles, and rhythms of editing. The classical Hollywood aesthetic preference for an objective, transparent window onto the characters in their story world does not apply here. One is always aware of the fact that these are stories being voiced by someone in a cinematic manifestation.

Given the Jewish subject matter and his eclectic, and masterful, command of storytelling and cinematic style, Daniel Burman has often been called "the Argentine Woody Allen." Yet apart from its value as a global marketing catch phrase for a theatrical poster, DVD cover, or Netflix description, how useful is this comparison? It turns out, in fact, to be quite instructive. By pairing the films of Daniel Burman with pertinent examples from the Balzac-like productivity of Woody Allen, one can explore not only the accomplishments of two singular artists but also their renderings of the multiple ways in which two New World Jewish communities use, produce, negotiate, and experience urban space. Importantly, neither filmmaker offers a closed answer to the question of who is a Jew in Buenos Aires or New York. As each film from Allen or Burman foregrounds "the Jewish question," it sorts and explores the multivalent issues through the experience of a strongly individualized protagonist. The character undergoes a crisis at a particular historical moment in his own life and that of his community. Neither artist encourages overly eager generalizations or broad allegorical readings. Indeed, both make fun of characters who partake of such practices.

The struggles of Burman's protagonists in twenty-first-century Buenos Aires find similar situations in key films by Allen in the 1970s and 1980s. Even so, Burman's works can by no means be considered remakes or even homages to Allen. Rather, they are parallel acts of narrative and cultural investigation. The concrete differences in the personalities of the protagonists and their immediate material environments are just as important as the more abstract shared features of New World urban Jewish experience. All of the films resist facile summary. Anti-didactic, they firmly reject reduction to straightforward tracts about Jewishness. What they offer about the Jewish experience of New World urban space is best understood by examining them in their narrative and cinematic specificity. The analyses that follow do so in agreement with the shrewd observation of Erin Graff Zivin: "Jewishness functions as a wandering signifier that, while not wholly empty, can be infused with meanings based on the needs of the textual project in question" (2). Let us turn now to six projects by Burman and Allen.

Waiting for the Messiah (2000) and *Annie Hall* (1977), for instance, each portray the love affair of a Jewish male with a Gentile female little familiar with the traditions of her lover. For the male protagonist in both films, the attempt to understand the Gentile turns out to be a profound journey of self-discovery about urban Jewishness. *Family Law* (2006) and *Crimes and Misdemeanors* (1989) tell stories about law and justice in the contemporary world. The Jewish protagonists are highly assimilated professionals in predominantly secular institutional settings far from neighborhoods defined by religious identity. Their individual crises raise questions about how ethical action finds grounding in their Jewish traditions. *The Tenth Man* (2015) and *Radio Days* (1987) are united by the theme of returning to a lost Jewishness. In the former, the Argentine Jewish protagonist returns from his professional life in Manhattan to Once, the historical center of Jewish life in Buenos Aires, where his father is a leading community activist. His planned brief visit is subverted by numerous challenges from within the Jewish neighborhood. In *Radio Days*, the protagonist exists as a voiceover narrator never visualized. His project is to return by memory and evocation to the Jewish community of his childhood in the 1940s, a largely working-class neighborhood—the Rockaways—whose relationship with the larger society is mediated by the omnipresence of radio. His task is balancing loss and retrieval.

Waiting for the Messiah is set in the wake of the disastrous 1999 meltdown of the Argentine economy. In his first iteration Ariel is the son of the owner of a restaurant—La Estrella de Simón—in Once, the largely Jewish unofficial zone full of small merchants and businesses just off the official corridor of Corrientes Avenue. Underemployed as a videographer chronicling the family and community activities of Jewish Buenos Aires, he resists his father's entreaties to join in the family business and the overtures of his childhood friend Estela to marry her. It is she who decides to work in the restaurant. While changing a flat tire in the shadow of the Obelisk Ariel shares with Estela his desperate need to get outside what he calls "the bubble," the world of Jewish Buenos Aires centered in Once. His dream of adventure outside his community takes a new direction when he gets a job at a TV station. There he meets a Gentile, bisexual producer-reporter, Laura, with whom he has an affair. His lover, in turn, is investigating the effects of the financial crisis. She takes as her subject a homeless, unemployed ex–bank clerk named Santamaría.

In spatial terms, the film alternates among three disparate locations: Jewish Once, Santamaría's homeless streets, and the virtual space created by television reportage. While it is easy for commentators to emphasize the portrait of Once, I wish to assert that the importance of the film lies in its coordination of the three senses of the city. The lives and discontents of Laura and Santamaría put into relief the doubts suffered by Ariel as he tests his commitment to his community. The Jewish community is seen as challenged but not defeated by the economic crisis. The members can turn to each other as a community for help to survive. No one is portrayed as unemployed or homeless. Even so, the visual treatment of the community emphasizes enclosure. For example, there are numerous repeated shots of the metal gate that serves as a façade for the restaurant while closed to protect it from theft or vandalism. Interior spaces are full of people. Indeed, so strong is the social impulse inside the community that it is hard to be alone. When she is not at the restaurant, Estela is at the Jewish community center coaching children in song.

This stands in stark contrast to the portrayal of Santamaría, who receives significant rather than modest screen time. The meltdown has left him unemployed and homeless. Carrying his modest belongings around the city, he does his best to maintain his dignity, which includes dealing with the pressing problem of hygiene. At a public lavatory he meets a middle-aged attendant, Elsa, who is trying to support herself while her husband is in prison for an unnamed crime. After several attempts, his overtures to the lonely woman are successful. By the end of the film they have formed a fragile new family that includes an abandoned baby. Their milieu is the opposite of Once, which may have no official designation as being Jewish but is recognized in practice by everyone and is supported by an active web of institutions, formal and informal. Santamaría and Elsa, by contrast, exist at the margins, visibly invisible. Everything they do is a daily improvisation imitating the world of middle-class prosperity that has been denied to them.

It is here that the reporter enters the story, as a link between the worlds of Ariel and Santamaría. As her well-appointed apartment suggests, Laura is free of immediate economic concerns. But like Santamaría, she is without a nuclear family. While Ariel has a family that wants to be too close, and Santamaría has no biological family present, Laura has a family that exists but can find no space in which to unite itself. Her father promises to visit for Christmas, but year after year fails to appear. Her regular female lover remains loyal, but retreats to the nest of her own family as they vacation in Uruguay. Laura points out to Ariel that her sexuality distances her from Argentine norms no less than his Jewishness positions him as an outsider. Her most comfortable space is virtual. If she can't have her own family, she can at least show the city to others in its many textures, including such aspects as the shantytowns, which are not part of the standard cartography proposed by the Obelisk. At a wedding in Once she is happy to take the camera from Ariel to capture his joy as he manifests his Jewishness in dance.

Thus Ariel's doubts must be positioned not according to the easy dichotomy of Jewish versus Catholic Argentina but in a much more nuanced urban space of multiple overlapping identities. Indeed, Ariel's career as videographer and editor adds another aspect to his growth and to the narrative texture of the film. His life puts him in contact with Santamaría and Laura, but the nature of his audiovisual profession pushes him to consider them as subjects that cannot be treated in the same way as the weddings and bar mitzvahs of Once. In textual terms, a self-consciousness about the powers and limits of cinematic representation threads through the film.

The film ends with an epilogue. Ariel and his old girlfriend Estela meet a year after he has left Once and settled in a bachelor apartment. The encounter is filled with tension, although not unfriendly. Ariel chain smokes as he offers a confession about the trials of separation from his native community. His terms of explanation are far from grand or theoretical. In becoming self-sufficient he must learn new skills, like ironing his own shirts. This is not frivolous. In fact, it is a discovery on his part of the social texture of his past—having his shirts ironed for him from within the family circle. His continued separation anxiety is underlined by jump cuts and the passing of heavy, noisy traffic. Estela, on the other hand, seems content with her own progress, excepting the departure of Ariel from her imagined future. She remains in the community but notes that she is learning new songs. The closure offered by the film is thus mixed and inconclusive.

While the film is structured around Ariel's trajectory out of the Jewish community as he explores additional aspects of his identity, the narrative is not centered exclusively on his experience. Most importantly, Santamaría and Laura appear in their own scenes without Ariel present. In terms of the narration, the scenes in which Ariel does not appear affirm a directorial agency—an implied Daniel Burman in the film—quite distinct from Ariel. Indeed, much of the film's gentle irony is created by the difference between Ariel's view of his life and how the film as a whole shows Buenos Aires. The Jewish creator, like his artistic godfather Woody Allen, should not be confused with the Jewish characters whom he creates on screen.

Recognizing the difference between the director's control of the overall patterning of all elements in a film and a protagonist's role as a narrator in the film is key to unlocking the vision of New York Jewish life in *An-*

nie Hall, one of Woody Allen's most praised and popular films. It is a work that would be named the definitive "Woody Allen film" by many people. The film's male protagonist is Alvy Singer, portrayed by Woody Allen himself, who is a successful, if nervously neurotic, Jewish comedian of national reputation who lives in Manhattan but was raised in lower-middle-class Coney Island, Brooklyn.

The film is structured as a memory piece as Alvy sorts out the ups and downs of his romance with Annie Hall, an aspiring singer from a prosperous Protestant family in Wisconsin. Even beyond the factor of romantic attraction, Alvy sees himself as a life tutor to Annie, her guide to cosmopolitan Manhattan and its Jewish components. Here is an important point of contact with Ariel in *Waiting for the Messiah* but with an inversion: Ariel doesn't play the role of tutor. Like Annie, Ariel is the object of tutoring, not the tutor. But what Alvy's ruminations reveal is that his curriculum as a tutor is flawed, although well intended. In the overall narrative arc there is a notable parallel with George Bernard Shaw's *Pygmalion*, in which Professor Henry Higgins seeks to transform working-class Eliza Doolittle into a proper lady. Higgins fails not because his pupil cannot perform the tasks for which she is trained but because her moral and intellectual growth move so far beyond his limited scheme that her whole vision of herself and life is transformed. In a like manner, Alvy's confessional inquiry into his relationship with Annie reveals as much about the complexity of his Jewish identity as it does about her induction into New York life. Just as Shaw was interested in the limitations imposed upon Professor Higgins by the British class system, so Allen reveals that Alvy lives within a world far smaller than the one he claims to have mastered. His Jewish identity both empowers and hinders him.

Manhattan is the anchor of the film's spatial dynamics. Alvy has lived there for many years, while Annie is a relatively recent arrival from the Midwest. Alvy shows Annie the bookstores, movie theaters, restaurants, sights, and public spaces that make up the lived texture of his assimilated, secular Jewish urban life. Yet in every case Alvy demonstrates that his pleasures can be easily twisted. As Annie observes, he only gives her books with the word "death" in the title. In the waiting area of a movie theater he is so angered by the pretentious banter of another patron that he fantasizes about achieving revenge by bringing media theorist Marshall McLuhan onto the scene to humiliate the offending party. At a cocktail party full of people from "the *New Yorker* magazine," as his second wife puts it, he retreats to a bedroom to watch basketball rather than mix with the guests. In a delicatessen he smirks as Annie orders mayonnaise with her corned beef.

Despite all of his presumed comfort as a cosmopolitan Jew in Manhattan, he harbors fears of anti-Semitism. He imagines that a passerby calls him "Jew!" and a companion corrects him by saying the words were "did you" and weren't even directed at him. Although he is a comedian who makes a living by public performance, he is uncomfortable being recognized and dealing with fans. If Manhattan itself presents challenges for Alvy, leaving it is even worse. A trip to meet Annie's family confirms his fears of what really lurks in non-Jewish America, in his phrase, behind a "Norman Rockwell portrait." Annie's grandmother "Grammy Hall," he thinks, is a "classic Jew hater" who makes him imagine himself as an ultra-Orthodox Jew in religious attire. The decorum of Annie's mother's table manners makes him remember the competitive, overlapping arguments of his own family dinners in Brooklyn. Annie's brother, he fears, is a suicidal and homicidal maniac who will kill them in a head-on collision.

If urban space can be a villain, then the city of Los Angeles is Alvy's nemesis. He needs to travel there for professional reasons and proves himself not merely skeptical of its more eccentric features but contemptuous of its totality. If New York is authenticity, then Los Angeles is everything false. Annie, by contrast, sees the city as distinct in every way from New York, yet just as rich in possibility if one has the flexibility to make use of the opportunities offered. She stays in California to record an album for laid-back producer Tony Lacey, an anti-artist incarnate, from Alvy's standpoint. Eventually, some years after their break up, Annie moves back to New York. She has become a self-possessed artist and master of multiple urban spaces.

While Alvy never achieves as broad and flexible a physical command of urban spaces as Annie does, he is able to find a way to navigate his Jewish presence in the city: through storytelling. His identity is defined by the wide range of stories about Jewish life in the city that he tells in a creatively dense mix of styles. Alvy, who grows very little in the plot in contrast to Annie, charms from the first moment he appears on screen. The film begins and ends with scenes in which Alvy, against a simple one-color backdrop, directly addresses the spectator. He tells humorous anecdotes that illustrate what he has learned from Annie. In fact, he narrates the entire film to the imagined offscreen spectator. His narration is highly inventive and inflected with self-deprecating humor. He offers memories and conjectures in multiple registers. The adult Alvy can walk into memory space and talk with the characters at his elementary school or at a distant family dinner. He visualizes himself as an animated character in debate with Annie. He imagines subtitles for what he and Annie are thinking, rather than what they are actually saying. He writes a play about his relationship with Annie but

In a memory sequence, Alvy Singer (Woody Allen) revisits the elementary school classroom of his dominantly Jewish neighborhood in Brooklyn in the 1940s. *Annie Hall* (1977), directed by Woody Allen. Still courtesy of Metro-Goldwyn-Mayer.

changes it to have a happy ending. He uses a split screen to illustrate how he and Annie interpret the same events in a different way. Examples could continue.

At the end of *Annie Hall* Alvy may be no more settled or comfortable in the physicality of non-Jewish New York than Ariel is in Buenos Aires, but he has found a permanent virtual refuge in the storytelling resources of Jewish tradition. The Argentine Ariel, fifteen years younger than Alvy in his first instantiation, will find stability, too, but only in a later avatar in a later film when he reaches Alvy's age. Above Alvy stands the directorial presence of Woody Allen. In his hands, the film maps both Alvy's foibles and his virtues, his broad curiosity and his self-censorship. As a New York–based Jewish director, he also proves that an "authentic" film can be shot in California, an idea that Alvy could never consider.

Authenticity is not at stake in *Family Law* and *Crimes and Misdemeanors*. The protagonists in both films have well-established professional lives in which their Jewish descent plays seemingly only a modest role. Their religion is not seen as putting them in conflict with any other ethnic or religious groups. Comfortable in how they enact their Jewishness, they lead a life of assimilation among friends and colleagues largely identified with the secular urban world. Yet in both films events transpire that raise the question of how the ethical dimension of Jewish theology relates to contemporary law and justice. Misdemeanors define the world of *Family Law*. Crimes and misdemeanors animate the plot of the film titled with the same words.

Family Law centers on how a young Jewish law professor in Buenos Aires, Ariel Perelman, comes to understand his successful lawyer father, Bernardo Perelman, who defends small clients using methods that are well adapted to how the legal system (mal)functions in Argentina. These methods are nothing that the son would ever teach in his courses. They trade propriety for positive results. As Ariel says of himself, "I didn't go for law. I went for justice." Bernardo has a room in his offices ready for his son, but as the film begins it is unoccupied. Ariel chooses to keep his distance. Both men have comfortable perches in society.

It is safe to say that Ariel protests too much. As he contemplates his father over the course of the film, he comes to realize how much his own love of justice derives from his father's practice of law and how much that transfer of deep values owes to the Polish Jewish tradition that crossed the Atlantic as his grandparents escaped the Nazis. Ariel's recovery of this Jewish aspect of his own formation does not put him in conflict with Argentine society but instead broadens and deepens his understanding of himself as a father, husband, and lawyer. This profound debt of son to father is something long recognized by everyone except Ariel. Indeed, throughout the film both men are referred to by all as simply "Perelman," with there being no need to mention to their first names.

Narrated by Ariel, the film develops in a linear manner. Its first two sections are heavy in exposition. In the first, we see the daily routines that Perelman Sr. has followed for more than forty years. In the second, we see how Ariel courted his wife, Sandra, an Argentine Catholic with whom he has a three-year-old son, Gastón. Ariel's description of his father is rendered in brisk montage editing. We witness, among many things, where he eats breakfast, how he avoids lines when filing courthouse papers, how he talks to clients in a wide range of settings, and how he returns to the office to work with his trusted assistant, Norita. Happy in his ability to achieve what his clients want, he skips rather than walks in moments of joy. He is so good at conforming to diverse needs that Ariel references a Woody Allen creation to call his father a "Zelig among lawyers."

Ariel's description of his courtship is no less cheerful. He notices Sandra as a student in his class. He finds out that she is a physical fitness instructor who teaches the Pilates Method. To get to know her he signs up for sessions. Eventually, he helps her with a lawsuit over the trademark name "Pilates Method." With his father's help as a silent partner, he wins the case. He and Sandra marry and settle into the middle-class life of Argentine professionals. It is told almost like a simple fairy tale of love, one in which their different Jewish and Christian family backgrounds create no tension. Indeed, several years later Sandra even describes them as "the typical Argentine Judeo-Christian married couple."

An absurd event upsets the balance that Ariel has constructed for his professional and domestic life. The courthouse where he tries his cases is temporarily shut down: the weight of the stored files in the building has made the structure unstable. A friend encourages him to see the time as a private vacation about which even his wife need not know. His father's view is different, because he sees it as a recruitment opportunity. What Ariel will not know until later is that his father's entreaties have a special urgency. Bernardo is terminally ill. Initially, however, what the time together means is that Ariel must open himself to the complexity of his father's role in his life. This includes reviewing fond memories of his childhood when he was following his father's rounds. As he rejoins his father, the montage of their activities matches in shot selection and pacing with the earlier portrait of Bernardo alone. Ariel and Bernardo skip down the courthouse steps together as if dancing in a chorus.

The time spent together also reminds Ariel why he chose to create a distance from his father. Bernardo's brother, Eduardo, is a debt collector who knows how to ruin lives by public shaming. Among Bernardo's clients is Uncle Mamuñe, who operates in a gray zone as a currency speculator. Among Bernardo's helpers is Ramón, a Paraguayan who is a "professional witness." His function is to testify in court—manifestly perjuring himself—about events in which he never participated. For Bernardo, these highly flexible tactics serve the end of a positive legal outcome in a flawed system. Abstract justice is meaningless to him. Individual relationships are more important than grand claims about justice.

Ariel's "vacation" also allows him to play a more active role as a father to his three-year-old. Sandra leaves for a professional retreat, her first time away from home since Gastón's birth. Ariel must take full charge of his son's care, something that he has never done before. It is not that he has been a bad or unloving father—Burman's view is too subtle for that—but that he has not been fully open to the pleasures and responsibilities of his role. Ariel's newly awakened sense of duties as a father leads him to take a new look at his son's school. He had never noticed that it was Swiss, although, as Sandra reminds him, he has known that all along. The particular trigger is seeing the Swiss cross on his son's uniform, which provokes him to make a remark about the morally compromised role of the Swiss in dealing with Jews in World War II.

Ariel's time with his father and his son compels him to consider what a father can and should give to his son. More concretely, he begins to pose the question in terms of what a Jewish father gives to his son. The homogeneous Argentine space of his life now manifests Jewish traces. Lost or repressed memory is reactivated. The two visual manifestations of this are Bernardo's large Jewish funeral and an elaborate montage of condolence messages in a Jewish newspaper. None of this leads Ariel to the idea that he must become a more observant Jew. What he does come to understand is that his father acted in accordance with Jewish traditions and did so on the material terms of his generation.

As a first-generation Argentine, Bernardo grew up with others struggling forward as he did. He remained deeply faithful to those who were not as successful as himself, whether Jewish or otherwise. Bernardo's life, as Ariel comes to understand, was dedicated to "repairing the world," in accordance with the set of Jewish values suggested by the Hebrew phrase *tikkun olam*. Ever relevant, these imperatives of making the world a better place manifest themselves in different ways as the material conditions of the world change. Bernardo's way of enacting them was through his small-time clients. Ariel does so by teaching law, a professional path not available to his pioneering father.

Ariel comes to recognize that he and his father represent not so much the opposition of law versus justice but a set of common Jewish values that inhabit different spheres of life in Buenos Aires. Ariel knows, too, that his son Gastón will need to grow on his own terms but should do so with his Jewish values as part of his identity. He may never live in a neighborhood as Jewish as Once, but his Jewish identity will help define the urban space that he makes his own. For now though, as a three-year-old, Gastón can simply be a Jewish boy in a Catholic country in a Swiss preschool.

Crimes and Misdemeanors begins with an image of assimilation. Dr. Judah Rosenthal, a successful ophthalmologist, is being feted at the elegant Tavern on the Green restaurant in Central Park. He is praised for his work as a physician, for his contributions to charity, and for his worth as a reliable friend and family man. He is at the pinnacle of Jewish accomplishment in New York. It should be the best night of his life, but that impression is immediately undermined by flashbacks. His mistress, Dolores Paley, a stewardess whom he met on a business trip, has threatened to reveal their affair to his wife and go public about some financial indiscretions that would tarnish his crown. While *Family Law* reveals its Jewish concerns by slow, incremental exposition, *Crimes and Misdemeanors* populates its story world with characters who openly debate their place in modern America as Jews.

There are multiple models of what success can be and multiple commentators about how Jews find meaning in success.

Among several storylines, the other most important one is about Cliff Stern, a filmmaker who wants to make documentaries about serious subjects. As his marriage falls to pieces, he tries to start a new relationship with a network producer, Halley Reed. With the connecting theme of adultery, Judah's plot leads to murder (the crime of the title), while Cliff's story results only in moral and emotional disappointment (the misdemeanor of the title). The film deftly intercuts between the two moral spheres. Judah fails to negotiate a settlement with Dolores, commissions her murder, falls into despair over his crime, searches for a moral compass, but eventually returns to a normal life as if he had just recovered from a nasty bout of the flu. Undiscovered and unpunished as a murderer, he is again at a pinnacle. Cliff's arc, by contrast, is from disappointment to hope to further disappointment. He meets Halley as he begins work on a documentary about his brother-in-law Lester, a wildly successful producer of sitcoms. Cliff sees Halley as his ally in a struggle against the self-serving, shallow values represented by Lester. When his documentary mocks rather than celebrates its subject, he is fired. What is worse, Halley falls for Lester. In the end Cliff is divorced, unemployed, and confused about his future prospects.

Whereas Ariel in *Family Law* had to uncover and recognize the traces of Jewish tradition in his life, Judah and Cliff are surrounded by fellow Jews. In their world it would be hard to find an urban space lacking a Jewish component. But Jewishness here is by no means a single or unified thing. New York City, past and present, young and old, downscale and upscale, is a forum for debate about moral structure as derived from Jewish theology.

Crimes and Misdemeanors is what the literary theorist Mikhail Bakhtin would call a dialogical text. The points of view of the different characters are put in conversation with each other but never resolved into a single dominant voice. Apart from Judah and Cliff, there are at least five other sources of commentary on the moral issues at hand. The first among these is the observant family from which Judah comes. He remembers with wonder the debates that animated their gatherings on High Holy Days. His brother Jack, who arranged for the hitman to murder Dolores, offers the advice of a cynical secular pragmatist. For him, there are no moral issues but only problems to be solved. By contrast, there is his patient, Ben, a calmly thoughtful rabbi who is going blind. For him, the quest for moral understanding, if not its achievement, is motive enough for a Jewish life. Also in the mix are two characters associated with Cliff's attempt to understand his sense of purpose in the city. His nemesis is Lester, whose specialty is reducing philosophical issues to sitcom-style one-liners. For instance, he brags that comedy is nothing more that "tragedy plus time." Case closed; no need for further inquiry. Cliff's hero is the subject of his unfinished documentary, an elderly philosopher named Leon Levy who is humane, subtle, and insightful. Unfortunately, he commits suicide, leaving a note that says only "I've gone out the window." Cliff is baffled rather than enlightened. Moreover, Levy's suicide destroys the intended moral light of Cliff's documentary.

The film ends as it begins, with a large Jewish celebration. This time it is the wedding of the daughter of the now-blind rabbi, Ben. The majority of the key commentators are there. Judah and Cliff briefly meet and chat, although neither knows the other's story. In terms of dramatic structure, the scene could be used easily to give the floor to a character whose point of view would achieve hegemony in the narrative. It is the "big speech" moment. Allen rejects that option and remains true to his dialogical aims. A complex montage of counterpointing image and words expresses his rejection of an essentialist Judaism. As the blind rabbi dances elegantly with his daughter, Allen intercuts images from key dramatic scenes in the film. In voiceover we hear a lecture by Professor Levy extolling the virtues of the simple pleasures in life that take precedence over large plans or ideas. The party, like New York City itself, cannot provide an overarching answer to Jewish theological questions, but it can provide a space in which the questions may be asked again and again.

The Tenth Man and *Radio Days* both feature characters who have lost touch with their roots in urban New World Jewish experience. The films test how they may recover what has been lost. In the former, the recovery takes place as a journey from contemporary Manhattan into the labyrinth of working-class Once in Buenos Aires. In the latter, an offscreen adult narrator considers the habits, hopes, and foibles of his Jewish family life in the outer boroughs of New York City in the era of World War II. Both films portray Jews at the economic margins of their societies yet celebrate with comic exuberance the vitality of those communities.

The overall plot of *The Tenth Man* can be described as a well-planned ambush. The latest of Daniel Burman's Ariels is an Argentine economist reared in Once, yet long resident in Manhattan as a secular professional. He has organized a trip to Buenos Aires to introduce his fiancée, Monica, an Argentine dancer also residing in New York, to his father, Usher, the director of a community services center in Once. Usher's plan is different. The trip is his opportunity to lure his son back into a life of caring and giving to the needy of his community. Every day Usher has a new trick to bring his son closer to the practical good that can be done on the ground. Each day is marked as a separate chapter in the film leading up to Purim, the most festive of all Jewish holidays. Each day takes Ariel deeper into the Jewish life of Once. What is remarkable about Usher's scheme is that he is able to execute it without being physically present. Busy with his own overextended obligations, he communicates by cellphone. He only appears in the penultimate scene of the film. By that time Ariel has been seduced back into the community. As Ariel leaves to be present as the tenth man of a *minyan*—the quorum necessary in Jewish tradition for certain religious obligations to be performed—Usher slyly smiles. He has succeeded.

Usher plots to keep Ariel busy with multiple tasks, each of which will bring him into contact with the "swarming activity" (to return to Certeau's phrase) of Once. An immersion in the material problems and experiences of the neighborhood, Usher bets, will defeat his son's intellectual reasons for keeping a distance. Each of the tasks seems simple enough, but they weave together into a strong cultural fabric. A young, mute Orthodox woman needs help sorting through the apartment of a recently deceased old man. A teenager awaiting brain surgery in a hospital needs new tennis shoes with Velcro rather than laces. And a butcher needs to donate much-needed meat for the Purim celebration. Objects and places are no less important than persons in Usher's campaign. Usher leaves crackers and dulce de leche, Ariel's favorite snacks as a child, in the apartment for his son. An Israel t-shirt is under his pillow. A trip to a local synagogue results in singing, recitation of Torah, ritual immersion, and donning *tefillin*. Usher's argument is experiential rather than overtly theological. Like Bernardo Perelman, Usher embodies the tradition of *tikkun olam*.

Ariel's reconversion to service to the Once community is made credible by the film's control of point of view. Everything is experienced through him. He is present in every scene. Images of the past are either his memories or materials that he discovers in family archives. Importantly, much of his wandering through Once is captured by a handheld camera closely aligned with his navigation of the crowded scene. There is a high frequency of optical point-of-view shots from his perspective. As Ariel is immersed in Usher's plan, so is the spectator. As the week progresses, Ariel's behavior changes step by step. At the crowded entrance to the community center he evolves from making excuses for his ability to enter rapidly to asserting his need to enter so he can help others. Inside the center, his body language adapts over the week to allow smooth passage amid its hive-like activities. He becomes proactive in seeking solutions. For instance, he finds a rabbi who will offer a bat mitzvah to a transgendered singer. Ariel began the journey as a harried economist in an antiseptic midtown Manhattan skyscraper dealing with the world on abstract terms. He ends reinserted into direct contact with Once at the level of repairing the world person by per-

In the Jewish neighborhood of Once in Buenos Aires, Argentina, Ariel, who has recently returned to his native city from Manhattan, runs a community service errand for his father, Usher. *El rey de Once* (*The King of Once*, shown in the USA as *The Tenth Man*), directed by Daniel Burman, 2015. Still courtesy of Kino-Lorber.

son, task by task, community service by community service. A childhood friend refers to Usher as the "King of Once." The film closes with Ariel wearing a festive crown while driving his father's dilapidated Renault through their neighborhood. He picks up his new girlfriend, Eva, the mute Orthodox woman who turns out to be the butcher's daughter—and not so mute and not so Orthodox. Jewish Once has as many surprises and mysteries as challenges and problems. But they are only knowable by direct contact. Ariel is ready to know in a Jewish way.

Direct contact with the events of the film is not available for the narrator-protagonist of *Radio Days*. As he observes, "It's all gone, except the memories." In struggling to recall scenes from his youth some forty years later, the narrator is unable to construct a linear, even if multistranded, narrative. Instead, the film is a receptacle of anecdotes, some longer or shorter than others, some addressing Jewish experiences and some not. There is no single image, truth, or lesson to be taken from the evocation of the era. There are, however, flashes of understanding that individual anecdotes can reveal, including insights into the many ways that lower-middle-class Jews of the 1940s in New York saw themselves in relationship to broader American society, especially as a constructed image of that society was produced and distributed by the mass culture of radio.

The narrator's family members are all ardent consumers of the many genres broadcast by radio. They live in the seaside neighborhood of the Rockaways in Queens, as much as an hour by subway from the cosmopolitan precincts of Manhattan. A multigenerational household, the family has no profound sense of exclusion from American society, nor are they overly obsessed with being Jewish. It is a fact, not a site of conflict. But anecdote by anecdote, the film paints a large canvas of the differences between how the Jewish family experiences America and the image of the country that radio creates.

Given that radio is an auditory medium, one of the first places that differences appear is in the accents of different classes and ethnic groups. The morning radio show "Breakfast with Irene and Roger" is delivered by speakers who could be imagined to reside closer to London than the outer boroughs, and radio heroes such as the Masked Avenger and Biff Baxter speak in flat Standard American English. And although the narrator's family and their neighbors speak in an English highly influenced by Yiddish in rhythm, intonation, and word order, that particular accent is never heard on the radio. Indeed, the narrator tells the story of a cigarette salesgirl from one of the Manhattan nightclubs, Sally White, who transforms her life with diction lessons. Her delivery of celebrity gossip with a "sophisticated" accent makes her a celebrity. The narrator's family, by contrast, is full of verbal invention, but such improvisation remains within the boundaries of their community. Harmless, bantering insults, for instance, include Uncle Abe advising his wife to "take the hose" (that is, to commit suicide by gassing herself). The moment in which the humor of Woody Allen, Mel Brooks, Carl Reiner, Neil Simon, and others transforms American popular culture has not arrived yet.

It is an era in which certain taboos begin to fall while others remain in place. As one anecdote claims, an elderly neighbor had a stroke when she saw a Jewish girl kiss a black boy. The narrator's man-hungry aunt, Bea, is confused when one of her dates breaks into tears over his deceased male lover. Still, Bea's quest for true love doesn't seem to be restricted to Jewish men. American modernity and a tolerant family give her choice, but within their tolerance reside mixed interpretations of what it means to be Jewish. On a High Holy Day Uncle Abe goes next door to complain to his neighbors that they are not being properly observant. He returns an hour or so later now imbued with a Marxist belief in the need to serve man rather than an abstract god. There is no serious implication that the rather simple man will become a revolutionary, but rather the suggestion that the same neighborhood contains many forms of Jewishness, each of which will evolve in its own way.

Indeed, the many forms of entertainment offered by radio are like a giant dressing room in which Jews and others can try on different versions of being American. The offerings may be very tempting, but there is no requirement to buy any selection. Imagined life, whether of fantasy or social reality, whether joyful or painful, is all there. The family can join America in awaiting the rescue of a small girl trapped in a well or dance through their own house in a conga line as if they were in Havana. What the adult narrator recognizes is that the particular configuration of Jewish immigration to New York, the conditions of World War II, and the pervasive presence of radio as a dominant mass medium were unique, limited, and fragile. To be Jewish in that era was to be so in an experientially rich way now impossible to recover. Cinema wed to memory may be the best hope for rescuing lost Jewish urban history but, as the narrator remarks in the closing moments of the film, "With the passing of each New Year's Eve, those memories grow dimmer and dimmer."

While the narrator's last thoughts in *Radio Days* sound melancholy, they should not be taken as a summary of Woody Allen's view of New World Jewish urban history, nor of that of his artistic godson, Daniel Burman. What binds their work together is more than common interest in New World Jewish experience. Their narrative and cinematic practices investigate the ways that individuals act within particular material circumstances. As such, their art is an active laboratory for testing the many expressions of Jewish life that make the cultures of the New World different from those of the Old World. There is no end to their exuberant art as they instantiate again and again the truth that being Jewish can never be reduced to a timeless unity. As long as they make movies, there will never be a final version. When we walk in their Jewish cities we will always find Certeau's "swarming activity."

Works Cited

Films

Allen, Woody, dir. *Annie Hall*. United Artists. 1977.
———. *Crimes and Misdemeanors*. Orion Pictures. 1989.
———. *Radio Days*. Orion Pictures. 1987.
Burman, Daniel, dir. *Derecho de familia* (*Family Law*). BD Cine. 2006.
———. *Esperando al Mesías* (*Waiting for the Messiah*). BD Cine. 2000.
———. *El rey del Once* (*The Tenth Man*). BD Cine. 2015.

Articles and Books

Bakhtin, M. M. *The Dialogic Imagination: Four Essays*. Ed. Michael Holquist. Trans. Caryl Emerson and Michael Holquist. Austin: University of Texas Press, 1982.
Certeau, Michel de. "Walking in the City" (1984). In *The Practice of Everyday Life*, 91–110. Trans. Steven Rendall. Berkeley: University of California Press, 1984.
Graff Zivin, Erin. *The Wandering Signifier: Rhetoric of Jewishness in the Latin American Imaginary*. Durham, NC: Duke University Press, 2008.

CHAPTER 15

Interfaith Relations between Jews and Gentiles in Argentine and US Cinema

NORA GLICKMAN

I want to see what life is like outside of the bubble.
WAITING FOR THE MESSIAH, 2000

What happens when a Jew falls in love with a Gentile? How does cinema represent the feelings of the couple, and of those around them? What is the impact of public events on a couple's relationship? In films addressing these questions, it is natural to expect a wide variety of approaches. These can be related to the personal style and sensibility of the directors, the autobiographical tendency of some of the films, the values they attribute to their subjects, the significance of the time when the films were produced, and how they relate to the historical period they represent.

This essay offers a panoramic, comparative survey of films from the United States and Argentina that grapple with these questions. These two countries were selected for being the richest providers of Jewish culture in North and South America, respectively, as well as the largest producers of films on interfaith relationships. In both there is a disproportion between the percentile of Jews in the population and their representation in films. The following essay examines some of the distinguishing circumstances that affect the lives of interfaith couples. The films on interfaith romances reviewed here were produced from the sixties to the present, with the exception of *The Jazz Singer*, which had its first production in 1927 and then a 1980 remake.[1] The list is extensive but certainly not exhaustive.[2] By juxtaposing Argentinean and US films according to the wide range of reactions by the couples, their parents, and their children, we can observe how their attitudes toward intermarriage have evolved.

Demographic statistics from both countries reveal a progressive trend among Jews toward assimilation, a drastic reduction of Jewish practices, and an increased integration into the fiber of society.[3] This essay raises questions about to what extent interfaith films reflect changes in attitude over time, how directors portray events that took place in earlier generations, how they succeed in reaching the sensibilities of their contemporary audiences, whether Jewish directors with a semi-autobiographical bent make any particular observation when reminiscing about interfaith roles, what their subjective views reveal about their choice of characters and situations, and how their films relate to more recent events.

The First Generation: Diaspora and Emigration to the Americas

Fiddler on the Roof, directed by Norman Jewison in 1971, and *The Jewish Gauchos*, directed by Juan José Jusid in 1975, are two films that showcase parents' inflexibility toward the concept of intermarriage. Both are musical adaptations from celebrated Jewish authors. *Fiddler on the Roof*, an adaptation from Sholem Aleichem's *Tevye the Dairyman* (1894), which so vividly depicts Jewish traditions, was first produced as a Broadway show in 1964 and moved to Hollywood seven years later. The film ends when Tevye and his family are being forced to flee from the pogroms in Russia. Having reconciled himself to marrying two of his daughters to poor Jews, Tevye never forgives his third daughter for marrying a non-Jew and forbids his family to talk to her as she leaves for Siberia with her husband.

Just a few years after *Fiddler on the Roof*, and strongly influenced by it, Jusid produced *The Jewish Gauchos*, an adaptation of the stories written in 1910 by Alberto Gerchunoff, who in turn was much affected by the writings of Sholem Aleichem. Gerchunoff himself had immigrated from Russia to the Argentine countryside as a child, as part of a resettlement project funded by philanthropist Baron Hirsch (1831–1896).[4] While *Fiddler* ends with Tevye's emigration to North America, *The Jewish Gauchos*, in celebration of Argentina's hundredth year of independence, opens with the arrival of Eastern European refugees to the agricultural colonies of Argentina. The saga of these Jewish pioneers, a particular historical phenomenon unequaled in scope, is not featured in US cinema, except for some animated films.[5]

Among the twenty-four stories that compose Gerchunoff's *The Jewish Gauchos*, one of them, also depicted in the film adaptation, is devoted to the romance between Rogelio Míguez and Myriam, whose only solution to her parents' objection to her marrying a gaucho is to elope with him. A more developed story, interspersed among the rest, is "Camacho's Wedding." In his film, José Jusid places it last, as the crowning segment of his film. It features the elaborate wedding between Pascual Liske, the richest and dumbest Jew of the colony, and Raquel, the prettiest and poorest girl—a wedding feast that ends in a dramatic elopement: riding a white horse, Raquel, still in her wedding gown, gallops away with Gabriel, in his best *gaucho* attire, leaving behind their astonished wedding guests posing for a photograph from which only the bride is missing. Enraged, the father of the groom curses the gaucho who stole the bride, curses the bride for being an adulteress, and curses his in-laws for having brought her up as a whore. After a chaotic scene in which the whole wedding feast collapses, the wise words of one of the town's elders restores order as he declares that the bride had the right to a divorce since she did not love her spouse and the wedding had not been consummated. The congregants leave in silence, saddened by the outcome. As Jusid must have expected, his 1975 contemporary audience cheered at the lovers' daring feat, and that is probably why he made it the climax of the entire film.

María Victoria Menis, who directed *La cámara oscura* (*Camera Obscura*, 2008) almost half a century later, expected the same reaction from her public as Jusid's. Like *The Jewish Gauchos*, her film unfolds during the same time and at the same place as the Jewish rural colonization of Eastern European Jews in the north of Argentina. Like *The Jewish Gauchos*, but centered on just one family, *La cámara oscura* moves toward the dramatic elopement of a Jewess with a Gentile. Here, however, it is not the parents who are shocked by the flight of the couple, since the bride is no longer a young girl. By the time Gertrudis leaves her family she is already a middle-aged woman with unfulfilled aspirations who rebels against her neglectful husband and her unappreciative, grown children. The fact that the photographer she elopes with is a Gentile, significantly named Jean Baptiste, does not seem to be as important as her daring action. Menis takes some liberties with the adaptation from the eponymous story by Angélica Gorodischer. Both the film and the story unfold in the early 1920s. However, the original story, written in 1993, is more poignant because it satirizes the *machista* behavior of Gertrudis's grandson who, two generations after the elopement took place, still condemns his grandmother for dishonoring his family.

Eastern European immigrant parents held the same negative attitudes toward intermarriage whether they settled in the rural areas of Argentina or in the urban centers of New York and Baltimore. Before World War II, as American Jews experienced problems of anti-Semitic discrimination in employment, housing, and entry to private universities, intermarriage was an uncommon phenomenon. On the screen, however, Hollywood directors gave a positive depiction of intermarriage during the initial period of immigration to the United States. In *Abie's Irish Rose*, directed by Victor Fleming in 1928, the love between two immigrants, a Jewish man and an Irish Catholic woman, erases all ethnic differences through assimilation and intermarriage.[6] From Hollywood's perspective, Americanization was reinforced by choosing a non-Jewish spouse or an individual career in defiance of parental pressure. In spite of actual statistics that pointed to a very low intermarriage rate from the mid-1920s on, there was a subgenre of films on relationships between Jewish and Irish families living under similarly disadvantaged economic circumstances, which often included romance and marriage. In defiance of parental opposition from one or both sides, the young couple overcame the obstacles.

This optimistic "melting pot" ideology probably reflected the desire of Jewish mogul producers and directors like Louis B. Meyer, Adolph Zukor, Max Ophüls, and Otto Preminger—all of them European immigrants—to depict happy outcomes for mixed marriages. One of their paths to success in America consisted of divorcing their Jewish spouses and remarrying Gentile women, thus presenting an image of bliss and harmony through intermarriage.

This accounts for the tremendous popular appeal of *The Jazz Singer*, directed by Alan Crosland in 1927, as it dealt with the generational conflicts that beset Jewish and other immigrant families. Here the protagonist, Jackie Rabinowitz (the memorable Al Jolson), the son of East European immigrants, provokes a devastating reaction from his father when he rebels against him and, instead of becoming a cantor as his father was, goes off in pursuit of a jazz-singing career after adopting the stage name Jack Robin. His romance with Mary Dale, a Gentile woman and the star of the Broadway review in which Jackie is a performer, will presumably lead to their marriage. The response of Jackie's father is bleak: he says *kaddish* for his son and later suffers a heart attack.

So successful was *The Jazz Singer* that it was produced again and again—in a remake by Danny Thomas in 1952, followed by a television adaptation by Jerry Lewis (NBC television series) in 1959, and another film remake by Richard Fleischer in 1980, each one reflecting the needs and dreams of its generation. In the 1980 version, Yussel Rabinowitz (Neil Diamond) defies his father's wishes and abandons New York City and his Orthodox wife in search of a singing career. Almost as soon as he reaches Los Angeles, he is spotted by the lively Gentile Molly Bell, an artistic agent who finds him an opening in a performance. Yussel's Jewish wife, resigned to losing him, gives him up without a struggle. As in the seminal 1927 version, Cantor Rabinowitz disowns Yussel for rejecting his traditional Jewish ways. Tearing his garment, he bellows: "I hef no son!" But finally, however, he reconciles to his loss when he finds out that he is to become a grandfather, that the baby will be called Chaim Rabinowitz, and that the child will carry his family name.[7]

Toward Integration

In contrast with the inflexibility and dogmatic traditionalism of first-generation immigrant parents, whether they settled in the country or in the city, cinematic portrayals of Jewish sons and daughters born either in the United States or in Argentina show more tolerance and a gradual acceptance of new values. Whereas in earlier American films the Gentile counterpart of the Jew tended to be a red-haired, Irish Catholic woman, second-generation films replace that model with one of a blond, blue-eyed WASP (White Anglo Saxon Protestant), male or female.

Director Sydney Pollack poses difficult questions in *The Way We Were* (1973), a film that spans the decades from the 1930s to the 1950s and is set against social unrest in the United States in 1973, when demonstrations against the Vietnam War were unfolding. Although Pollack's film was conceived as a sentimental romance between a Jewess and a Gentile, what distinguishes it are its political overtones. *The Way We Were* features Katie Morosky (Barbra Streisand), a political activist who is entranced when she first meets her opposite, Hubbell Gardiner (Robert Redford), a WASP—upper class, preppy, and an accomplished athlete. Although Katie immediately realizes that Hubbell's lifestyle is far removed from her radical politics, she does not rest until he marries her. And once married, when his first novel fails, she still encourages him to become a novelist.

During the McCarthy period and the witch hunts of the 1950s, Katie pronounces herself publicly in defense of the jailed victims ("The Hollywood 10"), while Hubbell remains indifferent. The couple splits after ten years, and when they meet again, Hubbel has "made it" as a screenwriter in Hollywood, whereas Katie is continuing her leftist activities, giving speeches in the street and on the radio. Their bittersweet reunion only confirms that they made the right decision in going their separate ways. *The Way We Were* is an example of Pollock's success in reconciling the "insoluble dilemma" of a mixed couple by confronting their private desires with their public awareness.

Similarly, Barry Levinson's semi-autobiographical comedy *Liberty Heights* (1999) serves as a stage for the director's ideas on ethnic integration and tolerance. In recreating his own suburb of Baltimore in the early 1950s, Levinson transcends ethnic boundaries and prejudices. During a Halloween party, young Van Kurtzman becomes infatuated with a mysterious, gorgeous blond girl disguised as Cinderella and devotes all of his time to attracting her. His dream, however, fades even before his parents find out about it, as he becomes aware of the girl's excessive flirtatiousness and her partiality to drinking. As will be discussed below, his younger brother, Ben, will go further in testing racial prejudices, as he befriends an African American girl.

A more positive outcome for an interfaith affair is experienced by Alby Sherman (Elliott Gould), the protagonist of *Over the Brooklyn Bridge* (1984), a lighthearted comedy that Menachem Golan, its director, originally intended to call *My Darling Shiksa*—perhaps a more accurate title. The film re-creates the gritty atmosphere of New York City in the 1980s. Alby's father is absent from the film, and the paternal influence of domineering Uncle Benjamin (Cid Caesar) almost succeeds in spoiling his chances of a happy future. At first, Alby, a diabetic nebbish (a timid or ineffectual person), is lured by the prospect of exchanging his drab Brooklyn candy store for a fancy restaurant in Manhattan on the condition that he marries "a nice Jewish woman."

But Levinson, romantically inclined, eventually redeems his anti-hero. Over the course of an unforgettable family dinner scene, Alby refuses his uncle's generous check and makes an eloquent speech in defense of true love, which culminates in his success in getting both his "darling *shiksa*" (Margaux Hemingway)—who, like Anne in Edward Norton's *Keeping the Faith* (2000), is prepared to convert to Judaism—and the fancy restaurant he had been eyeing.[8] The uncle's final generous gesture, despite his prejudice, shows that societal and cultural changes can win out over inflexibility.

More attuned to the religious interactions and influences that his contemporary audience experience, Norton's *Keeping the Faith* highlights how dramatically mainstream American attitudes toward minorities have changed over the course of one century in the treatment of ethnic and racial relations. In his insightful comparison of *Keeping the Faith* with *The Jazz Singer*, Lawrence Baron points to significant parallels in the narrative structure and the content of both films.[9] For example, Norton inverts the message delivered in *The Jazz Singer*. The heroes of the 1927 and the 1980 versions of *The Jazz Singer* believe they can attain the American dream by abandoning religious traditions and placing their careers as entertainers above everything else, including their love for a non-Jew. As a modern rabbi, Jake (*Keeping the Faith*) privileges religious diversity and spiritual fulfillment over material success.

He feels that "the best way for the Jewish community to respond to the high rate of Jewish intermarriage is to make Jewish traditions and Judaism as relevant as possible and to help those who are in interfaith marriages to be part of the Jewish community."

In *The Jazz Singer*, the old cantor announces that he no longer has a son because that son defied the laws of his religion. In *Keeping the Faith*, the director plays it safe on all counts: Jake's father disowns him when he realizes Jake will not follow in his footsteps and join him as a partner in his banking firm but will instead become a rabbi. Once he has become a rabbi, Jake and his best friend, Brian, a Protestant priest, fall in love with the same woman, a beautiful WASP whom they've known since they were children. Their relationship does not turn into a *ménage à trois* (as in Paul Mazursky's *Willie and Phil* [1972]), fortunately, becoming instead a conventional relationship of an interfaith couple, Jake and Anne, with Brian's blessing. When Jake realizes that Anne is willing to give up her career for his sake, he fears losing his mother's approval, as she had already broken her ties with her older son when he married "out." No less important is Jake's fear of alienating his congregation. As a rabbi, he assumes that by marrying outside the faith he would not serve as a positive role model for other Jews of marriageable age. He finally reaches out to his congregation by risking his career when he confesses, fittingly during his Yom Kippur sermon, that he is in a relationship with a non-Jewish woman whom he loves and asks to be forgiven for having had too little faith in their understanding and compassion. His sincerity wins them over.

Baron observes another interesting parallel: while in the earlier version of *The Jazz Singer* the father's grief over his son contributed to his heart attack before he was finally reconciled by the arrival of a grandson, in *Keeping the Faith* Ruth's concern over her son's future gives her a mild stroke, but it also causes her to soften her attitude and to encourage Jake to follow his heart.

In spite of Norton's obvious intention of crafting a multicultural, pluralistic message suggesting that religious continuity depends more on adaptation and reciprocity than on the dogmatic traditionalism of someone like Cantor Rabinowitz (or for that matter, of Liske's parents in *The Jewish Gauchos*), he does not take the situation to its natural conclusion. Success seems to come too easily to Jesse: he is reappointed as a rabbi and also learns that Anne is preparing to convert to Judaism. A more pertinent question for *Keeping the Faith* in the twenty-first century would be: What if Anne does not convert? Would Jake be able to hold his position as a rabbi? Norton does not attempt to entertain that problematic possibility.

Preconceptions about Passing

On the other hand, in *Sol de otoño* (*Autumn Sun*, 1996), Argentine director Eduardo Mignogna delves into misconceptions about ethnic and cultural customs held by partners of different religious backgrounds. Just as Jewish men are portrayed as romanticizing Gentile women of "goyish" appearance, and Jewish women fantasize about their Gentile partners, Gentile men and women express similar preconceptions about their Jewish mates.

Mignogna's *Autumn Sun* is set against the backdrop of Buenos Aires in the late 1970s, when the climate of economic insecurity had infiltrated the lives of individuals.[10] The film connects two seemingly separate incidents. At the outset the protagonist has her wallet snatched away from her on a busy street of Buenos Aires, an apparently minor detail that illustrates the contrasting gap between different social classes living in the same pluralistic metropolis. Clara (Norma Aleandro) is a middle-class Jewish professional woman whose life centers around her friends and clients, while Raúl Ferraro (Federico Luppi) is a working-class Argentine artisan of Italian descent, sharing his house and workshop in a *porteño* neighborhood with an unemployed neighbor and his grandchildren. As it turns out, the petty thief who assailed Clara is the grandson of Raúl's neighbor and lives in the same household.

In this light comedy of errors, Mignogna plays with the ambiguities of his protagonists' sentiments, as both Clara and Raúl practice deceit in order to achieve their aims. Clara places an ad in the classified section of a newspaper stating that she wishes to meet a gentleman with whom to enter a "serious friendship" and indicates her religion by including a Star of David. Her intention is to find a man who will play the part of her Jewish husband, so that she can impress her brother on his visit from America. Raúl, her respondent, only pretends to be a Jew and calls himself Saul Levine because he fancies the idea of dating a Jewish woman. Clara immediately sees through him because he mispronounces the Yiddish word *varenikes*, meaning "patties": "No Jew," she explains, "would say *marenikes* instead of *varenikes*."

When Clara finds out that her brother has canceled his visit (we never know if such a visit was the product of Clara's fantasy or not), she doesn't have to pretend to be married to a Jew any longer. But rather than reject Raúl, since she has become attached to him, she offers him a crash course on traditional Jewish foods, celebrations, and Yiddish expressions so that he can pass for a Jew when he meets her friends. Raúl's masterful performance wins her over.

Expecting Clara to conform to his notion of what a Jewish woman fan-

A last chance for a romantic relationship: Clara Goldstein (Norma Aleandro) is Jewish, and Raúl Ferraro (Federico Luppi) is a Gentile pretending to be a Jew. *Sol de otoño* (*Autumn Sun*) (1996), directed by Eduardo Mignogna.

cies for breakfast, Raúl serves her an elaborate combination of borscht, matzah, and lox. In her effort to eat a healthy diet for his sake, however, she does not respond to his efforts as readily as he had hoped. For her part, Clara expects Raúl to demonstrate his non-Jewish "machismo." When she overhears a man verbally abusing the waiter at a restaurant, she fantasizes that Raúl will teach the bully a lesson—an unlikely behavior from a Jewish man, whom Clara conceives as shy and retiring. At the end of this sentimental comedy, Clara's behavior is that of a stereotypical Jewish woman who makes every sacrifice for her man when she finds out that he is seriously ill.

In a lighter vein—but using the same technique as Raúl, who pretends to be someone else in his search for the ideal Jewish partner—Christian O'Connell, the protagonist of *Jewtopia* (dir. Brian Fogel, 2012), has definite ideas about what his future wife should be like. He believes he has found his ideal bride in a Jewish girl, the rabbi's daughter, and that she could make all the proper decisions for him. Like Raúl, Christian claims he's Jewish. He says his name is Avi Rosenberg, and he takes lessons from his neurotic Jewish friend Adam Lipschitz on how to "act Jewish." Adam himself, going through pre-wedding arrangements with his Jewish bride, encounters no fewer troubles than if he were marrying out of his faith. The tricks Christian learns, like compulsively ordering many different dishes at a restaurant and immediately changing his order, over and over, account for his shallowness, as well as for the weak humor of the film.

The (Un)settling Pressure from Jewish Parents

When it comes to delivering their message, Jewish parents' approval or rejection of interfaith relations need not be explicit. In fact, in two important films of this kind, the Jewish parents are not physically present, yet the influence they exert on their sons is just as strong. In the most memorable segment of *Annie Hall* (1977), Woody Allen's comedy of urban love and incompatibility, Alvy Singer (Woody Allen) experiences a surreal fantasy about a dinner party at his girlfriend's Wisconsin house. He imagines his own religious Hassidic family—complete with side-locks and large black hats—sitting opposite Annie's WASPish relatives, under the scrutiny of her judgmental grandmother. Alvy's neurotic fear of sinning against his religion and of going against his parental dogma is manifested in his daydreaming. The internalized guilt-generating parent within him cannot be easily exorcised. The deep contrast between Alvy's and Annie's parents reveals the unbridgeable gulf that separates the couple. The outcome is that after a few intense yet failed encounters back and forth between New York and Los Angeles, the relationship ends.

Argentina, a Catholic country, does not depict the figure of the WASP in its cinema, but the nebbish type sometimes appears in Argentine interfaith movies. Sammy Goldstein (Ricardo Darín), the protagonist of *Samy y yo* (*Sammy and I*), directed by Eduardo Milewicz in 2002, resembles Woody Allen's hero in many respects. Sammy has the same ungainly appearance as Alvy Singer, and he shares his profession as a struggling comedian. Sammy's flashback about himself, like Alvy's fantasy about facing Annie's WASPish family, reveals his worst fears about becoming like his own parents. In a retrospective segment, Alvy appears as a child holding his father's hand and listening to his bitter complaints, in uninterrupted Yiddishized Spanish, against his situation, his life, and his domineering spouse. In consequence, Sammy grows up looking for parental models that differ from his. Unhappy with his first fiancée, a Jewish, snobbish sex therapist, Sammy becomes gradually attracted to Mary, a gorgeous Colombian *shiksa* half his age, who is determined to turn him into a successful comedian. In spite of their differences in taste, character, and age, Mary and Sammy do not express any concern about their ethnic backgrounds. After two years in an on and off relationship, they meet again and both of them have matured. Sammy has become a successful novelist, free from his mother's suffocating influence, and has shaken off his paranoia, while Mary has turned into a responsible single mother (her baby is not Sammy's). In Argentina, three decades after the US production of *Annie Hall*, this reunion, though seemingly contrived, is the director's way of forecasting an enduring romance.

A more concrete presentation of Jewish parents affecting the romantic decisions of their children can be found in the Argentine film *Esperando al Mesías* (*Waiting for the Messiah*), directed by Daniel Burman in 2000, and in the American film *Two Lovers*, directed by James Gray in 2008. Both portray nebbishes who long to abandon their Jewish milieu to explore a relationship outside the confines of their tribe. Ariel Goldstein (Daniel Hendler), from the neighborhood of Once, and Leonard Kraditor (Joaquin Phoenix), from Brooklyn, are amateur cameramen who work at weddings and bar mitzvahs and help their parents in their modest business.

Both are certain they could have an ideal relationship with a smart and beautiful Jewish girl. Despite this, or maybe precisely because of it, they reject them, seeking excitement elsewhere. Leonard becomes infatuated with Michelle (Gwyneth Paltrow)—a glamorous WASP—and neglects his Jewish girlfriend, Sandra. Ariel, like Leonard, abandons his steady Jewish fiancée, Estela, in favor of his mysterious Gentile coworker, Elsa. In his awkward attempt to impress another character, Laura, when he tells her he is Jewish, Ariel cannot distinguish whether he said "soy gay" ("I'm gay") or "soy goy" ("I'm a Gentile"). Unlike Ariel, who is in his early twenties, Leonard is in his thirties and more intensely dramatic. He survived a suicide attempt after a breakup with a previous fiancée, is dependent on medication, and has moved back in with his parents.

Their respective parents react differently. Ariel's father (Héctor Alterio), in mourning for his recently deceased wife, leans on Estela, his son's Jewish girlfriend, who comforts him as she patiently waits for Ariel's return to her and to her steadfast Judaism. But Ariel's father is also capable of showing tenderness toward Elsa. Their brief encounter partly compensates for Elsa's yearning for her own absent father. In fact, Ariel's father's reluctance to interfere in his son's decision concerning his return to the Jewish "bubble" only increases Ariel's respect for him.

Eight years after *Esperando al Mesías* came *Two Lovers*, a film, directed by James Gray, whose complex characters provide a singular take on this romantic genre.[11] Both sets of parents hold divided opinions about Leonard's future. His prospective Jewish father-in-law, like Alby's Uncle Benjamin in

In this Brooklyn-set romantic drama, a Jewish bachelor (Joaquin Phoenix) is torn between his family's arranged marriage to a Jewish girl (Moni Moshonov) and his beautiful WASP neighbor (Gwyneth Paltrow). *Two Lovers* (2008), directed by James Gray.

Over the Brooklyn Bridge, aggressively arranges a match between Leonard and Sandra, his daughter, claiming it will be advantageous to both parties—a match that only intimidates Leonard even further. On the other hand, the subdued behavior of Leonard's mother (Roberta Rosselini) breaks from the Jewish mother stereotype. Whether or not she approves of her son's behavior, she always sides with him. After being repeatedly rejected by Michelle, Leonard reconciles himself to a more congenial, albeit less exciting, life with Sandra, his Jewish fiancée. His mother's tacit understanding of his situation contributes to his return to Judaism.

Non-Jewish Parental Reactions

Non-Jewish parents in interfaith films do not express as many definitive opinions about their children's decisions as Jewish parents do. Some of them[12] are portrayed with less detail and less sympathy than Jewish parents, while others express their prejudices in a veiled manner. In *Esperando al Mesías*, Laura's father, whom she always idealizes, sends her money and keeps promising he will visit her but never does. Laura's brief contact with Ariel's father compensates for the lack of affection from her own father. Laura's lesbian relationship might also be a response to her mistrust of the role her father plays in her life. Michelle's father in Gray's *Two Lovers* has drunken outbursts that cause his daughter to seek shelter in the corridor of her apartment, where Leonard finds and rescues her. These violent episodes naturally play a part in Michelle's risqué behavior, including her pregnancy by her married lover, her abortion, and her drug use.

Ariel Winograd's *Mi primera boda* (*My First Wedding*, 2011) tests a mixed couple's capacity to endure premarital pressure just hours before their wedding ceremony. The bride's Gentile mother is portrayed in a negative light. She is a narcissist and an alcoholic, and the bride's Aunt Marta is a zealous Catholic. Adrián Meier's Jewish mother, on the other hand, is pragmatic. She expresses her doubts as to the outcome of mixed marriages and cites the high rate of divorce in such cases. Perhaps the only impartial voices in this film come from the philosophical disquisitions about life and religion held between two paternal figures, the priest and the rabbi, during their adventurous car ride on their way to conduct the Jewish/Catholic ceremony.

In the romantic comedy *The Heartbreak Kid* (1972), director Elaine May successfully translates Mr. Corcoran's feelings of rage and frustration toward Lenny, his Jewish son-in-law. As a wealthy Minnesotan, Corcoran regards Lenny as the stereotype of the unscrupulous, ambitious New Yorker. Lenny may have succeeded in entering the upper-class Minnesota circle, but at a high price. From the moment he sets eyes upon the ravishing Kelly (Cybill Shepherd), right in the middle of his honeymoon, he tries every drastic maneuver possible to get rid of his new spouse. With the excuse that Lila is severely sunburned, he confines her to their hotel room, while he relentlessly pursues Kelly.[13] Lenny's "prize" turns out to be a beautiful WASP whose intelligence can be epitomized in one question: "How do you expect me to think when I'm listening?"

In his coming-of-age comedy *Liberty Heights* (1999), previously discussed, Barry Levinson transcends social boundaries by re-creating the atmosphere of Baltimore in the early 1950s, when the city's neighborhoods were still ethnically divided and racial integration began to be implemented in American schools. The Kurtzman family, of modest means, is depicted as bigoted and snobbish. Ada, the mother, is convinced that Jews are "a unique kind of people," and when she hears her son Ben fancies a "Negro" classmate from school, she is appalled and moans: "Oh, my God, my God! Just kill me now!" In contrast, Sylvia's African American family is sophisticated and affluent. Her father, a doctor, remains calm when he comes home unexpectedly and discovers a stranger hiding in his daughter's bedroom. After he finds out Ben's full name, he appraises the situation and courteously asks, "Mr. Kurtzman, would you please come out of the closet?" He then gives Ben a ride back home, since the boy is under age and cannot drive. And yet, in spite of his politeness, Levinson makes it clear that Sylvia's father is adamantly opposed to his daughter's relationship with a white boy, whether or not he is Jewish. At the end of the film, the passionate good-bye kiss that Ben gives Sylvia at their high school graduation, right in front of their shocked parents, reveals the director's optimism about the progress in social integration that will take place in the years to follow.

Like Levinson, director Paul Mazursky makes an original and humorous statement about the capacity for tolerance that non-Jewish parents display when dealing with their children's independent lifestyles. Mazursky's *Willie and Phil* (1980) reflects the mood of America during the 1970s, a decade that offered choices of cults, radical politics, and alternative lifestyles. The reactions of Willie's and Phil's parents when they visit their sons in Greenwich Village combine a mixture of resentment, love, anger, and confusion. In spite of her initial shock at her son's bohemian lifestyle, Willie's Jewish mother is prepared to tolerate it. The *ménage à trois* of Willie, Phil, and Jeannette develops into a marriage between Willie and Jeannette (a WASP) that produces a son. By the time of Willie's mother's visit, Jeannette has a new lover and all of them are living under the same roof. In contrast, Phil's Italian mother is not so receptive to what she finds; in fact, she is so baffled at her son's outrageous choices that she wastes no time before picking up her suitcase, taking a taxi to the airport, and flying back home with her husband.

The Offspring of Interfaith Couples

When considering the interfaith relations of couples from the perspective of children and of grandchildren, US cinema is mostly inclined to analyze the social and psychological behavior of its characters. By contrast, Argentine cinema maintains a strong link with historical and political issues. This can be best appreciated in two Argentine films, *Pobre mariposa* (*Poor Butterfly*), directed by Raúl de la Torre in 1986, and *Un lugar en el mundo* (*A Place in the World*), directed by Adolfo Aristarain in 1992.

In *Pobre mariposa*, de la Torre draws attention to his country's recent history (the post–military rule years that ended in 1983) by setting his story in 1945, right after the end of World War II and only months before the rise of Perón to power. Clara Samonoff de Merino, the daughter of a Jewish immigrant father and an Argentine Catholic mother, is distressed when she hears that her school-age daughters were accused of being Jewish, when in fact they are practicing Catholics. Clara avoids giving them a straight answer regarding their identity. She chides them and then reassures them that Argentina was never involved in the war: "Aquí no ha pasado nada [Nothing's happened here]." Clara realizes, however, that her father's unresolved murder after his discovery of a list of Nazi war criminals entering Argentina has indirectly put her own future at risk. Being happily married to a Catholic surgeon and enjoying a privileged social position do not prevent Clara from undertaking a search into her own suppressed Jewish past. She learns from those around her (her communist cousin, her Jewish relatives, her father's socialist comrades in exile after the Spanish Civil War) what it means to be both Jewish and Catholic. At the end of the film, along with the list of credits, a newscaster's voiceover announces that Clara had been "accidentally" killed in a street skirmish as she was about to enter her radio station. In 1945 Argentina was not ready for an interfaith marriage without consequences. In 1986 de la Torre is asking: Is Argentina finally ready for a true democracy?

Produced six years after *Pobre mariposa*, and nine years after the "Dirty War" (1976–1983) was over, Adolfo Aristarain's *Un lugar en el mundo* examines the circumstances of a local crisis. The film comments on the recent past through the tension that grows between capitalism and the social justice the protagonists seek for the townsfolk. As in De la Torre's *Poor Butterfly*, in which the interfaith couple believed that it was possible to lead a "normal" life, undisturbed by outside corruption, Aristarain's film establishes a clear contrast between the private harmony enjoyed within the intimate circle of an intermarried couple and their inability to control the tragic circumstances unfolding around them in the public sphere. Through a series of flashbacks, their son Ernesto, a medical student, recalls his childhood in the village of San Luis; he goes back there to visit his father's grave. Ernesto holds fond childhood memories of Luciana—a twelve-year-old Catholic girl who could not understand why he had refused to enter a church. To her question about his faith, "What are you, then?" he replied, "I am nothing." Yet Ernesto's precarious Jewish upbringing somehow lingers on, as he retains knowledge of the Yiddish songs and the Hebrew alphabet learned from his grandmother. After his parents' return from exile in Spain, their noble aspirations were cut short by the personal interests of Andrada (Rodolfo Ranni), the landowner who exploits the small community they are trying to help through education and cooperative organization. Ernesto's father, Mario Dominicci (Federico Luppi) a community organizer of Italian descent, dies of a heart attack provoked by increasing harassment. Disheartened, his mother (Cecilia Roth), a Jewish doctor who has devoted herself to helping poor people, gives up on her dreams of social change in the province and moves with Ernesto to Buenos Aires.

Argentina's dramatic films involving politically motivated conflicts affect the lives of interfaith couples and their offspring, but ethnicity does not affect the internal relationship of the couple. In *Derecho de familia* (*Family Law*, 2006)—part of Daniel Burman's semi-autobiographical cycle of films, which also includes *Esperando al Mesías* (*Waiting for the Messiah*, 2000) and *El abrazo partido* (*Lost Embrace*, 2004)—Bernardo Perelman gives his father a traditional Jewish burial, although he does not identify himself as a Jew, except for his surname; he, his Gentile wife, Sandra, and their child are secular Argentines.

In contrast, the United States tends to produce comedies that accentuate the Jewish distinctiveness of their characters and highlight subcultural differences in their daily practices, speech patterns, and gestures. At the beginning of the twenty-first century, one of the most pressing concerns of American Jews, having moved from the social margins of American society to its mainstream, was whether their offspring would identify themselves as Jews. Lawrence Baron observes a curious paradox that is reflected in American cinema. The steady attrition in the commitment of American Jews to Judaism coincides with a shift away from the melting-pot model of Americanization, to a multicultural model that celebrates ethnic, racial, and religious pluralism. This can be appreciated in recent films such as *Meet the Fockers* (Paul Weitz, 2004), part of the trilogy that includes *Meet the Parents* (Jay Roach, 2000) and *Little Fockers* (Paul Weitz, 2010).

In *Meet the Fockers* the interfaith romance between Jewish Greg Focker and Pam Byrnes, a WASP, is not affected by their different ethnic backgrounds. The satire is focused instead on the distinctive idiosyncrasies of their parents and in-laws, Jack and Dina Byrnes, and Roz and Berney Focker. What stands out here are the personality, the compatibility, and the particular lifestyle of each family. Roz Focker (Barbra Streisand), a Jewish sex therapist with liberal ideas, proudly shows off to her in-laws her son's photo album containing a nylon envelope with the foreskin from his *bris*. For his part, the snobbishness and prejudiced remarks displayed by Jack Byrnes (Robert De Niro) are directed not against his son-in-law's religion but against his lower social status as a nurse. He feels his daughter deserves to have married a doctor rather than a male nurse.

Whereas the offspring of American couples such as those in the *Meet the Fockers* have no conflict in their interfaith relationship, their parents and in-laws visibly display cultural and ethnic differences. In *This Is 40* (2012), the latest comedy of this subgenre, Judd Apatow sets the stage for a confrontational scene in which financial issues concerning the parents interfere with the personal relationship of the couple, to the point that racial biases are exposed. Larry, the Jewish grandfather, a man with a garrulous and aggressive nature, openly collides with Debbie, his WASP daughter-in-law, and with her father's detached behavior. His paranoia makes him overreact to remarks that he interprets as anti-Semitic. Larry, for instance, considers himself entitled to be involved in his married son's family affairs, while he secretly receives financial assistance from him—a behavior that Debbie regards as plain interference.

From Mamas to Drag Queens

Perhaps the most challenging films to classify in this subgenre are those related to homosexuality, since social taboos against homosexuals are stronger than against mixed marriages. Argentina's film *Cohen vs. Rosi*, directed by Daniel Barone, was produced in 1988, the same year as America's *Torch Song Trilogy*, directed by Paul Bogart. The latter, an adaptation of a successful Broadway play by the same name, was created and interpreted by Harvey Fierstein. Written as a nostalgic reflection on the problems that gays experienced during the 1970s, before the AIDS epidemic, the movie focuses on the intimate life of Arnold Beckhoff (Harvey Fierstein), who—in spite of having accepted his homosexuality from an early age—has been unable to rid himself of insecurity and loneliness. Arnold's love for his Jewish mother (Anne Bancroft) leads him to spend his life tolerating her insults and recriminations for being gay, which include forbidding him to say *kaddish* at his father's grave, hinting that Arnold's sexual orientation was the cause of her husband's death, and telling him that she would have rather remained childless than give birth to a homosexual son. Arnold's mother is so incensed at his homosexuality that the fact that both of his lovers are not Jewish is not even in her list of objections.

After the murder of his lover, who was killed by a gang of homophobes, Arnold finds a new Gentile partner with whom to raise the gay adolescent son he adopted. By now Arnold has become a sensitive and reasonable person, as well as a successful drag queen and New York comedian; he will no longer make concessions. Now he demands "love and respect" from those close to him—in particular from his own mother. Ironically, in raising his son, Arnold adopts the same nagging Jewish mannerisms as his mother, with added sarcasm and wit: "When I bring him up," he tells her, "I think of you, and then I do the opposite."

Against a background of Jewish klezmer and Italian tarantella music, as the title of the film proclaims, *Cohen vs. Rosi* is about the long-term quarrel between two opponents living in a country overwhelmed by political and economic corruption. Ariel Cohen and Carla Rosi engage in a family feud that began years earlier, between their respective parents. Contrary to the concept of the *grotesco criollo*, the early-twentieth-century dramatic genre from which this film draws, this family farce has a happy rather than a tragic ending.[14] A flashback to Ariel and Carla's grandparents' first meeting reveals a secret and passionate affair between the immigrants—an East European Jew and an Italian—on the ship that brought them to Buenos Aires in the 1920s. The final twist involves the renewal of the liaison between the two men in their old age, after Rosi, dressed as a female impersonator, announces on public television that he does not regard himself just as the father of a politician or the grandfather of a journalist, but as "la nonna," or "grandmother," and that he is, in fact, "a woman in a man's body." Following this shocking revelation the reality of the interfaith romance between Carla and Ariel, the grandchildren of the immigrant lovers, seems conventional. At the end, these rival, dysfunctional families become reconciled, and they face a harmonious future. In spite of Barone's intended message about successful interfaith relations in Argentina, the happy ending of this farcical film is so staged and melodramatic as to appear inauthentic.

Conclusion

Demographic data from Argentina and the United States over the past sixty years confirm a trend toward increased integration of Jews into the fiber of society, from parental condemnation of interfaith relations among first-generation immigrants to full acceptance in the present. In fact, a number of sources predict that the increasingly high trend toward intermarriage may eventually lead to the demise of Jewishness in these countries.[15] Films related to the early immigration period, both in rural Argentina and in the urban United States, reveal the directors' efforts to speak to their own contemporaries. There are some noticeable differences: Argentine films reflect the impact of ongoing political and economic factors that rocked the country at crucial historical moments and had a negative impact on the private lives of individuals. Argentine rural settings, where first-generation immigrant Jews interact romantically with Gentiles, eventually leading to elopement, have no equivalent in US cinema.

US movies involving interfaith relations are more concerned with the behavioral traits and lifestyles of the characters, and with the preservation of Jewish traditions. While stock figures such as the nebbish, the dominant Jewish mother, and the biased Gentile parent-in-law (absent, prone to drinking, prejudiced) are featured in both Argentine and US films, cinematic portrayals of the WASP and his/her romantic attachment to the Jew are exclusive to American films. In the twenty-first century some of the racial and ethnic differences persist, but they do not threaten the solidity of the couples' attachments. On the contrary, personal compatibilities tend to override all other differences.

Notes

1. The cast of the films included here are listed at the end of this essay according to the directors' names, along with the films' names and dates of production.

2. Many of the US films that center on interfaith romantic relations do so directly or indirectly, with varying degrees of success, as some of them follow stereotypes: *Exodus* (dir. Elia Kazan, 1960); *The King of the Roaring Twenties* (dir. Joseph Newman, 1961); *Cast a Giant Shadow* (dir. Sidney Lumets, 1964); *No Way to Treat a Lady* (dir. Jack Smight, 1968); *Portnoy's Complaint* (dir. Ernest Lehman, 1972); *American Pop* (dir. Raph Bakshi, 1981); *Eyewitness* (dir. Peter Yates, 1981); *Chariots of Fire* (dir. Hugh Hudson, 1981), *Sopie's Choice* (dir. Alan J. Pakula, 1982); *The Big Chill* (dir. Lawrence Kasdan, 1983); *Keeping the Faith* (dir. Edward Norton, 2000).

3. Intermarriage rates in the United States: before 1970, 13 percent; 1997–2011, 47 percent. Of all married Jews, 31 percent are intermarried, and 33 percent of children in intermarriages are raised as Jews. According to "Key Jewish Population Statistics," Jews make up roughly 2 percent of the (US) population. Of the 14.4 million Jews throughout the world, around 6.5 million live in the United States and 5.7 million live in Israel. http://www.interfaithfamily.com/news_and_opinion/synagogues_and_the_jewish_community/Jewish_Intermarriage_Statistics. Then, in descending order, are France, Canada, the United Kingdom, Russia, and Argentina (*Interfaith*, Spring 2011).

4. Baron Maurice de Hirsch (1831–1896) was the founder of the Jewish Colonization Association (JCA or ICA), created in 1891 to facilitate the mass emigration of Jews from Russia and other East European countries by settling them in agricultural colonies on lands purchased by the committee in North and South America, especially Argentina and Brazil. In 1889 the ICA sought to assist Jewish immigrants in Argentina by creating a number of agricultural settlements in the north of the country.

5. *An American Tail*, directed by Don Bluth in 1986. While emigrating to the United States, a young Russian mouse gets separated from his family and must search for them while trying to survive in a new country. Its sequel, *An American Tail 2: Fievel Goes West*, is a 1991 animated Western produced by Steven Spielberg. The film follows the story of a family of Jewish Russian mice who emigrate to the Wild West.

6. Adapted from a successful Broadway play by Anne Nichols, the film was immensely popular, although it received poor reviews at the time.

7. *The Jolson Story* (1946), with Larry Parks, has a similar plot. Sam Raphaelson transformed his story "The Day of Atonement" (1922) into a successful Broadway play, *The Jazz Singer* (1925). It was adapted for the screen in 1927 as *The Jazz Singer*, directed by Alan Crosland and starring Al Jolson. Later adaptations were directed by Michael Curtiz in 1952, with Danny Thomas; Ralph Nelson in 1959, with Jerry Lewis and Molly Picon (a television version); and Fred Sears in 1956 (a looser version titled *Don't Knock the Rock*). See Goldman, *An American Jewish Story through Cinema*.

8. A number of films on this topic center around food and dinner table conversations.

9. Baron, "*Keeping the Faith*: A Multicultural *Jazz Singer*."

10. Daniel Burman's *Waiting for the Messiah* (2000) interweaves a similar scene, in which Ariel's mother has her purse snatched away in broad daylight, with a parallel story of Santamaría (not discussed in this paper), a clerk who loses his job in a bank and survives by returning stolen wallets for a voluntary fee. Both stories relate to the damaging effects of globalization.

11. *Two Lovers* was inspired by a story by Fyodor Dostoyevsky ("White Nights"). It was directed by James Gray and adapted from a screenplay by James Gray and Richard Menello.

12. Of the movie directors, five out of the twelve Argentines are Jewish, while all the American directors are Jewish.

13. The original version of *The Heartbreak Kid* is based on a story by Jay Friedman and a screenplay by Neil Simon. The 1990 remake is very different from the original.

14. This farce features exaggerated characters exhibiting some of the peculiarities drawn from the *grotesco criollo*—a century-old Argentine theater subgenre that acquired new meaning in subsequent historical periods. Here we find a preoccupation with personal identity, Mafia entanglements, sexual maneuvers, and rampant corruption, displayed in a lavish crescendo. Armando Discépolo, the highest exponent of *grotesco criollo*, in musing about his characters, said that "upon knowing the smallness of their destinies, the enormity of their pretensions seemed absurd" (*La Nación*, 1934).

15. See www.simpletoremember.com/vitals/world-jewish-population.htm. See also https://en.wikipedia.org/wiki/Jewish_population_by_country.

Works Cited

Argentine Films

Aristarian, Adolfo, dir. *Un lugar en el mundo* (*A Place in the World*). Perf. Federico Luppi and Cecilia Roth. 1992.
Barone, Daniel, dir. *Cohen vs. Rosi* (*Cohen vs. Rossi*). Perf. Ariel Cohen and Carla Rosi. 1988.
Burman, Daniel, dir. *Derecho de Familia* (*Family Law*). Perf. Daniel Hendler, Arturo Goetz, and Adriana Aizemberg. 2006.
———. *Esperando al Mesías* (*Waiting for the Messiah*). Perf. Daniel Hendler, Héctor Alterio, Melina Petriella. 2000.

de la Torre, Raúl, dir. *Pobre mariposa* (*Poor Butterfly*). Perf. Graciela Borges and Fernando Fernán Gómez. 1986.
Jusid, Juan José, dir. *Los gauchos judíos* (*The Jewish Gauchos*). Perf. Pepe Soriano and China Zorrilla. 1975.
Menis, María Victoria, dir. *La cámara oscura* (*Camera Obscura*). Perf. Mirta Bogdasarian and Fernando Arman. 2008.
Mignogna, Eduardo, dir. *Sol de otoño* (*Autumn Sun*). Perf. Norma Aleandro and Federico Luppi. 1996.
Milewicz, Eduardo, dir. *Samy y yo* (*Sammy and I*). Perf. Ricardo Darín and Angie Cepeda. 2002.
Winograd, Ariel, dir. *Mi primera boda* (*My First Wedding*). Perf. Natalia Oreiro and Daniel Hendler. 2011.

US Films

Allen, Woody, dir. *Annie Hall*. Perf. Woody Allen and Diane Keaton. 1977.
Apatow, Judd, dir. *This Is 40*. Perf. Paul Rudd and Leslie Mann. 2012.
Crosland, Alan, dir. *The Jazz Singer*. Perf. Al Jolson and Richard Tucker. 1927.
Fleischer, Richard, dir. *The Jazz Singer*. Perf. Neil Diamond, Lucy Arnaz, and Lawrence Olivier. 1980.
Fogel, Brian, dir. *Jewtopia*. Perf. Ivan Sergei and Joel More. 2012.
Golan, Menachem, dir. *Over the Brooklyn Bridge*. Perf. Elliott Gould, Cid Caesar, and Margaux Hemingway. 1984.
Gray, James, dir. *Two Lovers*. Perf. Joaquin Phoenix, Gwyneth Paltrow, and Roberta Rosselini. 2008.
Jewison, Norman, dir. *Fiddler on the Roof*. Perf. Chaim Topol and Norma Crane. 1971.
Levinson, Barry, dir. *Liberty Heights*. Perf. Joe Mantegna, Adrien Brody, and Ben Foster. 1999.
May, Elaine, dir. *The Heartbreak Kid*. Perf. Cybill Shepherd and Charles Grodin. 1972.
Mazursky, Paul, dir. *Willie and Phil*. Perf. Michael Ontkean, Ray Sharkey, and Margot Kidder. 1980.
Pollack, Sidney, dir. *The Way We Were*. Perf. Barbra Streisand and Robert Redford. 1973.
Weitz, Paul, dir. *Meet the Fockers*. Perf. Barbra Streisand, Dustin Hoffman, Robert De Niro, Blythe Danner, Ben Stiller, and Terry Polo. 2004.

Articles and Books

Baron, Lawrence. "*Keeping the Faith*: A Multicultural *Jazz Singer*." In *The Modern Jewish Experience in World Cinema*, ed. Lawrence Baron, 412–419. Hanover, NH: Brandeis University Press, 2011.
Goldman, Eric C. *An American Jewish Story through Cinema*. Austin: University of Texas Press, 2013.

AFTERWORD

Film Studies, Jewish Studies, Latin American Studies

NAOMI LINDSTROM

The essays in this volume cover a still-emerging category of cinema. The films discussed appeared between 1974 and 2012; these dates are a reminder of just how recent a development is the treatment of Jewish themes in Latin American film. The fifteen authors—who to varying degrees represent film studies, Jewish studies, and Latin American studies—have examined a selection of movies in Spanish, Portuguese, English, and German, with some Yiddish and Ladino. The movies are in most cases professionally made fiction films but also include three outright documentaries, some films on the border between fiction and documentary, and a collection of homemade movies. The films that the authors have chosen for analysis are, with few exceptions, made along realistic lines, a point to which I will return later. Read together, the essays provide readers with an informative and wide-ranging view of Jewish Latin American filmmaking up to the present.

 The title of the volume may prompt the reader to wonder in what sense a motion picture may be considered Jewish. Is the fundamental criterion the prominent appearance of figures—whether fictional characters or the human beings portrayed in a documentary—identified as Jews? What if the characters are identified as Jewish, perhaps by their names or other characters' assertions, but their Jewishness never becomes a theme of the movie (a question whose complexities are brought to the fore by Amy Kaminsky in her essay on "incidental" Jewishness)? Does the director's background figure into the equation? (Graciela Michelotti points out the non-Jewish identity of the director of the film she discusses.) Conversely, would a film be Jewish if it focused on the struggle of a non-Jew to become a Talmudist? Do the audience and the circumstances of a film's reception affect its Jewishness? For example, did *The Ten Commandments* (1956) become a more Christian film when shown as a fundraiser for churches and a more Jewish film when Jewish families went to see it? What if a film explains to viewers all its Jewish cultural references, in what Amy Kaminsky in her essay calls a "pedagogy of Jewishness"? Does that make it less Jewish than a film whose scriptwriters assume that their audience will be familiar with Jewish culture?

Each contributor could be said to be operating with a different implicit definition of what constitutes Jewish film. In some cases, the authors select films that make Jewishness an overt theme. Jerry Carlson, for example, studies three linked films by Daniel Burman (Argentina) in which the various complications of the protagonist's Jewish identity provide much of the subject matter. Carlson analyzes Burman's work together with three equally "Jewishly marked" films by Woody Allen. Some other contributors follow the same strategy of examining movies that continuously signal the Jewishness of their characters and settings.

At the same time, many of the other scholars in this collection prefer to study films in which Jewish references draw less attention to themselves. In a number of instances, Jewish matters are important, but share the stage with multiple thematic concerns. Of the topics that coexist with Jewishness, among the most prominent throughout the volume are the shaping and reshaping of memories and the relations between history and memory. The contributors consider how memories are constructed, function within a family or society, and are transmitted across generations, edited, and revised over time. Another topic that surfaces repeatedly in the volume is the significance attributed to items of material culture, especially photographs, Jewish books, and ritual objects. As might be expected, the perennial question of "Who is a Jew?" is either an overt or an underlying concern in a number of the essays.

The volume opened with "Out of the Shadows: María Victoria Menis's *Camera Obscura*," by Graciela Michelotti. This critic focuses on the 2008 Argentine film, based on a short story by Angélica Gorodischer, in which the Jewish agricultural colonies of Argentina serve as a backdrop for the story of a woman who overcomes a lifetime of being kept out of the picture. Both the protagonist's family of origin and her husband and children define her as an example of physical ugliness who should remain as invisible as possible. A visiting photographer recognizes her inner beauty and long-suppressed independence of spirit; he first draws her out as a luminous portrait subject and then escapes with her, to the astonishment of her family.

In the original short fiction, an image that the photographer made of the wife before eloping with her becomes charged with varying meanings decades later. A conformist male grandchild believes that the photograph should be hidden, along with his grandmother's forbidden love, while his spouse, more appreciative of the oppressed wife's rebellion, has it framed and displayed. Michelotti compares the film and the short story with a particular focus on photographs and the meanings that viewers assign to them. Her analysis is greatly strengthened by drawing on such theoretical studies as *Family Photographs* by Julia Hirsch and *Family Frames* by Marianne Hirsch.

Elissa J. Rashkin in her "Intercultural Dilemmas: Performing Jewish Identities in Contemporary Mexican Cinema," adapted to the study of Jewishness the concepts of performance developed by Judith Butler in her much-cited *Gender Trouble* and by other theorists working along similar lines. She analyzed how competing definitions of Jewishness are performed in two Mexican films, *My Mexican Shivah* (2007; dir. Alejandro Springall), which quickly became a fixture of Jewish film series in the United States, and the 2008 *Nora's Will* (dir. Mariana Chenillo). Both movies combine somber and comedic elements, though in very different ways, and center on rituals of mourning. Rashkin's discussion of the performance of Jewishness is among the most carefully executed in the volume; of the contributors, she and Vohnsen have paid the closest attention to the specifically cinematic aspects of the films that they discuss. While Rashkin's analysis focuses on the similarities between the two films, they also diverge in significant ways. *Nora's Will* unfolds more slowly and is more sentimental than the rambunctious *My Mexican Shivah*. In addition, the latter, which has magical-realist moments, is the only film discussed in the volume to depart significantly from the conventions of realism.

In one of the most conceptually stimulating of the essays, Amy Kaminsky has drawn out some of the complications surrounding Jewish film by studying examples that strain, and quite possibly expand, the periphery of the category. She begins with some reflections on the difficulty of defining Jewish film. In her own analyses, Kaminsky veers away from the overtly Jewish-themed films favored by many of the contributors and instead proposes that even fleeting allusions may generate significance in a film. She cites an unexpected test case, the 2013 *Thesis on a Homicide* by the Jewish Argentine director Hernán Goldfrid, in which the mere utterance of the surname of a minor character can "function as a reminder that Jews, too, live here." In two other Argentine films, Jewish directors Paula Markovich and Julia Solomonoff focus primarily on sexual and political marginalization, but weave in a subtheme of the occasional awkwardness of being Jewish in a society where Catholicism is widely assumed to be the norm. Kaminsky then goes on to analyze in greater detail the work of Fabián Bielinsky, the Argentine director known for *Nine Queens* (2000), an ingenious tale of con artists. In Kaminsky's viewing, a brief scene in *Nine Queens* "is highly suggestive of the ways that Jewishness both permeates Argentina and yet remains inassimilable." The acute observations in this essay could beneficially serve as the point of departure for future analyses of films that are subtly tinged with Jewishness.

Jeanine Meerapfel, who was born in Argentina to German Jewish parents and has pursued a successful directorial and screenwriting career in Germany, is the only filmmaker to have two essays in this volume devoted in their entirety to her work, which tends to feature the aftereffects of collective trauma. Daniela Goldfine, in her "*My German Friend* and the Jewish Argentine/German 'Mnemo-Historic' Context," examines Meerapfel's semi-autobiographical *My German Friend* (2012), applying Daniel Levy's concept of mnemo-history, which has to do with how memories of particular aspects of history are created and evolve over time. The film, whose plot follows a friendship and love affair through three decades and two continents, brings together the phenomena of Jews seeking refuge from Nazism and ex-Nazis seeking refuge from justice, both in Argentina. The central characters, the daughter of German Jewish émigrés and the son of an SS officer, are driven by a need to distance themselves from the familial past, moving between Argentina and Germany and throwing themselves into causes. Goldfine praises Meerapfel for her success in locating *My German Friend* at a "crossroads where languages, nationalities, cultures, identities, temporalities, and geographies intersect" and for applying, through creative means, the concept of mnemo-history to second-generation survivors and the "born guilty" descendants of Nazis.

In "Dispersed Friendships: Jeanine Meerapfel's *The Girlfriend*," Patricia Nuriel analyzes a 1998 film in which the Jewish identity of one of the two main characters is used as a theme, but this is only one element in a broader picture. Nuriel examines how the film links two outstanding examples of traumatic injustices and their persistence in memory: the Holocaust (and current-day anti-Semitism) and the Proceso launched by the Argentine military dictatorship of 1976–1983, during which thousands of citizens were detained, tortured, and "disappeared." Here both Meerapfel as filmmaker and Nuriel as critic enter into the expanding comparative study of how disturbing and unjust events become processed over time in a society's memory and continue to exert influence decades later. The Holocaust and the Proceso are examined jointly in, to cite a scholarly example, the essays in the 2001 volume edited by Pablo M. Dreizik, *Memoria de las cenizas* (*Memory of the Ashes*); the much-noted novel *Daughter of Silence* (original *Hija del si-*

lencio, 1999; English translation by Darrell B. Lockhart, 2012) by Manuela Fingueret of Argentina is a creative juxtaposition of the two events.

In "Revisiting the AMIA Bombing in Marcos Carnevale's *Anita*," Mirna Vohnsen examines a well-received 2009 film particularly memorable for the performance of the lead actress, a nonprofessional with Down syndrome. Much of the film takes place the day of, and the first few chaotic days after, a car bomb destroyed the AMIA, the Jewish community center in central Buenos Aires. While *Anita* has often been screened in specifically Jewish spaces and the protagonist's family is Jewish, Vohnsen's analysis on the whole shifts attention away from the film's Jewish themes. She shows that in the film the characters' search for missing relatives following the AMIA bombing parallels family members' quest to locate those "disappeared" during the 1976–1983 military dictatorship. In this way the destruction of the AMIA becomes understood as a nationwide trauma, not just one affecting the Jewish community.

In "*The Year My Parents Went on Vacation*: A Jewish Journey in the Land of Soccer," Alejandro Meter discusses the 2006 Brazilian film (dir. Cao Hamburger) that earned international acclaim, showing the links between two of its themes, Jewish identity and soccer. (The film opens in the lead-up to the 1970 World Cup and ends shortly after Brazil's victory.) For the purposes of this particular analysis, Meter accords lesser prominence to the film's other great topic, the repression exercised by the Brazilian military government. He advances the idea that, for the child protagonist, "The recovery of his Jewish roots . . . [is] directly linked to his passion for football." The resulting essay is unmistakably the work of a soccer aficionado. Meter draws upon soccer scholarship, which has experienced exponential growth in recent years, and his essay includes considerable information about the game in its many variants, from a toy version through different amateur levels and on to the World Cup, in order to show how the protagonist discovers his Jewishness through the sport that is considered a national religion in Brazil: soccer.

In "Coming of Age in Two Films from Argentina and Uruguay," Carolina Rocha discusses jointly two similar films, one Argentine and one Uruguayan: *Cheesehead: My First Ghetto* (2006), directed by Ariel Winograd, and *Acne* (2008), whose director was Federico Veiroj. Each film follows a series of events that contribute to the maturation of a male adolescent from a well-off Jewish household. In both cases, the adult characters are consistently faulted for their reluctance to face troubling issues and their willingness to sacrifice their values for a conflict-free existence; in contrast, the central adolescents still maintain their sense of justice and ethics untarnished.

The two films' portrayal of adolescents struggling toward maturity and dealing with moral dilemmas and questions of self-esteem are not outstandingly original, though both movies appear to have been respectfully received by critics. Nonetheless, this essay is notable as a very clear example of a specific approach, and it follows this particular critic's characteristic strategy of approaching Jewish Latin American film by selecting for examination movies in which the director is Jewish and the central characters, settings, and themes are all stamped as Jewish; in the two films discussed here, the identity of the male adolescents is quickly established through the well-worn strategy of a scene set in a restroom. Rocha makes a point of the similarity between the lives of the directors and the fictional existence of the main characters, asserting that "the young characters are first and foremost alter egos of the directors themselves." Besides evincing Rocha's predilection for realistic films with unambiguous markers of Jewishness, this essay exemplifies another of this critic's favored procedures, studying jointly a selection of films whose protagonists share some feature, such as childhood, adolescence, Jewishness, or a complicated masculinity.

The essay by Ernesto Livon-Grosman, "Waiting for the Messiah: The Super 8mm Films of Alberto Salomón," has offered an unexpected reminder that filmmaking is a broad phenomenon that extends beyond the institutionally distributed films that we usually think of as film. Livon-Grosman, who is a documentary maker as well as a scholar, expanded his research on visual representations of 1960s–1970s Argentine families to include, among other sources, home movies shot in Super 8mm. His search led him to the films of Alberto Salomón, which, although homemade and originally screened only for family and friends, developed fictional narratives and were "intensively choreographed and edited." In the work of Salomón, a Jewish Greek immigrant to Argentina, Livon-Grosman has discovered an effort to process private turmoil, including the filmmaker's difficult relationship with his father and his alcohol dependency, while bringing in elements of social critique, most notably a jaundiced outlook on Judaism and organized religion generally. In his discussion of Salomón's homemade films, Livon-Grosman explores a number of issues, including the coming together of public and private spheres, hybridity in art (footage from borrowed and rented films is spliced into Salomón's scripted narratives), Jewish immigrant identities, filmmaking as therapy, and the constantly shifting interrelations between memory and social history. Livon-Grosman's "Waiting for the Messiah" is unique among the essays in this volume in its focus on cinematic production that is not merely independent but a clear example of outsider art. The article offers not only a thoughtful analysis of an unusual body of work but also an excellent basic introduction to an area of scholarly inquiry—research on home and amateur film—that will be unfamiliar to many readers.

Ariana Huberman's "Geographic Isolation and Jewish Religious Revival in Two Contemporary Latin American Documentaries" brings together several thematic concerns. As well as analyzing the two documentaries that are the announced topic of her essay, she discusses print publications by the directors of both films. They are the Cuban American anthropologist Ruth Behar, who in her 2002 documentary *Adió kerida* (*Goodbye Dear Love*) follows her familial connection to the Sephardic community of Cuba, and the Peruvian photographer Lorry Salcedo Mitrani, best known internationally for the 2009 *El fuego eterno* (*The Fire Within* in US release), which follows the struggle of an Amazonian community to be recognized as Jews by the established Jewish world. While examining the work of Behar and Salcedo, Huberman introduces isolated Jewish communities whose members' identity may be questioned because of patrilineal descent, syncretistic observances, and, to put it bluntly, mestizo ancestry. The essay looks at the portrayal of objects and photographs in both the films and the books produced by the authors to highlight the problem of exoticism in the process of telling the story of these communities' survival and their religious revival.

Taking a comparative and highly evaluative and critical approach, Tzvi Tal in his "Negotiating Jewish and Palestinian Identities in Latin American Cinema" has examined *Legado* (*Legacy*), an Argentine documentary about Eastern European Jewish immigrants to the agricultural colonies and their subsequent history, presented as a story of success achieved despite hardship; a film by renowned Chilean director Miguel Littin that combines invented and documentary elements to tell the story of the sizable Palestinian community of Chile; and, finally, a Spanish comedy about a family of Jewish oddballs in Spain and the daughter's Palestinian suitor, who heartwarmingly earns acceptance in the household.

The unstated premise underlying Tal's discussion is that film should deliver a social critique, sharpen awareness of historical processes, and encourage a demand for structural change where needed. By these criteria, all three films have been weighed and found wanting. While the first two films show Jews and Palestinians very differently—the Jews are depicted as the quintessence of book learning, while the Palestinians are portrayed as the bearers of a purely oral folkloric culture—in both cases the result is to show the immigrants and their descendants as innocuous and plucky. The broader historical background, whether in the old country or the new, is edited out, and the new arrivals to Argentina and Chile appear as humble people devoted to the unobjectionable goals of persevering in the face of adversity and building a better life for their families. The Spanish film combines madcap comedy with the promotion of intercultural tolerance. Tal nonetheless faults the film, asserting that, in the course of endorsing the brotherhood of humanity, it employs stereotypes that are the residue of imperialistic ways of thought.

Tal's verdicts are consistent with his criteria for evaluating films, but one may still wonder whether he is setting a requirement not well suited to films from utilitarian genres. The documentary *Legado* (*Legacy*), clearly created for use in classrooms and community centers, appears to have as its goals the education of audiences, including schoolchildren or those unfamiliar with the subject matter, and the preservation of a visual and audio record of the memories of the Argentine immigrants' children while they are still living. Perhaps the standards should be made more flexible to take into account what a given film is striving to accomplish.

In "From a Dream to Reality: Representations of Israel in Contemporary Jewish Latin American Film," Amalia Ran argues that, as decades and conflicts grind on, Israel is losing its monolithic status as the touchstone for Jewish identity, yet continues to play many diverse roles in the diasporic imagination. Ran briefly discusses four films, noting various trends. She finds that Latin American directors and screenwriters have been persistently depicting Israel as an exotic land with wish-fulfilling properties. An example is their propensity to represent the Dead Sea and other desert filming locations as "meditative and healing places, dominated by serenity and solitude." Though Ran shows the range of views of Israel to be broader than in the past, she ended her essay by expressing disappointment over the paucity of critical analyses of relations between Jews in the diaspora and the current-day state of Israel.

"On Becoming a Movie" is an intensely personal account, by the noted novelist and essayist Ilan Stavans, of the emergence of Jewish themes in Mexican film. Stavans situates himself as the son of the celebrated Mexican actor Abraham Stavchansky, a denizen of the Mexican cultural scene, and a writer whose work has been adapted for the screen (the 2007 film *My Mexican Shivah*, analyzed by Elissa J. Rashkin in her essay "Intercultural Dilemmas" in this volume). He writes from the perspective of an involved and strongly opinionated insider. His essay chronicles a journey from an era in which Mexican film was nearly devoid of Jewish themes, through an early introduction of the subject matter that left him only partially satisfied (Arturo Ripstein's 1974 Inquisition drama *The Holy Office*), and the gradual appearance of more complex treatments.

The final section of the volume offers two comparative examinations of

Argentine and US films. "Jewish Urban Space in the Films of Daniel Burman and Woody Allen," by the film scholar and director Jerry Carlson, zeroes in on the two artists who most quickly spring to mind when one thinks of Jewish directors in Argentina and the United States; Burman has at times been introduced to Anglophone audiences, in a very approximate analogy, as "the Argentine Woody Allen." Both artists have long attracted notice for the markedly Jewish identity of their main characters, but Carlson explores the more subtle phenomenon of Jewish urban space in the filmmakers' work. He draws on Michel de Certeau's conceptualization of living "down below," amid the "swarming activity" of the city, where boundaries and norms often break down. He then links three of Burman's films from the early twenty-first century with three thematically similar Woody Allen movies from the 1970s and 1980s and proceeds to analyze them in a side-by-side arrangement.

While the comparative approach is the most obvious feature of Carlson's essay, perhaps its most original contribution is its ability to shift readers' focus away from the perplexed and conflicted male protagonists, who so often appear on screen or are heard in voiceover and can easily monopolize attention, and toward the broader concept of Jewish urban space. The author examines a variety of Jewish spaces: private, public, poor, posh, recent post-immigrant, and assimilated, as well as Jewish characters venturing insecurely into milieux that are not at all Jewish. The essay exhibits an outlook that is decidedly more media studies in tone than most of the other contributions, with the added element of spatial studies.

"Interfaith Relations between Jews and Gentiles in Argentine and US Cinema," by Nora Glickman, a pioneering figure in the study of Jewish Latin American film, stands somewhat apart from the rest of the contributions to the volume. While the other collaborators draw upon theory and analyze a very limited number of films, Glickman's article presents a historical chronology that includes twenty-five movies featuring Jewish/non-Jewish couples. She compares selected US films with Argentine movies that feature a similar generation, period, or theme. Glickman has identified films as Jewish by their characters and the perennial Jewish concern over intermarriage. She regards films as an indicator of the social outlook on this phenomenon, which over the decades has come to seem less fraught with trouble. The films Glickman's article covers span the early twentieth century to the present; they show how attitudes toward intermarriage have evolved over time from parental condemnation of interfaith relations to progressive Jewish assimilation and increased integration into society. One important difference she notices is that while Argentine films reflect the impact of ongoing political and economic factors during crucial historical moments, US films involving interfaith relations are more concerned with the behavioral lifestyles of the characters and with the preservation of Jewish traditions. Glickman has taken pains to be inclusive, discussing same-sex couples as well as straight relationships ranging from contented to strife-ridden, and Jewish characters paired with genetically and culturally diverse partners, from African Americans, though various ethnicities, to blonde and blue-eyed WASPs.

A look back at all the essays together reveals a variety of approaches but also some commonalities. With the exception of *My Mexican Shivah*, in which two spirits, visible only to the viewer, comment upon the human characters, the films discussed are essentially realistic. Yet not all Jewish Latin American filmmakers are realists; the cult favorite Alejandro Jodorowsky (1929; Chile and France) favors an allegorical approach tinged with surrealism, yet both his origin and his kabbalistic learning identify him as a Jewish creator, though his Jewishness is not an overt theme in his films. Here one might pause to wonder whether in the future the discussion of Jewish Latin American films will eventually branch out more into the study of subterranean currents of Jewish thought or outlook in films without the overt markers of Jewishness that it is easy for realist movies to supply.

This volume not only has presented readers with an abundant supply of information about Jewish Latin American film from its emergence in the 1970s to the present day but also has provided them with a good sense of the principal issues being developed and debated by scholars of the phenomenon. Readers should also find the filmography at the end of the volume invaluable as they seek to expand their firsthand knowledge of this emerging body of film.

Works Cited

Dreizik, Pablo M., ed. *Memoria de las cenizas*. Buenos Aires: Patrimonio Argentino, 2001.

Fingueret, Manuela. *Daughter of Silence*. Trans. Darrell B. Lockhart. Lubbock: Texas Tech University Press, 2012.

Jewish Latin American Filmography

Argentina

18-J. Dir. Israel Adrián Caetano, Carlos Sorín, Daniel Burman, Alberto Lecchi, Alejandro Doria, Lucía Cedrón, Juan Bautista Stagnaro, Mauricio Wainrot, Marcelo Schapces, Adrián Suar. Aleph Productions. 2004.

36 justos, Los (*36 Righteous Men*). Dir. Daniel Burman. 2011.

abrazo partido, El (*Lost Embrace*). Dir. Daniel Burman. BD Cine/Wanda Visión S.A./Instituto Nacional de Cine y Artes Audiovisuales (INCAA)/Paradis Films/Stories. 2004.

amiga, La (*The Girlfriend*). Dir. Jeanine Meerapfel. Jupiter Communications. 1988.

amigo alemán, El (*My German Friend*). Dir. Jeanine Meerapfel. Geißendörfer Film- und Fernsehproduktion/Jempsa/Malena Filmproduktion/Westdeutscher Rundfunk. 2012.

Anita. Dir. Marcos Carnevale. Millecento Cine/INCAA/Shazam S.A. 2009.

antena, La (*The Aerial*). Dir. Esteban Sapir. LaDopleA. 2007.

aura, El (*The Aura*). Dir. Fabián Bielinsky. Buena Vista. 2005.

Bajo bandera (*Under Flag*). Dir. Juan José Jusid. Film Suez/INCAA/Prisma Films/Surf Films. 1997.

Bessarabia a Entre Ríos, De. Dir. Pedro Banchik. 2014.

cámara oscura, La (*Camera Obscura*). Dir. María Victoria Menis. Sophie Dulac Productions/Todo Cine S.A. 2008.

camino del sur, El (*The Road South*). Dir. Juan Bautista Stagnaro. Art Film 80/CFS. 1988.

Cara de queso: Mi primer ghetto (*Cheese Head: My First Ghetto*). Dir. Ariel Winograd. Tresplanos Cine/Tornasol Films. 2006.

Cartas para Jenny (*Letters for Jenny*). Dir. Diego Musiak. INCAA/San Luis Cine. 2007.

Cohen vs. Rosi. Dir. Daniel Barone. Patagonik Film Group/Pol-Ka Producciones. 1988.

Cómo ganar enemigos (*How to Win Enemies*). Dir. Gabriel Lichtmann. 2015.

crisantemo estalla en cinco esquinas, Un (*A Chrysanthemum Bursts in Cincoesquinas*). Dir. Daniel Burman. BD Cine. 1998.

Debajo del mundo (*Under the Earth*). Dir. Beda Docampo Feijoo, Juan Bautista Stagnaro. 1988.

Derecho de familia (*Family Law*). Dir. Daniel Burman. BD Cine/Classic Film/INCAA/Paradis Films/Wanda Visión S.A. 2006.
Diablo (*Devil*). Dir. Nicanor Loreti. 2011.
Diapasón (*Metronome*). Dir. Jorge Polaco. 1986.
espera, La (*The Wait*). Dir. Fabián Bielinsky. 1983.
Esperando al Mesías (*Waiting for the Messiah*). Dir. Daniel Burman. Astrolabio Producciones/Classic Films/BD Cine. 2000.
Esta es mi vida (*This Is My Life*). Dir. Román Viñoly Barreto. Argentina Sono Film. 1952.
Felicidades (*Congratulations*). Dir. Lucho Bender. Bendercine S.A./Tango Films. 2000.
Gatica "el mono" (*Gatica "the Ape"*). Dir. Leonardo Favio. Choila S.R.L. 1993.
gauchos judíos, Los (*The Jewish Gauchos*). Dir. Juan José Jusid. Film Cuatro. 1975.
gusto a rabia, Con (*The Taste of Rage*). Dir. Fernando Ayala. Aries Cinematográfica Argentina/Artistas Argentinos Asociados. 1965.
Hacer patria (*Forging a Nation*). David Blaustein. Zafra Difusión S.A./Tornasol Films. 2007.
Hermanas (*Sisters*). Dir. Julia Solomonoff. Cruzdelsur Zona Audiovisual/Tornasol Films/Patagonik Film Group/VideoFilmes. 2005.
hijo de la novia, El (*Son of the Bride*). Dir. Juan José Campanella. Pol-Ka Producciones/Jempsa/Patagonik Film Group/Tornasol Films. 2001.
Jevel Katz y sus paisanos (*Chevel Katz and his Landsmen*). Dir. Alejandro Vagnenkos. 2005.
Judíos en el espacio (*Jews in Space*). Dir. Gabriel Lichtmann. INCAA/Primer Plano Film Group. 2005.
Judíos por elección (*Jews by Choice*). Dir. Matilde Michanié. INCAA/2011.
Legado (*Legacy*). Dir. Vivian Imar, Marcelo Trotta. INCAA/Centro de Investigación Cinematográfica (CIC)/Internacional Raoul Wallenberg. 2004.
lugar en el mundo, Un (*A Place in the World*). Dir. Adolfo Aristarain. Cooperative/Transmundo Films. 1992.
Mar del Plata. Dir. Sebastian Dietsch, Ionathan Klajman. INCAA/Rebecca Films/Ovidio Cine. 2012.
Mi primera boda (*My First Wedding*). Dir. Ariel Winograd. Tresplanos Cine/Telefe Cine. 2011.
Mujeres de la Shoa (*Women of the Shoa*). Universidad de la Matanza/Museo del Holocausto—Buenos Aires. 2008.
Neró. Dir. Alberto Salomón. Arghellas Producciones. 1987.
NEY, nosotros, ellos y yo (*NEY, Us, Them and Me*). Dir. Nicolás Avruj. El Campo Cine S.R.L. 2015.
nido vacío, El (*Empty Nest*). Dir. Daniel Burman. BD Cine/Wanda Visión S.A. 2008.
Novias—Madrinas—15 años (*Brides—Mothers of the Bride—Sweet Fifteens*). Dir. Pablo Levy and Diego Levy. 2012.
Nueve reinas (*Nine Queens*). Dir. Fabián Bielinsky. SONY Pictures Classic. 2000.
Otro entre otros (*Another among Others*). Dir. Maximiliano Pelosi. WAP Productora. 2010.
Papirosen. Dir. Gastón Solnicki. Filmy Wiktora. 2011.
Pelota de trapo (*Ragged Ball*). Dir. Leopoldo Torres Ríos. Sociedad Independiente Filmadora Argentina. 1948.

Pobre mariposa (*Poor Butterfly*). Dir. Raúl de la Torre. Bensil Productions/Raúl de la Torre Producciones. 1986.
pogrom en Buenos Aires, Un (*A Pogrom in Buenos Aires*). Dir. Herman Szwarcbart. 2007.
Relatos salvajes (*Wild Tales*). Dir. Damián Szifron. Corner Producciones/El Deseo/INCAA/Instituto de la Cinematografía y de las Artes Audiovisuales/Kramer & Sigman/Telefe Cine. 2014.
rey del Once, El (*The Tenth Man*). Dir. Daniel Burman. BD Cine/Pasto/Telefe Cine/INCAA. 2016.
Samy y yo (*Sammy and I*). Dir. Eduardo Milewicz. Bulevares Producciones. 2002.
Simón, el hijo del pueblo (*Simon, the Son of the People*). Dir. Rolando Goldman, Julian Troksberg. 2013.
Sol de otoño (*Autumn Sun*). Dir. Eduardo Mignogna. V.C.C. 1996.
Subte-Polska. Dir. Alejandro Magnone. Asa Nisi Masa/INCAA/Stigliani & Mouriño Cine. 2016.
suerte en tus manos, La (*Luck Is in Your Hands*). Dir. Daniel Burman. Gullane Filmes/BD Cine/INCAA/Telefe Cine/Tornasol Films. 2011.
Tango: Una historia con judíos (*Tango: A Story with Jews*). Dir. Gabriel Pomeraniec. 25p Films. 2009.
Tiempo de valientes (*On Probation*). Dir. Damián Szifron. 20th Century Fox de Argentina/Chemo/INCAA/Kramer & Sigman Films/OK Films/Shok Films Argentina. 2005.
último traje, El (*The Last Suit*). Dir. Pablo Solarz. 2017.
Valentín. Dir. Alejandro Agresti. First Floor Features/De Productie/RWA/Patagonik Film Group/DMVB Films/Duque Films/Castelao Producciones/Surf Film/INCAA/Nederlands Fonds voor de Film/Rotterdams Fonds voor de Film en Audiovisuele Media. 2002.

Brazil

About Sugar Cane and Homecoming. Dir. Shaul Kesslassi. Ruth Diskin Films. 2008.
ano em que meus pais saíram de férias, O (*The Year My Parents Went on Vacation*). Dir. Cao Hamburger. Gullane Films/City Lights. 2006.
Judeu, O (*The Jew*). Dir. Jom Tob Azulay. Ministério da Cultura do Brasil/Embrafilme e Instituto Português de Arte Cinematográfica e Audiovisual/IPACA. 1996.
Novos Lares—Judeus de Nilópolis (*New Places—Jews from Nilopolis*). Dir. Radamés Vieira. Pro Sol. 2009.
Olga. Dir. Jayme Monjardim. Europa Filmes/Globo Filmes/Lumière/Nexus Cinema e Vídeo. 2004.
Tempos de Paz (*Peacetime*). Dir. Daniel Filho. Lereby Productions. 2009.

Chile

brindis, El (*To Life*). Dir. Shai Agosín. Agosin Films/Goliat Films. 2007.
Judíos en Chile: Emigrantes en el tiempo (*Jews in Chile: Emigrants in Time*). Dir. Cristian Leighton. 2002.

Mi vida con Carlos (*My Life with Carlos*). Dir. Germán Berger-Hertz. 2010.
viaje de Ana, El (*Anna's Journey*). Dir. Pamela Varela. 2002.

Israel/Argentina

Año que viene... en Argentina, El (*Next Year... in Argentina*). Dir. Jorge Gurvich, Shlomo Slutzky. 2005.
Like a Fish out of Water. Dir. Leonid Prudovsky. Television film. 2007.
Nekuda, psik. Dir. Shlomo Slutzky. Ruth Diskin Films. 2011.
Sin punto y aparte. Dir. Shlomo Slutzky. 2012.
Tercero en camino, El (*The Third One Is on Its Way*). Dir. Shlomo Slutzky. Ruth Diskin Films. 2008.

Mexico

beso a esta tierra, Un (*A Kiss to This Land*). Dir. Daniel Goldberg. National Center for Jewish Film (NCJF). 1995.
Cinco días sin Nora (*Nora's Will*). Dir. Mariana Chenillo. Cacerola Films/Fidecine/IMCINE. 2008.
Laberintos de la memoria (*Labyrinths of Memory*). Dir. Guita Schyfter. Producciones Arte Nuevo. 2007.
Morirse está en hebreo (*My Mexican Shivah*). Dir. Alejandro Springall. Goliat Films/Elevation Filmworks/IMCINE. 2007.
Novia que te vea (*Like a Bride*). Dir. Guita Schyfter. Fondo de Fomento a la Calidad Cinematográfica/Instituto Mexicano de Cinematografía (IMCINE)/Producciones Arte Nuevo. 1993.
Ocho candelas (*Eight Candles*). Dir. Sandro Halphen. Goliat Films/NXFLIX/Setton Sun Productions. 2002.
premio, El (*The Prize*). Dir. Paula Marcovitch. Fondo para la Producción Cinematográfica de Calidad (FOPROCINE)/IZ Films/Kung Works/Mille et Une Productions/Niko Film/Staron Film. 2011.
santo Oficio, El (*The Holy Inquisition*). Dir. Arturo Ripstein. IMCINE. 1973.
Te extraño (*I Miss You*). Dir. Fabián Hofman. IMCINE/FIDECINE/Fílmele Producciones/INCAA/IBERMEDIA. 2010.

Spain

Seres queridos (*Only Human*). Dir. Teresa de Pelegri and Dominic Harari. Tornasol Films. 2004.
último sefardí, El (*The Last Sephardic Jew*). Dir. Miguel Angelo Nieto. 2005.

United States

Abraham and Eugenia: Stories from Jewish Cuba. Dir. Bonnie Burt. Bonnie Burt Productions. 1995.

Adio Kerida. Dir. Ruth Behar. Women Make Movies. 2002.
Believers: Stories from Jewish Havana, The. Dir. Bonnie Burt. Bonnie Burt Productions. 1994.
Between Revolution and Tradition. Dir. Ruth Diskin. Ruth Diskin Films. 2001.
Expulsion and Memory: Descendants of the Hidden Jews. Dir. Simcha Jacobovici, Roger Pyke. National Center for Jewish Film. 1996.
Fire Within, The: Jews in the Amazonian Forest. Dir. Lorry Salcedo Mitrani. Ruth Diskin Films. 2008.
Glass House, The. Dir. Brad Marlowe. Write Angle Productions. 2006.
Havana Nagila: The Jews in Cuba. Dir. Laura Paull. Ergo Media Incorporated. 1995.
Jubanos: The Jews of Cuba. Dir. Milos S. Silber. Ruth Diskin Films. 2010.
Longing, The: The Forgotten Jews of South America. Dir. Gabriela Bohm. 2007.
Nuestros Desaparecidos (*Our Disappeared*). Dir. Juan Mandelbaum. New Day Films. 2008.
Tango desnudo (*Naked Tango*). Dir. Leonard Shrader. 1990.
Tijuana Jews. Dir. Isaac Artenstein. Cinewest. 2005.

Uruguay

Acné (*Acne*). Dir. Federico Veiroj. Control Z/Avalon Productions/Rizoma Films. 2008.
barrio de los judíos, El (*The Jewish Barrio*). Dir. Gonzalo Rodríguez Fábregas. 2011.
Mr. Kaplan. Dir. Álvaro Brechner. 2014.
Reus. Dir. Pablo Fernández, Alejandro Pi, and Eduardo Piñero. 2011.
Whisky. Dir. Juan Pablo Rebella, Pablo Stoll. Rizoma Films/Wanda Visión S.A. 2004.

Contributors

JERRY CARLSON is a specialist in narrative theory, global independent film, and the cinemas of the Americas. Professor Carlson is director of the Cinema Studies Program in the department of media and communication arts at City College CUNY. In addition, at the CUNY Graduate Center he is a member of the doctoral faculties of French, film studies, and comparative literature and a senior fellow at the Bildner Center for Western Hemispheric Studies. His current research is focused on how slavery and its legacy in the New World have been represented in film, literature, and music. He was educated at Williams College (BA) and the University of Chicago (MA and PhD).

NORA GLICKMAN is professor of Latin American literature at Queens College and at the Graduate Center, CUNY. Her latest book of narrative fiction, *Hilván de instantes*, follows *Uno de sus Juanes* and *Mujeres, memorias, malogros*. A few of her plays are collected in her *Bilingual Anthology of Theatre*. She is co-author of *Presencia del "inglés" en el teatro y el cine argentinos, Tradition and Innovation: Reflections on Latin American Jewish Writing, Argentine Jewish Theatre: A Critical Anthology,* and *Bridging Continents: Cinematic and Literary Representations of Spanish and Latin American Themes*. Nora Glickman is presently co-editor of *Enclave: Revista de creación literaria en español* and *Latin American Jewish Studies*.

DANIELA GOLDFINE is visiting assistant professor at the University of Wisconsin–River Falls. Her work has been published in several journals, and she is currently working on a manuscript on contemporary Jewish Argentine female artists. She is also co-editing a volume about gender and sexuality in Jewish Latin American cultural production. She received her

PhD from the department of Spanish and Portuguese studies, with a minor in feminist and critical sexuality studies, at the University of Minnesota.

ARIANA HUBERMAN is associate professor of Spanish at Haverford College. She has co-edited a book, *Memoria y representación: Configuraciones culturales y literarias en el imaginario judío latinoamericano*, with Alejandro Meter (2006). Her book *Gauchos and Foreigners: Glossing Culture and Identity in the Argentine Countryside* was published in 2011. She is co-editor of *Latin American Jewish Studies*. She is currently working on a manuscript on the presence of Jewish mysticism in Latin American cultural production.

AMY KAMINSKY is professor emerita of gender, women, and sexuality studies at the University of Minnesota. Trained in Spanish and Latin American literature, she is an interdisciplinary feminist scholar. Her books include *Reading the Body Politic* (1992), *Waterlilies: An Anthology of Spanish Women Writers* (1995), *After Exile: Writing the Latin American Diaspora* (1999), and *Argentina: Stories for a Nation* (2008).

NAOMI LINDSTROM is the Gale Family Foundation Professor in Jewish Arts and Culture, is professor of Spanish and Portuguese, and directs the Gale Collaborative for the Study of Jewish Life in the Americas at the Schusterman Center for Jewish Studies of the University of Texas at Austin. Her books include *The Social Conscience of Latin American Writing* and *Jewish Issues in Argentine Literature*. She is the coordinator of the electronic mailing list of the Latin American Jewish Studies Association (LAJSA).

ERNESTO LIVON-GROSMAN, who was born in Buenos Aires, Argentina, lives in the United States, where he teaches film and literature at Boston College. He has directed several documentaries: *Cartoneros* (http://www.der.org/films/cartoneros.html), *Brascó* (www.brascodoc.com), *Salomón* (http://vimeo.com/surynorth/salomonen), and, more recently, *MADI* (https://vimeo.com/surynorth/madien). Livon-Grosman is the editor of *Lezama Lima: Selections* (2005) and is co-editor with Cecilia Vicuña of the *Oxford Anthology of Latin American Poetry* (2010). He is now working on a feature documentary on the work of American composer Christian Wolff.

ALEJANDRO METER received his PhD from the University of Pittsburgh. His specializations include dictatorial and postdictatorial fiction of the Southern Cone, migration and exile, and Jewish Latin American studies. His research focuses primarily on Jewish Latin America, with an emphasis on Southern Cone cultural production. He edited *Literatura judía en América Latina* (2001) and a special volume of *Revista Iberoamericana*, and co-edited *Memoria y representación: Configuraciones culturales y literarias en el imaginario judío latinoamericano* (2006) with Ariana Huberman.

GRACIELA MICHELOTTI teaches in the Haverford College Spanish department. She received her PhD from the University of Pennsylvania, writing a dissertation on the new historical Latin American novel. Her research interests are the connections between twentieth-century literature and history, Latin American film studies, women writers, actors and directors from Latin America and Spain, and twentieth-century theater. In 2008 she published an annotated edition of *La Quijotita y su prima* by José Joaquín Fernández de Lizardi.

PATRICIA NURIEL is associate professor of Spanish in the department of modern languages, literatures, and cultures at Wofford College. She obtained her PhD from Arizona State University and her MA from the Hebrew University of Jerusalem, Israel. Her research work and publications focus on twentieth-century Latin American literature and culture, in particular Jewish Latin American fiction.

AMALIA RAN is a research fellow at the Sverdlin Institute for Latin American History and Culture at Tel Aviv University. She received her PhD from the department of Spanish and Portuguese at the University of Maryland, College Park, and worked as an assistant professor in the department of modern languages and literatures at the University of Nebraska in Lincoln, where she specialized in contemporary Latin American literature and Jewish Latin American culture. From 2009 to 2011 she was a research fellow at the S. Daniel Abraham Center for International and Regional Studies at Tel Aviv University. Ran is the author of *Made of Shores: Judeo Argentinean Fiction Revisited* (2001) and editor of *Returning to Babel: Jewish Latin American Experiences and Representations* (2011) and *Mazal Tov Amigos! Jews and Popular Music in the Americas* (2016).

ELISSA RASHKIN is a research professor in cultural and communication studies at the Universidad Veracruzana, Mexico. Her publications include *The Stridentist Movement in Mexico: The Avant-Garde and Cultural Change in the 1920s* (2009; published by the Fondo de Cultura Económica as *La aventura estridentista: Historia cultural de una vanguardia* in 2014), *Atanasio D. Vázquez, fotógrafo de la posrevolución en Veracruz* (2015), and *Women Filmmakers in Mexico: The Country of Which We Dream* (2001; published by the Universidad Veracruzana as *Mujeres cineastas en México: El otro cine* in 2015).

CAROLINA ROCHA is associate professor at Southern Illinois University Edwardsville. She specializes in contemporary Southern Cone literature and film. She is the author of *Masculinities in Contemporary Popular Cinema* (2012), co-editor with Elizabeth Montes Garcés of *Violence in Contemporary Argentine Literature and Film* (2010), and co-editor with Cacilda Rêgo of *New Trends in Argentine and Brazilian Cinema* (2011). She also published, with Georgia Seminet, *Representing History, Class, and Gender in Spain and Latin America: Children and Adolescents in Film* (2012) and *Screening Minors in Latin American Film* (2014).

ILAN STAVANS is Lewis-Sebring Professor in Latin American and Latino Culture at Amherst College and publisher of Restless Books. His story "Morirse está en hebreo" (*The Disappearance: A Novella and Stories*, 2006) is the source of the film *My Mexican Shivah* (2007). He is the author, most recently, of the graphic novel *El Iluminado* (2012, with Steve Sheinkin), *Thirteen Ways of Looking at Latino Art* (2014, with Jorge J. E. Gracia), *Quixote: The Novel and the World* (2015), and a new translation of *Lazarillo de Tormes* (2016).

TZVI TAL is a senior lecturer at the School of Sound and Screen Arts, Sapir College, Israel. His research focuses on the relationship between cinema and the processes of national identity, ethnicity, history, and discourses in the Ibero–Latin American area. He has published *Screens and Revolution—A Comparative Study of Argentina Liberation Cinema and Brazil New Cinema* (2005).

MIRNA VOHNSEN received her PhD from the School of Languages, Cultures, and Linguistics at University College Dublin in 2015, and is an assistant lecturer in Spanish and Latin American studies at Maynooth University. Her research explores the interplay between the cinematic representation of the Argentine Jewish community and the concept of *argentinidad*. She has published in *Aigne* and contributed to the *Directory of World Cinema: Argentina*, volume 2.

Index

Page numbers in italics represent people, places, and topics mentioned in photograph captions.

Abie's Irish Rose, 207
Abrams, Nathan, 105
abrazo partido, El (*Lost Embrace*), 37, 103, 175, 219
Acné (*Acne*), 103–106, 110–114, 229–230
"Adio Kerida" (folk song, from Verdi), 137
Adio Kerida (*Goodbye Dear Love*), 133, 137–138, 141–142, 231
African Americans, 96, 216–217
After Such Knowledge (Hoffman), 59n11
Agosín, Shai, 164, 166
Aizenberg, Edna, 11–12, 79
alcoholism, 82, 84, 119–120, 124, 125, 216, 230
Aleandro, Norma, 73, *76*, 156, 211, *212*
Aleichem, Sholem, 205
Alemann, Marie Louise, 128n13
Alfonsín, Raúl, 62
alienation/marginalization, 14, 16–17, 56, 83–84, 92. *See also* displacement
aliyah: and diasporic displacement, 5; as escape, 182; and geographic isolation, 6, 133–137, 138; modern paradigms of, 166
Allen, Woody, 188–189, 191–194, 213
Almodóvar, Pedro, 157
amateur film, definition of, 119–120

Americanization of Jews, 207. *See also* integration (ethnic), evolution toward
American Jewish Joint Distribution Committee (JDC), 142–143n1
American Tail, An, series, 222n5
AMIA (Asociación Mutual Israelita Argentina) bombing 1994, Buenos Aires, 5, 37, 149, 174–175, 229. *See also Anita*; *18-J*
amiga, La (*The Girlfriend*), 4–5, 62, 81, 228
amnesty programs, post-dictatorship Argentina, 63, 68–69
Anita, 37; bombing experience, 78–80; character background, 76–78; and cultural memory construction, 73–74, 85–86; overviews, 5, 37, 74–76, 229; post-bombing search and discovery, 80–85
Annie Hall, 189, 192–194, 213
ano em que meus pais saíram de férias, O (*The Year My Parents Went on Vacation*), 3, 5, 91–100, 103
anthropological perspectives, 139, 142
Antigone (Sophocles), 63–65, 67, 69
anti-Semitism, 25, 36, 56, 65, 99, 155, 165, 184, 193, 206, 228

Antonioni, Michaelangelo, 123
Apatow, Judd, 219–220
Aquellos años locos (*Those Crazy Years*), 166
Archetti, Eduardo, 99
Argentina: cultural memory, 51–58; national culture and Jewish presence, 11–12, 149; national identity, 18, 62; Palestinians, support for, 165. *See also* Buenos Aires, Argentina; dictatorships and state terrorism
Argentinian film industry: democratic era, 12; experimental film, 122–123, 125, 150; filmography, 235–237, 238; historical overview, 2; interfaith relations theme, 214–222; Jewish characterizations in, 103–104, 213–214, 217–218; New Argentine Cinema (2000s), 36; Salomón, Alberto, 117–127, 230–231
Ariel films (Burman), 6, 103, 219
Aristarain, Adolfo, 217
art films, 122–123
Asociación Judía de Beneficencia y Culto, 135
Asociación Mutual Israelita Argentina (AMIA) bombing 1994, Buenos Aires, 5, 37, 149, 174–175, 229. See also *Anita*; *18-J*
assimilation/integration, 204–205, 208–210, 221
Assmann, Jan, 51
aura, El (*The Aura*), 36, 42–44
"autobiographical pact," 43
autoethnography and Jewish cinema, 38–39
Autumn Sun (*Sol de otoño*), 37, 211–212
Avni, Haim, 56
award-winning films, 63, 74, 105
Azulay, Jom Tob, 3

Babenco, Hector, 3
Bakhtin, Mikhail, 198
baldío, 98–99
Baron, Lawrence, 209, 210, 219
Barone, Daniel, 220
Barthes, Roland, 44

beauty, perceptions of, 13, 14, 16–17
Behar, Ruth, 133, 231. See also *Adio Kerida* (*Goodbye Dear Love*)
Bejarano, Margalit, 143n1
Bemberg, María Luisa, 21n7, 21n11
beso a esta tierra, Un (*A Kiss to This Land*), 181–182, 184
Bet Jacob, 136
Bettinger-López, Caroline, 146n33
Bielinsky, Fabián, 4, 36, 38–39, 227–228
Bluth, Don, 222n5
Bodanzky, Jorge, 3
Bogart, Paul, 220
Bom Retiro neighborhood, São Paulo, 92, 96–98
Bonafini, Hebe de, 68
Borges, Jorge Luis, 36
Boston Jewish Film Festival, 181–182
boundaries, social, and constructed identity, 26, 33, 77–78
Bourdieu, Pierre, 94
Brazil: film industry in, 3; filmography, 237; national identity, 91–100, 229; Palestinians, support for, 165
Brecht, Bertolt, 64
Bregman, el siguiente (*As Follows*), 105
Breve historia del cine argentino (Maranghello), 2
brindis, El (*To Life*), 164, 166–169
Bronstein, Guillermo, 135, 144n11, 144n13
Bronstein, Marcelo, 144n9
Buenos Aires, Argentina: Obelisk of Buenos Aires, 187; Once neighborhood, 6, 77, 79, 175, 189–194, 199–201; representations of, 41, 80–81; urban experience and symbolism, 188–189. See also AMIA (Asociación Mutual Israelita Argentina) bombing 1994, Buenos Aires
Buñuel, Luis, 123, 179
burials, symbolism of, 64–65, 68, 92. See also cemeteries; death and ritual
Burman, Daniel, 2, 37–38, 77, 103, 164, 172, 226. See also *abrazo partido, El* (*Lost Embrace*); *Derecho de familia* (*Family Law*); *Esperando al Me-*

sías (*Waiting for the Messiah*); urban imagery and Burman/Allen film comparisons
Butler, Judith, 26, 227

Caillois, Roger, 98
Calvo-Roth, Fortuna, 140
cámara oscura, La (*Camera Obscura*). See *Camera Obscura*
Camera Lucida (Barthes), 44
Camera Obscura, 4, 12, 13, 14–18, 19–21, 206, 227–228
"Camera Obscura" (short story) (Gorodischer), 4, 12–15, 20, 206, 227–228
Camus, Albert, 99
Canadian Jewish Congress, 138, 143n1
capitalism/consumerism, critique of in film, 39, 124
Cara de queso: Mi primer ghetto (*Cheesehead*), 103–110, 229–230
Carlson, Jerry, 6, 187, 226, 232
Carnevale, Marcos, 37, 73, 74–75, 229. See also *Anita*
Cartas para Jenny (*Letters for Jenny*), 164, 171–172, 173
Carvajal, Luis de (the Younger), 179–180, 184
castillo de la pureza, El (*The Castle of Purity*), 179
Castle of Purity, The (*El castillo de la pureza*), 179
Castro, Fidel, 133, 137
Catholic Church: Catholic/Jewish intercultural themes, 28–30, 59n13, 195–196, 217–218; Irish Gentile persona, 208; religious intolerance of, 60n21; and Spanish colonial persecutions, 24–25. See also interfaith relations
Cedrón, Lucía, 174. See also *18-J*
Celan, Paul, 54
cemeteries, 64–65, 66, 69, 77. See also burials, symbolism of; death and ritual
censorship, 124
Center for Documentation and Information on Argentinean Jewry, Marc Turkow, 87n8

Centro Sefaradí, Havana, Cuba, 138
Certeau, Michel de, 187, 200, 233
Chávez, Hugo, 165
Cheesehead (*Cara de queso: Mi primer ghetto*), 103–110, 229–230
Chenillo, Mariana, 31, 183
Chevra Kedusha Ashkenazi (Jewish Mutual Aid and Burial Society), 86n1
Chiesa, Alcides, 63
Chile: filmography, 237–238; Palestinians in, 148, 149–150, 151–153, 158–159, 231–232
Cinco días sin Nora (*Nora's Will*), 3, 25, 31–33, 183, 227
Cinco horas con Mario (*Five Hours with Mario*), 183
"Cinema Novo," 3
Clarín, 74–75, 107
class discrimination/bias, 29
Cohen vs. Rosi, 220–221
comedy and hegemonic discourse, 153–154, 155
coming-of-age themes, 91–100, 104–106, 106–110, 110–114, 229–230
Comité Central Israelita de México, 29
community identity, production/construction of, 26, 30–31, 33, 96–98, 99, 190, 202–203
contextualization techniques, 49–50, 120–121, 122
conversions to Judaism, official, 133, 134–137
Copertari, Gabriela, 41–42
country club, symbology of, 106–110
Crimes and Misdemeanors, 189, 194–195, 197–199
Crosland, Alan, 207–208
Cuba, 133, 137–142, 180–181, 231
cultural identity: clichés of, 165; community identity, production/construction of, 26, 30–31, 33, 96–98, 99, 190, 202–203; and "difference," 25, 26; Palestinian, 148, 149–150, 151–153, 158–159, 231–232; performance (construction) of, 26–33, 66–68, 149, 151–152; and ritual, 28–33, 92, 134,

cultural identity (*continued*)
138–140, 199–200, 226. *See also* "Jewishness"; national identity
cultural memory, construction of, 73–74, 79–86
Czach, Liz, 119

DaMatta, Roberto, 94–95
Darín, Ricardo, 36, 43
Da Silva, António José, 3
Daughter of Silence (Fingueret), 228–229
"Day of Atonement, The" (Raphaelson), 222–223n7
Dead Sea, 172, 173
death and ritual, 4, 26, 28–33, 169–170, 178–179, 183, 227. *See also* cemeteries
De eso no se habla (*I Don't Want to Talk about It*), 21–22n11
de-familiarizing view, 106
De la Torre, Raúl, 217
Delibes, Miguel, 183
demographic statistics, 1, 86n1, 133, 143n1, 149, 187, 204–205, 207
depoliticization of memory, 151
Derecho de familia (*Family Law*), 37, 103, 189, 219
Deutsche Freund, Der (*My German Friend/El amigo alemán*), 49–58, 228
Diario Judío, 25
diaspora: and cultural identity, 149; Hirsch's colonization plan, 11, 39–40, 149, 150, 205; and identity as "other," 70; and identity misplacement, 14; overviews, 5–6. *See also* displacement
dictatorships and state terrorism: Brazil, 91–92, 93–96; disappeared/disappearances, 34n3, 68–69, 73–74, 80–85, 229; films during, 2; post-dictatorship identity, 62–71, 168. *See also* Dirty War
difference and cultural identity, 25, 26
Dirty War, 4–5, 80, 217–218. *See also* AMIA (Asociación Mutual Israelita Argentina) bombing 1994, Buenos Aires; disappeared/disappearances

Disappearance, The: A Novella and Stories (Stavans), 178
disappeared/disappearances, 34n3, 68–69, 73–74, 80–85, 229
Discépolo, Armando, 223
disidentification, 31
displacement, 5–6, 74, 106, 126, 157–158. *See also* alienation/marginalization; diaspora
documentary films, 6, 133–138, 141–142, 150–151, 181–182, 231–232
Dreizik, Pablo M., 228–229
Drowned and the Saved, The (Levi), 67
drugs in movie themes, 28, 165, 169, 170, 216

economic crises, Argentina, 63, 119, 175, 189–190
Edery, Victor, Sr., 133
18-J, 37, 77, 160n19, 174
8mm film, 117–127
elopement, 13, 14, 19, 205–206
El Universal, 30
Empty Nest (*El nido vacío*), 164, 172–173
Entre Ríos province, Argentina, 11, 14
espera, La (*The Wait*), 36
Esperando al Mesías (*Waiting for the Messiah*), 103, 189–194, 214–215, 215–216, 223n10
eterno retorno, El: Retrato de la comunidad judío-peruana (Salcedo), 140–141
ethics, 29, 195–199, 200–201
ethnic memory, 149–150. *See also* cultural memory, construction of
European ethnic comedy, 153–154
exaggeration techniques, 124–125, 173
exoticism, 134
expanded cinema, 120
experimental film, 120, 122–123, 124, 150
"eye among the blind," 106

Falicov, Tamara, 114–115n8
Family Frames (Hirsch), 227
Family Law (*Derecho de familia*), 37, 103, 189, 219
Family Photographs (Hirsch, J), 227

Feierstein, Ricardo, 115n13
feminist perspectives, 12, 20, 26, 62
Fiddler on the Roof, 2, 205
Fierstein, Harvey, 220
Fingueret, Manuela, 228–229
Fire Within, The (*El fuego eterno*), 133, 134–137, 141–142, 231
Five Hours with Mario (*Cinco horas con Mario*), 183
Fleming, Victor, 207
Forgács, Péter, 128n13, 128n16
Fox, Vicente, 178–179
Franco, Francisco, 154–155
Frías, Miguel, 107, 110
Frydemberg, Julio, 98
fuego eterno, El (*The Fire Within*), 133, 134–137, 141–142, 231
Full Stop Law (Ley de Punto Final), 63
funerals. *See* death and ritual
futebol de botão, 92

Galeano, Eduardo, 95, 96–97
Garage Olimpo, 80, 81, 82
gauchos judíos, Los (*The Jewish Gauchos*). *See Jewish Gauchos, The* (film); *Jewish Gauchos, The* (Gerchunoff)
gender roles and identity, 4, 16, 26, 28, 83, 156, 157, 172–173. *See also* homosexuality/bisexuality; women
Gender Trouble: Feminism and the Subversion of Identity (Butler), 26, 227
Gerchunoff, Alberto, 4, 11–12, 13, 40, 41, 151, 205–206
Gerdes, Dick, 180
Germany: Jewish marginalization in (post-war), 55–56; post-Nazi cultural identity quests, 4–5, 51–52, 55–57, 66–68
Girlfriend, The (*La amiga*), 4–5, 62, 81, 228
Glickman, Nora, 6, 204, 233–234
globalization and cinematographical modes, 148–149
Godard, Jean-Luc, 123
Goebbels, Joseph, 100n3
Goethe-Institut, 128n13
Golan, Menachem, 209

Goldberg, Daniel, 181. *See also beso a esta tierra, Un* (*A Kiss to This Land*)
Goldberg, Florinda, 66–67
Goldblatt, David, 94
Goldemberg, Isaac, 140, 143n3
Golden Age of Mexican cinema, 2–3
Goldenberg, Jorge, 27
Goldfine, Daniela, 4–5, 49, 228
Goldfrid, Hernán, 38, 227
Gómez Moragas, Cristina, 39, 45n4
Goodbye Dear Love (*Adio Kerida*), 133, 137–138, 141–142, 231
Gorodischer, Angélica, 4, 12, 13–15, 20, 206, 226–227
Graff Zivin, Erin, 188–189
Grant, Catherine, 67, 69
graveyards. *See* cemeteries
Gray, James, 214
grotesco criollo, 221
Gruenberg, George, 144n11
guilt, survivor's, 67, 228
Gundermann, Christian, 65, 68

Halbwachs, Maurice, 50
Hamburger, Cao, 3, 91, 103. *See also Year My Parents Went on Vacation, The* (*O ano em que meus pais saíram de férias*)
Harari, Dominic, 155
Harguindeguy, Albano, 65
Har-Paled, Misgav, 24
Heartbreak Kid, The, 216
He Came to Steal (*Vino para robar*), 105
Herzl, Theodor, 164
Hiriart, Hugo, 180
Hirsch, Julia, 13, 16, 20
Hirsch, Marianne, 15
Hirsch, Maurice de, 11, 39–40, 149, 150, 205
Hirzman, Leon, 3
Hisho que te nazca (*Like a Mother*) (Nissán), 180
Hispanic hegemony and homogonization of identity, 154–157
Historia de los judíos argentinos (Feierstein), 115n13

history and memory. *See* mnemo-history; relics, ritual, and memory
Hoffman, Eva, 59n11
Holmes, Amanda, 77–78
Holocaust, 49, 66–68, 168, 228–229. *See also* Shoah
"home" concepts, 157–158, 165–166. *See also* national identity
home movies, 117–122, 126–127, 230–231
Homo Ludens (Huizinga), 98
homosexuality/bisexuality, 120, 189, 202, 215–216, 220–221
Hospital de Clínicas, 81
Huberman, Ariana, 6, 133, 231
Huerta, César, 30
Huizinga, Johan, 98
humor, 28, 107, 120, 125, 193, 202. *See also* comedy and hegemonic discourse

identity, personal: awareness and self-discovery, 75, 91–100, 227; coming-of-age themes, 91–100, 104–106, 106–110, 110–114, 229–230; construction/discovery, 4, 27–33, 227; and intelligibility, 26–27. *See also* cultural identity
I Don't Want to Talk about It (*De eso no se habla*), 21–22n11
"I Found It at the Movies" (Stavans), 178
Im Land meiner Eltern (*In the Country of My Parents*), 55
indigenous peoples, 24, 25, 29, 133–134, 136–137, 144n11, 231
innocence and intuitive wisdom, 106, 107
integration (ethnic), evolution toward, 149–150, 204–205, 208–210, 221
intelligibility, 26–27, 30, 33
intercultural encounters/reconciliations: interracial, 202, 216–217; Jewish/Catholic, 27–30, 31–33, 63–71; personal/sexual relationships, 167; post-Nazi era encounters, 4–5, 53–55, 228; solidarity, nationalistic, 81, 94–95; tradition (dogma) *vs.* integration (adaptation), 3, 18, 31, 189, 194–203, 208–210, 234. *See also* interfaith relations; multicultural concepts
interfaith relations: diasporic era traditionalism, 205–208, 210; homosexual, 220–221; integration, evolution toward, 208–210, 219; offspring of, 217–220; overviews, 6, 204–205, 233–234; parental aspects, 213–217, 219–220, 220–221; preconceptions and stereotyping, 211–213. *See also* intercultural encounters/reconciliations
intermarriage, 205, 206–207, 222n3, 233. *See also* interfaith relations
international film festivals, 25, 63
interracial relations, 202, 216–217. *See also* intercultural encounters/reconciliations
In the Country of My Parents (*Im Land meiner Eltern*), 55
Iquitos, Peru, 133–137
Irish Catholic Gentile persona, 208
Island Called Home, An (Behar), 139
Israel and symbolism: contextual implication of, 174–175; as cultural and personal haven, 170–174, 182–183; Jewish cultural identity *vs.* humanism/universalism, 166–170; locations filmed in, 170–172, 173; overviews, 6, 164–166, 176, 232. *See also* aliyah
Israeli embassy attack 1992, 149

Jaffa, Tel Aviv, Israel, 171
Jazz Singer, The, 207–208, 209–210, 222–223n7
Jehovah's Witnesses, 137
Jerusalem, Israel, 171
Jewish Colonization Association, 11, 39–40
"Jewish film," defining, 1–4, 225–234. *See also* "Jewishness"
Jewish Gauchos, The (film), 2, 37, 151, 160n19, 205, 206
Jewish Gauchos, The (Gerchunoff), 4, 11–12, 13, 18–21, 40, 151, 205–206
Jewish mother character, 103, 108
"Jewishness": awareness and self-discovery, 75, 91–100, 166–169; ex-

ternalization of, 28; and geographic isolation, 135–137, 141–142; and "Jewish cinema," defining, 36–44, 225–234; *Judeo-latinoamericanidad* ("Judeo-Latin Americanness"), 166; and personal identity construction/discovery, 24–26, 27–33, 227; preconceived stereotypes, 211–213; prejudice of conservative sects, 135–137; relics, ritual, and memory, 28–30, 92, 134, 138–140, 226; and urban experience, 187–189, 233. *See also* cultural identity; interfaith relations; Israel and symbolism
Jewish princess character, 103
Jewison, Norman, 205
Jews in Latin America, numbers of, 1, 86n1, 133, 143n1, 149, 187
Jews of the Amazon (Segal), 135, 136
Jewtopia, 212–213
Jodorowsky, Alejandro, 234
"Joint, El," 142–143n1
Jolson Story, The, 223n7
Judeo-latinoamericanidad ("Judeo-Latin Americanness"), 166
judeu, O (*The Jew*), 3
Judíos en el espacio (*Jews in Space*), 103
Jusid, Juan José, 2, 205
justice, perspectives on, 195–197

Kael, Pauline, 178
Kaminsky, Amy, 4, 36, 225–226, 227–228
Keeping the Faith, 209–210
King, John, 64, 65
King of Once, The (*El rey del Once*, also *The Tenth Man*), 201
Kiss to This Land, A (*Un beso a esta tierra*), 181–182, 184
Klezmatics (band), 33
Kluge, Alexander, 62

LaCapra, Dominick, 85
Lamborghini, Osvaldo, 128n11
La Nación, 75, 107
language and identity, 37, 92, 202, 211
Last Moon, The (*La última luna*), 148, 151–153, 158, 231–232

Last Summer of La Boyita (*El último verano de La Boyita*), 39
Law of Due Obedience (Ley de Obediencia Debida), 63
Leen, Catherine, 81
Legado (*Legacy*), 148, 150–151, 153, 158, 231–232
Lejeune, Philippe, 43
Lerer, Diego, 74–75
lesbian relationships, 120, 215–216
Lesko, Nancy, 104
Letters for Jenny (*Cartas para Jenny*), 164, 171–172, 173
Levi, Primo, 67
Levinson, Barry, 208–209, 216
Levy, Danayda, 137–138
Levy, Daniel, 51, 58n6, 228
Liberty Heights, 208–209, 216–217
Lichtmann, Gabriel, 103
Like a Bride (*Novia que te vea*) (Nissán) (also film), 3, 180–181, 182, 184
Lima, Peru, 135, 140
Lincovsky, Cipe, 63
Lindstrom, Naomi, 225
Littin, Miguel, 151, 231
Livon-Grosman, Ernesto, 117, 230
Los Angeles, California, 193
Lost Embrace (*El abrazo partido*), 37, 103, 175, 219
love themes, 15, 52–55, 56
lugar en el mundo, Un (*A Place in the World*), 217, 218
Luppi, Federico, 63, 105, 107, 212, 218
Lury, Karen, 76

Madres de Plaza de Mayo (Mothers of Plaza de Mayo), 63–64, 68, 74, 80
Magee, Shawn, 55–56
magic and mysticism, 136
Manzo, Alejandra, 76
Maranghello, César, 2
Marker, Chris, 122
Markovich, Paula, 39, 227
Martín, Marina, 45n6
Martínez, Adolfo, 75, 107
Marxism, 94, 202
Masiello, Francine, 12

May, Elaine, 216
Mayol, Humberto, 139
Mazursky, Paul, 217
McLuhan, Marshall, 192
Meerapfel, Jeanine, 4–5, 49–58, 62, 228–229. See also *amiga, La* (*The Girlfriend*); *Deutsche Freund, Der* (*My German Friend/El amigo alemán*)
Meet the Fockers trilogy, 219
"melting pot" ideology, 207, 219. See also multicultural concepts
Memoria de las cenizas (*Memory of the Ashes*) (Dreizik), 228–229
memory: Argentine cultural memory, 51–58; collective, 51; depoliticization of, 151; ethnic, 149–150; global cultural, 168, 228–229; Jewish cultural, 40, 73–74, 79–86, 226; reproductive view of, 40–41; revisiting and directorial technique, 193–194; survivors', 85; validation of, 15–16, 20–21. See also mnemo-history; relics, ritual, and memory
Menemism, 45n4, 83
Menis, María Victoria, 4, 12, 206
men's roles and neoliberal destabilization, 82–83
Merliner, Max, 156
mestizo ancestry, 133–134, 137, 231
Meter, Alejandro, 91
Mexico: democracy, transition to, 178–179; European Conquest period, 24–25; film industry, 2–3; filmography, 238; independence from Spain, 180; Jewish cultural identity in, 25–26, 29, 179–184
Meyer, Louis B., 207
Michelotti, Graciela, 4, 11, 226
Mignogna, Eduardo, 37
Milewicz, Eduardo, 213–214
Miller, José, 133, 142n1
Mi primera boda (*My First Wedding*), 105, 216
Mitrani Reaño, Henry, 140
Mizraje, María Gabriela, 64
mnemo-history: concept overviews, 49–51, 57–58, 58n6, 228; and narrative construction, 53–55; and reconstructive imagination, 51–52, 121–122
Moguillansky, Marina, 115n10
Momentos, 21
Monjardim, Jayme, 3
morality themes, 110, 123–126, 197–199. See also sexuality
Morirse está en hebreo (*My Mexican Shiva*), 3, 25, 27–31, 164, 169–170, 178–179, 182–184, 227, 232
"Morirse está en hebreo" ("To die" is in Hebrew) (Stavans), 179
Moses, 93
Mothers of Plaza de Mayo (Madres de Plaza de Mayo), 63–64, 68, 74, 80
multicultural concepts, 27, 84, 96, 148–149, 158–159, 207, 219
Museo Tolerancia y Memoria, Mexico City, 25, 26
Musiak, Diego, 164, 171
music in film, 137, 138, 157, 205
Muslims, 149–150, 154–157, 158–159. See also Palestine/Palestinians
Mussolini, Benito, 100n3
My Big Fat Greek Wedding, 27
My First Ghetto. See *Cheesehead* (*Cara de queso: Mi primer ghetto*)
My First Wedding (*Mi primera boda*), 105, 216
My German Friend (*Der Deutsche Freund/El amigo alemán*), 49–58, 228
My Mexican Shiva (*Morirse está en hebreo*), 3, 25, 27–31, 164, 169–170, 178–179, 182–184, 227, 232
mysticism and magic, 136
myths: Antigone, parallels to, 64, 67, 69; Argentine Jewish origin, 39–40, 41; of Jewish/native savagery, 24, 155

narrative techniques, 124–126, 193–194, 195, 199, 201–203
Nasab, Homa, 58n1, 59n14
national identity, 18–19, 62–71, 93–96, 98, 100n3. See also coming-of-age themes; cultural identity; multicultural concepts

National Institute of Cinematography and Audiovisual Arts (INCAA), 62–63, 159n7
Nazis, 43, 49, 56, 66–67, 100n3. *See also* Holocaust
nebbish, definition, 209
neoliberalism, 2, 82–83, 106, 107, 115n17
Neró, 124–126
Neugeboren, Jay, 52
New Argentine Cinema (NAC), 2, 36, 150
New German Cinema, 62
New York City Jewish experience, 192–194, 197–199, 201–203, 209
nido vacío, El (*Empty Nest*), 164, 172–173
Nine Queens (*Nueve reinas*), 36, 38–39, 40–42, 44, 228
Nissán, Rosa, 180
Nora's Will (*Cinco días sin Nora*), 3, 25, 31–33, 183, 227
"Nora's Will" (Stavans), 184
Norton, Edward, 209–210
Novia que te vea (*Like a Bride*) (Nissán) (also film), 2, 180–181, 182, 184
Nueve reinas (*Nine Queens*), 36, 38–39, 40–42, 44, 228
Nuriel, Patricia, 54–55, 62, 228

Obelisk of Buenos Aires, 187, 189
Official Story, The (*La historia oficial*), 63, 73, 86
Olga, 3
Once neighborhood, Buenos Aires, 6, 77, 79, 175, 189–194, 199–201
Only Human (*Seres queridos*), 6, 148, 153–157, 158–159, 231–232
Ophüls, Max, 207
Organizacion para la Liberacion de la Palestina (OLP) (Palestine Liberation Organization, PLO), 148, 150, 158
Other, conceptualizations of: and colonial Catholic persecution, 24; and contemporary diversity, 25; and diasporic identity, 70; gaze of and self-liberation, 12, 17–18; and "home" concept, 157–158; isolation from, 106;

Jews in postwar Germany, 55–56; and performative intelligibility, 30; and repressive dictatorships, 66
Over the Brooklyn Bridge, 209

Pagoaga, Francisco Victoriano, 34n3
Palestine Liberation Organization (PLO), 148, 150, 158
Palestine/Palestinians: and Cuban Jews, 143n1; cultural identity in Chile, 148, 149–150, 151–153, 158–159, 231–232; Latin American support of, 165; Middle East conflict, Hispanic view on, 154–157
Partido de Accion Nacional (PAN), 179
Partido Revolucionario Institucional (PRI), 178–179
patriarchal repression, 16, 21–22n11
Pelé, 95–96
Pelegri, Teresa, 155
Peres, Shimon, 144n9, 165
performative acts, 26–28, 30–33, 120–121, 122. *See also* mnemo-history
Perón, Juan, 53, 217, 218
persecution, universality of, 54–55
Peru, 133–137, 140–141, 165, 231
perversion, 128n11
Pinfold, Debbie, 106, 107
Pinochet, Augusto, 153
Place in the World, A (*Un lugar en el mundo*), 217, 218
play and identity formation, 98–99
Pobre mariposa (*Poor Butterfly*), 217–218
political activism: and Jewish Mexican identity, 180–182; Mothers of Plaza de Mayo, 63–64, 68, 74, 80; in second generation film themes, 208
Pollack, Sydney, 208
Poor Butterfly (*Pobre mariposa*), 217–218
porteño, 187
Prats, Arturo, 153
Prats, Carlos, 153
Preminger, Otto, 207
premio, El (*The Prize*), 39
Prize, The (*El premio*), 39
Proceso, 228. *See also* Dirty War

public/private spheres, representation of, 123–124. *See also* contextualization techniques
Puenzo, Luis, 63
punctum, photographic *vs.* cinematic, 44
Pygmalion, 192

racism: anti-Semitism, 25, 36, 56, 65, 99, 155, 165, 184, 193, 206, 228; against indigenous peoples, 24, 25, 29, 144n11, 231. *See also* terrorism/violence
Radio Days, 189, 201–203
Ran, Amalia, 6, 164, 232
Ranni, Rodolfo, 218
Raoul Wallenberg Foundation, 159n7
Raphaelson, Sam, 222–223n7
Rashkin, Elissa J., 4, 24, 227
Reátegui Levi, Ronald, 144n11
Rebella, Juan Pablo, 103
Rein, Raanan, 1, 104
Reitz, Edgar, 62
relics, ritual, and memory, 28–30, 53–54, 92, 134, 138–140, 226. *See also* ritual and cultural identity
religion: and characterization of film culture, 225–226; critique of, in film, 124–126; ethics *vs.* doctrine, 29, 195–199; and intermarriage stresses, 209–210; religious hybridity, 136–137, 137–139, 141–142. *See also* Catholic Church; interfaith relations; "Jewishness"
repetition techniques, 124, 125–126
representational strategies. *See* contextualization techniques
resemantization techniques, 121
"restored" behavior, 30
rey del Once, El (*The King of Once*, also *The Tenth Man*), 201
Ripstein, Arturo, 2–3, 179, 180, 184
ritual and cultural identity, 28–33, 92, 134, 138–140, 199–200, 226. *See also* relics, ritual, and memory
Roach, Joseph, 26, 27, 33
Robson, Dave, 75
Rocha, Carolina, 38, 84, 103, 229

rubber industry, 133, 144n10
Russian pogroms, 11, 18–19, 39, 205. *See also* diaspora

Saferstein, Rubén, 144n13
Said, Edward, 156
Salcedo Mitrani, Lorry, 133, 134–137, 140–142, 231
Sales, John, 178
Salomón, Alberto, 117–127, 230–231
Samy y yo (*Sammy and I*), 213–214
San Sebastian International Film Festival, 63
Sans soleil, 122
Santería religion, 137
Santitos, 27
santo oficio, O (*The Holy Inquisition*), 2, 179–180, 184
São Paulo, Brazil, 92
Schechner, Richard, 30
schlemiel character, 103, 108
Schyfter, Guita, 2, 180
Segal, Ariel, 135, 136
self-determination themes. *See* coming-of-age themes
Seminet, Georgia, 84
Sephardic Center, Havana, Cuba, 138
Seres queridos (*Only Human*), 6, 148, 153–157, 158–159, 231–232
sexuality: adultery, 197–198; coming-of-age themes, 111, 113; extramarital, 189; and home movie aesthetic, 119–120, 125; homosexuality/bisexuality, 120, 189, 190–191, 202, 215–216, 220–221; and identity misplacement, 39, 156, 157, 227; promiscuity, 215–216, 217
Shaw, George Bernard, 192
shivah ritual, 28–31, 169–170, 178–179, 183, 227
Shoah, 4–5, 49, 55, 66–68, 85. *See also* Holocaust
Sicart, Miguel, 99, 101n21, 101n24
Silva, António José da. *See* Da Silva, António José
Singer's Typewriter and Mine (Stavans), 178

Sirota, Graciela Narcisa, 60n20
Six-Day War, 143n1, 164
16mm film, 118, 119, 122
small-gauge film, 117, 122
soccer and national/cultural identity, 91–100, 229
Sol de otoño (*Autumn Sun*), 37, 211–212
Solomonoff, Julia, 39, 227
Sound on Sight, 75
souvenirs (cultural), 134, 139
Spanish film industry, 148, 231–232, 238
sports and national identity, 94–95, 229
Springall, Alejandro, 2–3, 27, 164, 169, 178, 182
Stavans, Ilan, 6, 27, 178, 232
Stavans (Stavchansky), Abraham, 179, 232
stereotypes, ethnic, 108, 111, 152, 154, 211–213, 221–222
Stewart, Susan, 134, 139
Stoll, Pablo, 103
Storni, Alfonsina, 19
success and Jewish tradition, 197–199
suicide and disidentification, 31, 199
Super 8mm film, 117–127, 230
surrogation, 27
"swarming activity" concept, 187, 200, 203, 233
Swiss, Jewish view of, 196
syncretism and religious hybridity, 136–137

Tal Tzvi, 6, 104, 106, 115n17, 148, 231–232
Tel Aviv, Israel, 171
Ten Commandments, The, 225–226
Tendler, Silvio, 3
Tenembaum, Baruch, 150
Tenth Man, The, 189, 199–203
terrorism/violence, 4, 165, 167, 168, 174–175, 228–229. See also AMIA (Asociación Mutual Israelita Argentina) bombing 1994, Buenos Aires; dictatorships and state terrorism; Holocaust
Tesis sobre un homicidio (*Thesis on a Homicide*), 38, 227
Tevye the Dairyman (Aleichem), 205

textile industry, 119
Thesis on a Homicide (*Tesis sobre un homicidio*), 38, 227
This Is 40, 219–220
tikkun olam concept, 197, 200–201
Toledo, Guillermo, 156
To Life (*El brindis*), 164, 166–169
Tomkins, Cynthia, 42
Torch Song Trilogy, 220
tradition (dogma) *vs.* integration (adaptation), 3, 18, 31, 189, 194–203, 208–210, 234
transcultural identification, 28. See also intercultural encounters/reconciliations
transnationality and cinema, 36, 57, 156
traumatic injustice. See anti-Semitism; terrorism/violence
Trotta, Marcelo, 150
"twice-behaved behavior," 30
Two Lovers, 214–215, 216

Ullmann, Liv, 63, 64
última luna, La (*The Last Moon*), 148, 151–153, 158, 231–232
último verano de La Boyita, El (*Last Summer of La Boyita*), 39
UNCIPAR (Unión de Cineastas de Paso Reducido) (Association of small-gauge filmmakers), 122
United States film industry, 3, 6, 138, 141, 219–220. See also urban imagery and Burman/Allen film comparisons
urban imagery and Burman/Allen film comparisons: *Family Law/Crimes and Misdemeanors*, 194–199; overviews, 6, 187–189, 203, 233; *Tenth Man/Radio Days*, 199–203; *Waiting for the Messiah/Annie Hall*, 189–194, 214
Uruguayan film industry, 103–104, 239
Useful Life, A (*La vida útil*), 105

Veiroj, Federico, 103, 105, 229
Venezuela, anti-Jewish activity in, 165
vida útil, La (*A Useful Life*), 105
Villa Clara settlement, 14, 19

Vino para robar (*He Came to Steal*), 105
violence. *See* terrorism/violence
Virgin of Guadalupe, 24
Vohnsen, Mirna, 73, 227, 229

Wailing Wall, Jerusalem, Israel, 172
Wait, The (*La espera*), 36
Waiting for the Messiah (*Esperando al Mesías*), 103, 189–194, 214–215, 215–216, 223n10
Walker, Harry, 95
"Walking in the City" (from *The Practice of Everyday Life*, Certeau), 187
Wallerstein, Gregorio, 2
WASP Gentile persona, 208, 210, 214, 217, 219
Way We Were, The, 208
Weinstein, Anita, 87–88n8

Whisky, 103
Willie and Phil, 217
Winograd, Ariel, 103, 104–105, 229
women: feminist perspectives, 12, 20, 26, 62; Gentile stereotypes, 207, 211; Jewish stereotypes, 103, 108–109; marginalization of, 14–16, 20–21, 26, 157. *See also* gender roles and identity
World Cup Soccer, 93–94
World War II, 3, 4, 51, 199, 203

Year My Parents Went on Vacation, The (*O ano em que meus pais saíram de férias*), 3, 5, 91–100, 103

"Zelig," 195
Zionist project, 164
Zukor, Adolph, 207